Praise for

SEXPLOITATIO

and

CINDY PIERCE

"Cindy Pierce's new book, *Sexploitation*, is a comprehensive, wise, and sometimes alarming look at the culture of porn that surrounds our kids. Pierce is a straight-talker on the subject of sex; she is also a compelling writer and she makes a strong case that parents have to be brave and talk to their kids before the Internet introduces them to sexuality. Her book will help parents to find that courage."

—Michael Thompson, coauthor of the *New York Times*
bestseller *Raising Cain: Protecting the Emotional Life of Boys*

"For every parent who's ever panicked about having 'the talk' with their child, Cindy Pierce has created a frank, honest resource to help—and more importantly, a reminder that this isn't a 'talk' at all but rather a conversation that evolves as our boys and girls become responsible, sexually active young men and women."

—Jodi Picoult, *New York Times* best-selling author of
Nineteen Minutes and *My Sister's Keeper*

"As parents, we wish our kids will grow up to have happy, healthy sex lives. Just 'wishing' won't help. We need to talk with them, otherwise their sex education will come from popular culture and the Internet. Whether we like it or not, all teens, even preteens have to confront pornography. Cindy's book will help parents find our voices to discuss challenging topics that weren't part of our own growing up."

—Dr. Michael L. Lyons MD, assistant clinical professor
of community and family medicine at
Geisel School of Medicine at Dartmouth College

"Here's a guide to having meaningful conversations on 'the other side of awkward' with our teenagers so that these young people we love so much might be safer and happier. Who doesn't need that?"

—Kelly Corrigan, *New York Times* best-selling author of
Glitter and Glue, Lift, and *The Middle Place*

"*Sexploitation: Helping Kids Develop Healthy Sexuality in a Porn-Driven World* is a phenomenal resource to help us guide our children in developing healthy sexual and social relationships within themselves and with others. Cindy is raw, real, and fantastic. Her approach will leave you educated and empowered—ready to have comfortable, adult conversations with your children."

—Stacy Nadeau, professional speaker,
coach, and Dove model

"Cindy Pierce's *Sexploitation* is a searing analysis of how hypersexualized messages in pop culture harm our children's emotional lives. She weaves her experiences together with the stories of others, compelling data, and expert opinions to offer practical advice for developing healthy social and sexual relationships. This book is a must-read for parents who are concerned about their children's happiness in a society saturated with social media and porn."

—Caroline Heldman, associate professor of
politics, Occidental College

"Cindy Pierce takes direct aim at the place where the tsunami of our culture and the heart of our humanity intersect. Her straight talk on the importance of having conversations with our teens about how to manage the bombardment of messages from the mass media while defining their own 'inner compass' is a helpful guide for families."

—Julie Metzger, RN, MN, cofounder,
Great Conversations www.greatconversations.com

SEXPLOITATION

SEXPLOITATION

HELPING KIDS DEVELOP HEALTHY SEXUALITY IN A PORN-DRIVEN WORLD

CINDY PIERCE

bibliomotion
inc.

First published by Bibliomotion, Inc.
39 Harvard Street
Brookline, MA 02445
Tel: 617-934-2427
www.bibliomotion.com

Printed in the United States of America

Library of Congress Cataloging-in-Publication Data

Pierce, Cindy, author.
  Sexploitation : helping kids develop healthy sexuality in a porn-driven world / Cindy Pierce.
    pages cm
    ISBN 978-1-62956-089-2 (paperback) — ISBN 978-1-62956-090-8 (ebook) — ISBN 978-1-62956-091-5 (enhanced ebook)
  1. Sexual ethics for youth. 2. Pornography. 3. Sex. 4. Sex instruction for children. 5. Parenting. I. Title.
  HQ32.P54 2015
  176'.40835—dc23
                    2015023207

To my husband, Bruce Lingelbach. Thank you for your belief in this message and your unending support.

To our children, Zander, Sadie, and Colter. You make us laugh and light up our lives.

I love you all.

CONTENTS

FOREWORD

I am often called upon to talk to graduate students who are studying to become sexuality educators. Their questions capture both the anxiety and the giddiness that come with the prospect of entering their own classroom. A question they always ask me is, "How do you deal with negative reactions from parents who might take exception to what you're teaching their kids?" My answer always surprises them: I don't get negative reactions from parents. In fact, in the twenty-five-plus years I've been a classroom sexuality educator, I can count on one hand the negative parental reactions I've gotten. The reason is quite simple. I treat parents as allies and not as adversaries, as partners and not as problems.

The prospective teachers sometimes need a minute to process that statement. I can understand why. We seldom see news stories about parents who are delighted with their children's teachers. Adversarial relationships make for better TV or blog posts in our "if it bleeds, it leads" media philosophy. But there's absolutely no reason that parents and teachers should be at odds—especially when it comes to something as important as sexuality education.

Kids today are immersed in a society that isn't all that interested in their sexual health. (It isn't much interested in our sexual health, either.) It's easy to see this if you sample the advertisements popping up on our kids' Facebook pages, the YouTube videos they're streaming on their cell phones and tablets, and the sexually explicit and/or pornographic material they encounter, intentionally or otherwise. The message they're getting from these sources isn't "Love yourself as you are!" It's much more likely to be: "Are you _____ enough? If you're not, we can fix that!" (Fill in the blank with *thin, sexy, pretty, strong, hung, hard,* etc.)

I firmly believe that parents are, and should be, the primary sexuality educators of their children. I believe just as strongly that they can't, and shouldn't be, the *only* sexuality educators of their children. It truly does take a village to raise a sexually healthy kid. When educators partner with parents, we can address more of our kids' needs more effectively.

Parents also need our help. I went into sexuality education, in part, because I have the ability to think about and talk about issues that many other people find daunting. Becoming parents does not automatically endow individuals with the ability to talk with their kids about healthy sexuality. Some parents *do* have this ability—and that's terrific—but many don't, and they aren't sure where to begin. Being an advocate to parents as they embark on the vital work of raising sexually healthy kids means helping them learn not just what to say, but *when* and *how* to say it—and what *not* to say as well.

When I talk to parents, I stress two messages. The first is: "Encourage your hopes, not your fears." It's so easy to think about all the mistakes and terrible things that can happen to our kids on their way to healthy sexuality. When we start from that place, though, the messages we tend to give are negative and defensive. "Don't have sex!" "Watch out for STDs!" "Don't get pregnant or get someone else pregnant!" "I don't want you to have a broken heart!" Rather than thinking about all the things they *don't* want for their kids, parents are better off starting with what they *do* want for them. In the 2011 *New York Times Magazine* cover story "Teaching Good Sex," I am quoted as saying to a group of parents, "What if our kids really believed we wanted them to have great sex?" If that is something we want for them (it's something I want for my students), how do we help them achieve that?

Great sex isn't just about having a pleasurable experience, although that's certainly part of it. It comes from knowing our values, being able to communicate with our partner, feeling good about our bodies, understanding what we want out of a sexual encounter and being able to ask for it, and feeling confident about being a sexual person. Great sex necessarily entails being protected from unintended pregnancies and STDs, as well as from emotional turmoil and confusion. All of these things are teachable, and I want to help parents feel more comfortable and confident in teaching their kids how to develop these skills. Such an approach is not defensive; it doesn't spring from fear. It isn't sex-negative; nor is it hedonistic. This all comes from what we hope for our kids rather than what we fear for them.

My second message to parents is: "Help your kid choose authenticity over popularity." That may not sound like a sex ed message, but it certainly is! Healthy sexuality isn't about what's popular; it's about what's real. While I am not a parent, I have been a teenager and know the allure of popularity. It's a siren song that's hard to resist at that age. But the desire to be popular leads us to betray our values and to work against our self-interest, and it often leads to self-loathing rather than self-love. It may not be easy to tell our kids, "It's okay to feel awkward because life *is* often awkward" or "The middle of the pack is where most people are; there's nothing wrong with not being the best," but it's honest. Knowing who we are, warts and wonders, is what authenticity is all about. It's one of the healthiest messages we can give kids. Authenticity is the true path to happiness, sexual and otherwise.

Just as I want to partner with parents to help kids achieve healthy sexuality, I want to partner with other professionals who are doing this as well. Cindy Pierce is certainly one of those people. She and I are both passionate about helping parents engage with young people in meaningful ways. We both have great respect for parents and great affection for kids. And we're both out there every day doing this good work.

In *Sexploitation*, Cindy casts a wide net, giving parents access to sound advice on everything from when to start talking to what to say about particular topics. Her book is incredibly well researched, and she calls upon a wide array of experts to enhance her own solid ideas about the best ways to help kids develop healthy sexuality. She confronts some of the scary realities of our time, like easy access to pornography and "hookup" culture, without being alarmist. She has no doubt that parents can talk about these topics with their kids, and she's got ideas about how to do that well. Her extensive experience talking with students means that her finger is on the pulse of what kids really think, want, and struggle with. She both challenges and encourages parents to be brave, to start talking, and to keep their eyes on the prize: helping their kids become sexually healthy adults.

I've written my own book for parents on how to talk with their kids about healthy sexuality, and here I am writing the foreword to a book that will compete with mine. Why would I do that? I'm doing it because when you truly believe in community and collaboration, when you give more than lip service to the idea that it takes a village to help parents raise sexually healthy kids, you join with others you admire and you lend your voice to theirs. I admire Cindy Pierce for many reasons: her good heart, her honesty, her tenacity, and her authenticity, among others. Our books don't replace one another, they complement one another.

Early in her book, Cindy talks about her "healthy crew." It's her "team of friends and role models who advise me about all aspects of life." I'm delighted to be a part of Cindy's healthy crew and to have her as a member of mine. I hope you'll join us in our efforts to help all kids move toward healthy sexuality. You as parents and trusted adults have a vital role to play. We want to help you do that. We're on the same team—allies not adversaries. Welcome to the village!

Al Vernacchio, MSEd
Sexuality educator, author, and speaker
Author of *For Goodness Sex: Changing the Way We Talk to Teens About Sexuality, Values, and Health*
www.alvernacchio.com

INTRODUCTION

Living in the digital age means that we inhabit a world where possibility expands continually. And while technological advances—and the cultural and social changes that accompany them—yield many amazing and positive things, they can also create a void inside us, an emptiness created by a lack of true human connection and by the myriad comparisons we're prone to make when we are bombarded daily by envy-inspiring images we see in conventional, new, and social media.

Young people today are confronted with alarming amounts of information, much of it coming from their online activities, and tamping down stress and anxiety as they manage the onslaught can be a daily challenge. Parents, educators, and coaches underestimate the amount of time and energy kids put into sifting through the distractions, and they also misjudge the worry kids feel as they manage their many tasks. While younger people are more practiced in dealing with technology, the nonstop input they receive as they juggle homework, school, music, language, religious commitments, dance, and athletics can be overwhelming. As parents, we may not encourage downtime for our kids because we fear they won't do all they need to do to succeed in today's competitive world, or that they will use their free time for unhealthy activities.

Filling our time—and teaching our kids to fill theirs—is the new norm. We all feel pressure to check our phones for texts, calls, posts, and e-mails between any and all of the day's activities—it's what we feel we need to do to stay apace socially and to keep up with obligations. But being constantly connected has reduced many of us to device addicts who feel the need to keep tabs on others and who must feed our own need to see who is paying attention to our online lives.

Developing deeper connections with our children means that we must find the courage to step into the void and have meaningful and ongoing conversations with them about all aspects of life—their feelings about school, friends, sports, busyness, and yes, about difficult topics like sexuality, drugs, and alcohol too. In order to impact our kids' personal choices as they go through life, we need to have conversations with them, ideally before they are exposed to media, peers, and the Internet. Even if you miss that window before they're influenced by friends and social media—or even if you wait until right before they go off to college or to live on their own—it's worth starting the conversation. Whenever you begin, you'll ensure that your perspective is one that they weigh as they make their decisions.

Parent education experts agree that teenagers wish they had more open communication with their parents. And while parents may wish for the same, many avoid talking with their kids about topics that may be awkward and instead try to connect by doing stuff for them. People convince themselves that good parents use their time making lunches, cooking meals, cleaning, and micromanaging their children's lives, even though their kids are capable of doing most of the tasks on their own.

My hope for this book is that it convinces you that your parenting time is better spent talking to your kids about all aspects of life and the influences that are, or will be, moving into their view as they grow up. By talking frankly with your kids about your opinions and beliefs, and by guiding them toward trusted resources when they have questions you need help answering, you'll give them the confidence to make healthy decisions based on a strong set of values they develop through experience, the influence of trusted adults, and exposure to accurate information. Helping them find their way means we should focus on our relationship with them rather than their messy room or unkempt hair. According to parent educator Vicki Hoefle, "If we want to raise thinking kids with the mental muscle to navigate an ever-changing world, then we have to provide them with daily opportunities to learn to construct a meaningful and satisfying life and teach them the skills necessary to manage that life."[1]

As parents, we say we want kids to play outside, but we feel hassled by the need to check up on them. We want kids off their screens, but the noise of fighting siblings or horseplay annoys us. We want kids to read and relax more, but then we can't help but remind them to get their homework done. We want our kids to have life skills, and we talk about how they should help in the kitchen and around the house, but we don't invest time in teaching them those skills, and we get impatient when they don't do things *just* the way we like them. We need to mean what we say—which means that we need to slow down and pay attention to our kids. Sorting through parents' mixed messages is exhausting for kids.

When you first start having difficult conversations with your children—especially talks about sexuality, drugs, and alcohol—you'll most likely feel awkward. The key is to keep having the conversations until both you and your kids have enough practice to get to the other side of awkward. Practice helps you develop the courage to keep at it and the resilience to endure even the most uncomfortable moments. Once you have established a connection that can withstand all flavors of awkward, your talks will get easier. Consider that making it through these conversations with you will contribute to your children's comfort when they have to address awkward topics with friends, coworkers, and sexual partners as they move through life. If you avoid tough conversations in your family, your kids will learn to avoid them outside your family. If we genuinely want our kids to be confident speaking up, challenging norms, and addressing difficult situations, we have to show them how that looks and that it is possible to recover even when the conversation doesn't go well. Taking risks, stumbling, and getting back in the game builds character and resilience.

I hope the awareness you gain from reading this book inspires you to dive right into conversations with your kids. Kids need to hear their parents talk about their values and beliefs regarding friendship, sex, homework, alcohol, drugs, relationships, conflict, extracurricular activities, and lots of other topics. My personal stories are included so you can see that being the primary sexuality educator for kids is messy, and that you can and will recover from the inevitable setbacks. I have included advice from the many mentors who have enlightened me along the way, in the hope that you will expand your understanding by reading their books and blogs, watching their TED Talks, and signing up for their newsletters. I believe the variety of insights confirms that we need to muster our courage, bust through doubt, and start those conversations with our kids. Information is power: being informed will help you develop the conviction to inform your kids. Know that your kids will likely resist your attempts to talk about uncomfortable topics, but if you hold to your belief in the long-term benefits and follow through, they will start to listen and respond. Give the gift of your example to other parents. Courage is contagious.

CHAPTER 1

Inner Compass

Children need to develop their capacity to engage in life. That's
how they develop resilience and self-motivation.
—Catherine Steiner-Adair, *The Big Disconnect: Protecting
Childhood and Family Relationships in the Digital Age*

Making healthy decisions requires listening to your heart, feeling
what is in your gut, knowing your own mind, and following your
instincts—when you do this, you are following your own inner compass,
keyed in to a guiding interior force that indicates the right direction for
you. Awareness, perspective, forethought, and reflection are more accessible when you are tapped into your inner compass, which helps you make
healthy choices and handle consequences.

Unfortunately, the number and type of influences young people are
managing in the digital age make it more challenging for them to listen
to their inner compass. Many young people have a hard time making the
distinction between what they value and what they think they *should* value,
based on what they see online and in social media. As a society, we have
reached a point where we need to actively teach kids and remind adults of
the value of slowing down, being alone, and paying attention to one another
and the world around us. Tapping into one's inner compass requires focus.

"Being present" and "staying in the moment" were once considered
swirly, hippie concepts but now are standard advice from medical doctors,
therapists, counselors, and life coaches. The fact that such a large number

of people suffer from physical and emotional health problems indicates that we are more unmoored than ever. People who feel out of balance in their lives have made meditation and yoga mainstream practices and fueled a booming self-help industry. Being caught up in the treadmill of life has led people to seek peace and harmony, search for a stronger sense of purpose, and take a step back to live in the moment. Teens are facing their own overwhelming versions of the treadmill. The many influences contributing to stress and pressure on kids as they enter their teens and grow to adulthood call for more direct guidance from the adults—parents, teachers, coaches, and others must step in and show them how to set priorities and maintain balance in their lives.

> "It took me a while to discover my own heart, but the pain of being disconnected from it was overwhelming and had obvious consequences. Fortunately, I learned to meditate with excellent guidance."
> —William Okin, Thacher School math teacher
> and practicing Buddhist

Parents struggle to reconcile the disparity between their own childhood social experience and their kids' experience, particularly with regard to screen time. Tuning in to one's inner compass was a much easier task before smartphones and social media. Life, choices, and relationships seemed simpler, because our access to our friends and to the wider network of acquaintances and friends' friends was more restricted, and we were less aware of what was going on in the lives of people who didn't go to our school or live in our neighborhoods. Our parents may have complained about how much TV we watched, even though we had a relatively limited number of channels and options, but Internet access and social media complicate the lives of kids today in ways that are making it difficult for us to know how to respond.

Finding My Own Inner Compass

As the youngest of seven children in a device-free age, I had the opportunity to observe a lot of the choices my siblings made and the consequences of those choices, both positive and negative. Initially, my parents attempted to shield the youngest of us from discipline situations and the relationship issues of the older kids, but it was impossible to contain the volume and emotional intensity of my siblings' interactions with our parents. Listening from the next room meant we only got part of the story, which was worse than the whole truth in some cases.

Our parents made an executive decision to invite us to the table of negotiation around the personal issues of our older siblings. It was a feast of learning about friendship, relationships, marriage, drug and alcohol use, academic challenges, and the importance of abiding by laws and following family rules. My parents made it clear to all of us that when we did something wrong, we had to pay the consequences in order to learn and grow. They viewed failures and setbacks as hidden gifts. In some cases, they pointed out explicitly all the lessons and positive aspects of difficult situations, but after seven kids, I can understand their need to move the process along. I remember one of my brothers sobbing after a difficult breakup with his longtime, live-in girlfriend. My parents processed with him for a while, but long before my brother was ready, they were exclaiming what a blessing it was that the relationship was over and how it was time to move on. Even at fifteen, I could tell he needed more time to cry.

By being present for these emotional conversations, I learned early on that finding one's way through life was an ongoing experience of setbacks, challenges, and adaptation. Witnessing the outcomes of my older siblings' decisions contributed to my own development of forethought, measure of risk, personal values, and strong inner compass.

The Void

With so many people spending so much time online and engaged in social media—with the relentless reminders, posts, and messages showing what could, should, or would be—we all have a broader view of other people's lives. It is not surprising that young people today experience deeper feelings of emptiness—of an internal void—than previous generations did. Knowledge of the specific details of other people's possessions and lifestyles can set an expectation and standard for anyone who spends a lot of time online or using social media. Intensive awareness of the many things that can be purchased, worn, seen, or done makes keeping up a constant scramble and can distance us from our own desires and thoughts. With so much stimulation readily available on phones, tablets, and computers, we are spending less time with our own thoughts and more time filling the void with technological input of one kind or another.

Boredom was once something people endured, and spent energy and creativity to move through. Now, people reach for a device at the first sign of restlessness and in the first moment of free time. Many college professors remark on what happens at the end of class now; instead of a murmur of conversation filling the room, silence remains, as students immediately zone in on their phones. When I ask college students what it would feel like to walk to their next class or back to the dorm without looking at their phone, "lonely" is a common response. A number of students readily admit that they have pretended to be reading texts while walking alone because they feel awkward otherwise.

When this tendency to focus on smartphones is brought up with young people, many are surprisingly willing to consider self-regulating their technology use. While young people rarely try to justify online communication as a healthy alternative to interacting face to face, they admit that the efficiency of communicating through devices is hard to resist or avoid. Catherine Steiner-Adair, author of *The Big Disconnect,* says, "With the infusion of computers, cell phones, and online activities at younger ages, elementary school also now has become the training ground for people relating to each other through tech. At a developmental time when children need to be learning how to effectively interact directly, the tech-mediated environment is not an adequate substitute for the human one."[1]

Screen Time, Texting, and Social Media

While social media connect people, spread inspiring stories, raise awareness about issues, and deepen genuine friendships, they can also breed envy and superficial connections. Social media will continue to evolve new forms of connection and sharing, and the social media platforms and apps in use today will ultimately go the way of MySpace, becoming irrelevant. Everything is hot until it is not. Facebook, Twitter, Yik Yak, Snapchat, and Instagram are used in varying degrees by different age groups and fluctuate in their popularity. Trends in use will continue to shift, and some of these popular sites will be substituted by new platforms, but most young people today, regardless of socioeconomic background, are using one, some, or all of these social media each day. Thirty years ago, kids felt pretty special if a handful of people considered them to be mildly interesting and called them on the phone occasionally. Imagine the pressure to be wildly interesting on a daily basis in multiple public forums that kids face today. Poring over other people's photos and posts can lead to feelings of inadequacy, jealousy, and resentment. A solid number of young people spend hours cultivating their image through posts and photos. Social media give people the opportunity to put their best face forward—and in some cases it's a completely false image. Many young people report that viewing their friends' feeds, with flattering photos and posts about their exciting lives and the fabulous places they visit, makes them feel boring, uninteresting, and pathetic sitting in their dorm room or family room in their sweatpants. People of all ages feel left out when they see posts about parties, events, or gatherings to which they were not invited. It is easy to get caught up in viewing for hours, reinforcing the warped perception that everyone else is having amazing and interesting lives.

"Two-Facebook" may be a more appropriate name for the ways some people use social media, however, and middle-aged people are just as likely as young people to present highly curated profiles, posting all the wonderful things going on in their lives, the successes of their children, and the kind deeds of their amazing spouses. If the "friends" actually *are* friends or acquaintances in real life, it doesn't take long to get a clear sense of who is authentic in their presentation. Within days of reading glowing posts, we read in the paper about the outstanding kid getting busted by the police or hear people griping about their spouses with a vengeance. Humans are complicated, with multiple dimensions, and have the capacity to be excellent people with flaws. Social media, however, isn't the venue in which our multidimensional selves, including our misgivings and foibles, are portrayed.

Texting

Texting is the way most young people communicate with a large number of friends and contacts. They pass information and interact with great frequency and at high speed. But texts, even when emojis and capital letters are used, fail to convey nuance, limiting texting as a reliable form of communication. People of all ages claim they avoid calling friends on the phone because the conversation would be "awkward." Reading social cues has become increasingly challenging for people who communicate on screens most of the time. Many people agree on the inappropriateness of texting to arrange a "hookup" with a stranger or to break up with someone, but these behaviors continue. In general, we have come to accept, as a society, that we will use these impersonal means to talk about personal issues and feelings.

Relationships of all kinds require people to read social cues by engaging with, listening to, and observing others, because we all communicate subtly through voice tone, eye contact, body language, and facial expressions. Beginning at a young age and continuing into adulthood, people need to practice reading these cues, and learning to negotiate disagreements and personal boundaries. Development of interpersonal skills begins in earnest when kids are three or four years old, when they attend preschool or have playdates and other social experiences. These environments give kids the opportunity to disagree, cooperate, negotiate, communicate, and resolve conflict. When computers became part of preschool classrooms, kids had less time interacting and working through conflict because they spent more time sitting in front of screens. There is a movement to remove computers from nursery schools because educators and psychologist are noticing changes in children's behavior and in their emotional well-being as a result of less time spent practicing their social skills.

> "After dinner, it was work time for all. When everyone was done with homework, one watched a movie with earbuds, one watched a show, and my husband goofed around on the computer. I suggested we all watch something together, but the kids wanted to do what they were doing—solo. It makes me sad."
> —Parent of two teenagers

According to a 2010 Kaiser Family Foundation study of kids ages eight to eighteen, kids spent an average of eight sedentary hours per day consuming media through a screen.[2] As technology has advanced over the past five years, this average is almost certainly increasing. Many experts agree that so much time devoted to screens is affecting children's physical health and attention span. Psychologist and author Dr. Aric Sigman claims that increased screen time is impacting kids on neurological, social, and physical levels, but that there is relatively little concern about these changes: "Perhaps because screen time is not a dangerous substance or a visibly risky activity, it has eluded the scrutiny that other health issues attract."[3] But some parents and schools are concerned, and are working to address the issue. Jenny Brundin of Colorado Public Radio reported on a Waldorf school in Denver that encouraged families to participate in a media fast for two weeks, and to follow the fast with a media diet. Brundin connects Waldorf founder Rudolf Steiner's idea that children think by creating mental pictures with her own observations of kids living in the digital age: "If those pictures are supplied ready-made—there's less opportunity to build the 'imaginative muscle.' It's based on this simple belief: technology is a tool. Introduced too early, it becomes a crutch, an addictive one at that."[4]

Graffiti in the Digital Age

I have noticed that there has been a drastic reduction in graffiti since texting, social media, and chat rooms have become part of daily life. Before the digital age, you could not drive your car by a bridge, walk around town, or use a public bathroom without being inundated with graffiti. Some graffiti authors signed their first names or initials, but typically their work was unsigned. A good amount of graffiti was boldly crude. Graffiti artists seemed to gain a sense of power from drawing or writing in places where many people would see their words, yet they didn't have to take responsibility. The common thread between writing graffiti, posting comments on social media, and engaging in online chats is anonymity, or at least a distance from the receiver of the message. People find a lot more courage to speak their minds in texts, in chat rooms, and on social media than they do when they are engaged in face-to-face conversations. There is emotional safety in writing from afar, because the reader can't respond immediately. When the writer presses "send," he just moves on.

Social skills are weakened and social courage is diminished when people depend on texts, posts, and e-mails to communicate. The sender does not have to take full responsibility for the reaction of the recipient because she does not witness it. If the recipient is hurt by a message or takes issue with it, she can respond with a text, also avoiding responsibility for how the message lands. In many cases, the recipient may feel hurt and want to think about her response; she may plan to tell the sender how she felt the next time they run into each other. But, even if the two see each other later that same day, the number of texts to and from other friends in the intervening time may make the upsetting text seem so long ago that it is truly awkward to confront the person. Everyone has moved on, because interactions are fast paced and topics shift quickly. Strong connections with other people and honest conversations about emotions may become casualties of the short attention spans that are the product of fast-moving virtual interactions.

Catherine Steiner-Adair, author of *The Big Disconnect,* makes the point that, in terms of content, texting for kids today is similar to meeting at the park for previous generations. She notes that the lack of depth in kids' texts is similar to the lack of depth in the conversation of a group of kids hanging out at a park. The difference is that kids who frequently spend time on a screen have less practice interacting face to face, and miss opportunities to develop strong social skills. Reading social cues takes practice. Noticing subtle shifts in body language, facial expression, and vocal tone is essential to effective communication. We talk to kids about how important it is to know that "no means no" and to be aware of a nonverbal "no," particularly in sexual situations. But if teens are missing these cues on Tuesday afternoon in broad daylight, how can we possibly expect them to pick up cues in the dark, in a state of optimistic arousal, and possibly under the influence of alcohol?

Sexual Disconnect

The tolerance for disconnected sex with unfamiliar partners is what the hookup scene is all about, and we'll go into this in more detail in chapter 10. Many young people consider communicating via social media and texts an acceptable way to get to know another person, and it is not uncommon for two people to hook up even though they've had very little face-to-face communication. Any kind of sexual encounter puts people in a position of vulnerability, both physically and emotionally. Sex can be awkward in the best of circumstances, and there is no app that can rescue us from the unease of being emotionally and physically naked with another person.

No matter how hard people work to justify hooking up with someone they don't know well, it is a recipe for a disconnected sexual experience. A healthy sexual encounter involves a strong connection between partners. Dr. Marty Klein, certified sex therapist and author of *Sexual Intelligence*, says, "I see an increasing number of people who don't feel comfortable doing one thing at a time anymore. And that's bad for sex. Because— assuming you're with someone you want to be with, and they're pleased to be with you—there's only (a few) things you actually need to enjoy sex: Focus. Attention. Engagement."[5] It has become a common idea that young people can't be encouraged to focus on and engage their attention on anything or anyone else for too long because they are busy with so many commitments. When I speak to groups of high school and college students about casual sex and the hookup scene, some of them ask questions about how to balance their desire to have sex with the fact that they don't want a committed relationship because they have such busy lives. I have heard junior high girls claim they couldn't possibly have sex in any sort of committed way because it will get the way of their desire for a career. This attitude that a meaningful relationship is incompatible with attaining other life goals contributes to the acceptance of hookups, and casual sex seems to have joined the list of extra-curriculars like sports, chess club, and the recycling committee.

Yik Yak Plus

Another way people keep emotional distance while engaging with others is by posting anonymously in chat rooms or through apps like Yik Yak. Posting and commenting when your identity is known requires courage. Today, however, there are many opportunities to post or comment anonymously. Several apps that make it possible to post abusive or hurtful comments without consequences are causing problems in high schools and colleges across the country.

Yik Yak is one example of an app that allows users to post comments anonymously. Often, the light-hearted and funny posts are taken too far and become malicious. Yik Yak is based on GPS location, so when a user logs in, he can read the many "yaks" of the people physically closest to him at the time. This makes the app a nightmare for schools, as students know that everyone who is yakking near them while they are at school is a classmate.

These types of platforms have led to an increase in anonymous harassment, accusations of rape and abuse, bomb threats, bullying, and racist and homophobic comments about specific people on campuses. Allegations of rape and abuse, as well as bomb threats, seem to be easier for schools to address than the cruelty and prejudices that undermine the sense of community. Anonymity seems to inspire users, particularly high school students, to unleash outrageously harsh posts and follow-up comments. One dean of an independent school said:

> The underlying issue that Yik Yak causes is paranoia. When you don't know who has written something terrible about you, it leaves you feeling alone and hated by everyone. You no longer want to go to class, and especially not the cafeteria for lunch. You feel like everyone is in on one big secret—except you. What I found most interesting about the situation was that students reading the app thought it was hilarious and say, "Come on, don't shut it down. It's all innocent fun." Minutes later when someone had yakked about them, they were the first to want to shut down the network, collect all student phones, and sign a petition to end Yik Yak altogether! It was wild to watch.

An alarming number of students jump right into the cruel exchanges, leading some school administrators to block the Yik Yak app on their campuses. Fortunately, Tyler Droll and Brooks Buffington, creators of the Yik Yak app, have responded in a responsible way in most cases. Because the app is GPS based and operates within a five-mile radius of the user, Yik Yak can set up a "geo-fence" that disables the app at schools that provide their coordinates. This tactic doesn't change what students do when they leave campus, but this blocking effort has reduced the issues on campuses where the administration has been proactive. Yik Yak is designed for people eighteen years of age or older, but colleges are facing many of the same issues that high schools are.

Boston College Addresses Anonymous Posting

The frequency of racist yaks around Boston College inspired the FACES Council—a committee dedicated to promoting appreciation of diversity at BC—to create a video to demonstrate the harmful effects of Yik Yak on campus. The video shows a series of students reading anonymous racist, sexist, homophobic, or disrespectful posts on their phones. After each person finishes, he or she looks directly at the camera for a silent moment to let the harshness of the yak sink in. The narrator ends by explaining, "Comments like these are the reason there are students at BC who are struggling to balance two cultures, struggling to maintain positive body image, and struggling to be comfortable with who they are...Yik Yak should be a red flag to the administration that there is a serious problem in the way students are being engaged in conversations about difference of race, sexual orientation, socioeconomic status, gender, and ability."[6]

The comments that follow the video online and the letter to the editor of *The Heights*, an independent student newspaper of Boston College that accompanied the video reveal a surprising mix of support for the message as well as dismissal and mockery of the message. Some students suggested that people who find comments offensive should stay off Yik Yak. Others made the point that Yik Yak is just one of many platforms used to express racist attitudes, and the racist yaks reveal that the campus is in need of more conversations about intolerance and bigotry. This kind of debate is going on in varying degrees on campuses everywhere, resulting in important conversations about respect and tolerance, as well as about freedom of speech and the responsibilities of different types of speech.

Advice on Using Anonymous Social Media

By Rachel Simmons, author of
Odd Girl Out: The Hidden Culture of Aggression in Girls

- When people post anonymously, there are no consequences or costs to what they do. People write things they would never say. They also lie, just because they can. They say things to get a rise out of other people visiting your page. You can't trust anonymous posters because you don't know their motive, or even who they are. Anonymity doesn't give people courage to say what they really think; it lets people say anything, true or false, which is why you can't trust it.

- By inviting people to say harmful things to you, and then reading and responding, you give them credit. No matter how clever a come-back you come up with, you make it seem like their words are worth responding to when you reply.

- You will never be someone who is 100 percent liked by everyone, so stop thinking you're going to be. This is why so many girls sign up for sites where people can comment on them; they believe they might be that person everyone loves. This is a useless waste of time. Focus on the relationships that bring you happiness and security, not people who tear you down. If you are worried about what other people think of you, ask the people you trust and who know you, not cowards who hide behind a cloak of anonymity to hurt you.[7]

Multitasking

Multitasking is the term people use to justify flying from task to task and device to device. People of all ages claim to be multitaskers. In an interview on NPR's *Talk of the Nation*, Clifford Nass, psychology professor at Stanford, said, "High multitaskers think of themselves as great at multitasking."[8] Research shows, however, that multitasking trains the brain to be more susceptible to distraction and causes the multitasker to lose the ability to focus. According to Nass's research, people who consider themselves "good at multitasking" are actually worse at it than those who are low multitaskers. The research offers a note of caution about what we see in the world: kids today are negotiating multiple devices from an early age.

According to a study conducted by Stephanie Englander of Bridgewater University for the Massachusetts Aggression Reduction Center, 83 percent of middle school students, 39 percent of fifth graders, and 20 percent of third graders have a mobile device.[9] Students of all ages sit down to write a paper on a computer or tablet with their phone on and multiple tabs open to social media sites, YouTube, e-mail, and homework. As they attempt to write a paper, they are also chatting online, reading and replying to texts, checking e-mails that pop up, seeing notifications from Facebook and

Twitter, and dealing with distracting ads in banners, sidebars, and pop-ups on their screens. For many, the temptation to engage continuously is difficult to resist. Yet most researchers agree that multitasking is not effective. Travis Bradberry, a psychologist and *Forbes* magazine contributor, summarized current research on the topic by saying, "Multitasking reduces your efficiency and performance because your brain can only focus on one thing at a time. When you try to do two things at once, your brain lacks the capacity to perform both tasks successfully."[10]

Not only is multitasking an unproductive way to work, it reinforces the tendency to be scattered in general. The implications for connection with others on social and sexual levels are unsettling. When young people interact, few of them listen to someone else complete a thought without looking at their phone, talking over the person, or losing interest in the conversation by drifting off or starting a new topic. The general lack of social patience among younger people is one result of the prevalence of one-sided communication—texting, tweeting, and posting.

Fear of missing out (FOMO) is also common in this fast-moving digital age. Multitasking to avoid missing out is leading to shorter attention spans. Kids are often gathered together but are actually connected to and engaged with a number of people who aren't present; they are in the habit of being at a distance together. We have all seen kids make a huge effort to get together with friends and then sit next to each other looking at their phones, interacting with other people. With my own kids, I just keep encouraging them to engage with the people who are with them. We discourage phones in the car. This means we have to endure arguments over which station will play on the radio and some recreational sibling bickering. For long road trips, we allow headphones, but an interesting audiobook or podcast will often catch their attention.

Surrendering to our kids' obsession with screen time is a mistake, even though it is the easiest thing to do. When kids don't have an opportunity to reflect and consider the impact of so much screen time, they will roll right into the habit of managing multiple devices, often at the same time. According to Steiner-Adair, kids "typically multitask on a computer, simultaneously instant messaging (IM), uploading YouTube videos, posting updates on Facebook, and continually searching the Web for fresh diversions. The so-called downtime they spend on computers is neurologically, psychologically, and often emotionally action packed. Stimulation, hyper-connectivity, and interactivity are, as the psychiatrist and creativity expert Gene Cohen put it, 'like chocolate to the brain.' We crave it."[11] If we are genuinely interested in our kids spending less time on their devices, we need to curb our own habit of multitasking and resist the temptation to stay in constant contact and check responses. We also need to keep having conversations with our kids about the benefits of taking a break from screen time.

Stuck with Yourself

When I was fifteen, I confessed to my mother that for the ten years she required me to attend church, I never listened to what the priest was talking about. Without hesitation, she responded, "That may be true, but you were also not watching TV, talking, playing, or running around. You were sitting still and in your own mind for an hour a week." Touché. There are fewer and fewer opportunities for any of us to be in our own minds for a stretch of time before our devices beckon us to engage. Author and psychotherapist Gunilla Norris teaches meditation and leads contemplative workshops, and summarizes the need to be in our own minds in this way: "Within each of us, there is a silence, a silence as vast as the universe. And when we experience that silence, we remember who we are."[12] We have a choice to stay unplugged when we are alone. We need to remind each other and ourselves to make that choice.

Unplugging from devices, action, outside influences, media, marketing, and obligations is important for people of all ages. Being able to hear your inner compass requires that you slow down and step away from the frenzy of pressures. Life serves up a lot of stress on its own. With the added intensity of input that comes with living in the digital age, parents need to actively seek opportunities to bring their pulses down and to remind children of specific ways to keep their lives balanced too.

CHAPTER 2

Unplugging

Being allowed to use a device or website can never be a simple "yes" or "no." As a child gets access to new privileges, it is not just to push buttons but to interact with others. There is a higher obligation to this sort of recreation, and a different measure of responsibility that must be met.

—Rachel Simmons, *Odd Girl Out:*
The Hidden Culture of Aggression in Girls

Parents are in a position to help their kids find their inner compass by helping them unplug and avoid the trap of constant digital multitasking. When faced with life decisions, major or minor, many young people feel hesitant and uncertain because they are so overwhelmed. For young adults, figuring out where to go to high school or college, what to study, where to live, which job to take, or what interests are worth pursuing can seem like impossible tasks—the stakes appear intensely high. Even when parents and educators aren't placing expectations on kids about these decisions, kids sometimes feel intense pressure because they have so much going on and are overly aware of the many options available to them. It is hard for kids to focus on what they really want or what feels right. Blocking out the noise around them—in both their immediate and their virtual environments—is difficult. With awareness and practice, however, they can improve their focus, become more relaxed, and learn to be happier.

Teaching Self-Regulation of Screen Time

As parents, we are our kids' primary source of information and their touch-stone for values surrounding sex, screen time, alcohol and drugs, friend-ship, and relationships of all kinds. Our ultimate goal should be to help our kids learn to self-regulate what they consume from our culture. The invisible world in which kids are engaging online without adult awareness is vast—they have increasing time without us around, and will be on their own before we know it. Just as we commit to conversations with our kids about sex, we need to develop the habit of ongoing conversations with our kids about why it is important for them to self-regulate and find a healthy balance of live time and screen time. Don't count on anything you say sinking in right away. During the few seconds your kid looks up to listen to you voice your frustration with the amount of time he spends looking at a screen, a number of his friends are waiting for responses to texts or posts. You are not alone in your irritation when your child goes right back to looking at his phone before you've even finished your sentence about limiting screen time. In all likelihood, the content of the text or post he couldn't resist is not even remotely urgent, interesting, or funny—at least to you.

Dr. Frances E. Jensen works in the Department of Neurology at the University of Pennsylvania Medical School and is the author of *The Teenage Brain: A Neuroscientist's Survival Guide to Raising Adolescents and Young Adults*. Jensen points out that the allure of the smartphone is clearly disrupting sleep patterns, and there is speculation that electronic distractions are changing brains. Experts wonder if people will adapt to these disruptions, but the evidence won't be in until the kids in this latest generation—who have used devices from babyhood—reach their thirties. When describing kids who spend a lot of time on devices, Jensen explains, "They are not mindful about how to manage this input."[1] Our kids need the benefit of our time and wisdom as they learn to manage a dual life of interacting through devices and in live time. Over time, more and more research will help us in guiding young people—who are pioneers in this new age of social media and rapidly advancing technology—in finding a healthy balance between real and virtual activities.

Shifting the amount of time kids spend connecting, keeping up, and obsessing on their devices can seem like a hopeless task, but your kids' viewpoints about screen-time guidelines may surprise you. First off, this conversation requires that both of you are offline and away from your devices. Like most adults, kids are not particularly aware of how easily they get sucked into chats, videos, photos, and iFunny stuff. The limits kids offer up regarding daily consumption don't seem to correlate with their apparent desperation to plug into a device at every free moment. It almost seems that they secretly hope for restrictions dictated by someone else. Your aim in these conversations, however, is to start building the awareness that will lead to self-regulation. Modeling self-regulation is a good start. Establish clear guidelines about when and where it is appropriate to turn off or put away your phone, and be sure adults follow those guidelines strictly. Keeping devices downstairs and turning them off during meals and conversations is a great way to set expectations and teach kids to value time together as a family and without access to devices.

> "We have had some battles and some great conversations about our values around technology. Just keep talking about it—sharing how it makes you feel and what you notice. It is so easy to give in and let them do what they want. I have noticed a battle doesn't color the mood of the house. Kids gripe and move on. It is worth pushing our point. This is why kids have parents!"
>
> —Parent of two kids

Monitoring Devices

Promoting self-regulation to your kids takes time and the ability to focus on the ultimate goal rather than on single events like the recent sketchy post made by your kid. There is a wide range of advice about how to ensure your kids are good digital citizens, but at the minimum parents should tune in to be sure their kids are not bullying, being bullied, sexting, or being otherwise inappropriate on their devices. Expert advice varies, from insisting kids share all their passwords to a more trusting approach involving ongoing, proactive conversations—there is no proven approach that guarantees a positive outcome.

We all know parents who spend hours scrolling through their kids' texts, and snooping, checking up on, and fretting about their kids' virtual lives. Kids have figured out how to elude their parents with alternative accounts and coded language in their posts. For example, girls whose parents have forbidden them to ask people to rate their bikini photos decide on a word or unrelated emoji to signal that they want a rating. If you figure out their code system, they will come up with another. That is a battle you can't really win, and it undermines your chances of developing a trusting, open relationship. Plus, you have better things to do with your time.

Vicki Hoefle, parent educator and author of *Duct Tape Parenting: A Less Is More Approach to Raising Respectful, Responsible, and Resilient Kids,* recommends an approach that our whole family agreed was fair. It requires some faith and the ability to invest in long-term outcomes; it also means we have to let our kids make some mistakes online. But when kids get feedback from peers and from trusted adults after making a few benign mistakes, they begin to learn good digital citizenship. Rather than trying to stamp out any trouble before it begins, my husband and I let the natural consequences of smaller mistakes guide and inform our kids. We agreed on a plan to occasionally ask to view our high school kids' Facebook pages, Snapchat accounts, texts, and e-mail exchanges. They have the right to say no. We respect their decision, but then we have a discussion about why our viewing their posts or exchanges would make them uncomfortable. If they say yes, we can have access and promise to not react strongly, yell, or scold. If we see anything we find inappropriate, we quell our immediate reaction and take a few deep breaths before following up with a conversation about our objections. With this approach, whether the kids say yes or no to their parents' viewing of their accounts, parents learn a lot about their kids' online lives.

It is important to have conversations about the fine line between funny and disrespectful posts, comments, and photos. Many adults think they can deter kids from posting anything dicey by telling them that colleges and future employers will have access to these posts, and inappropriate content may affect whether they are accepted to a school or hired for a position. While it is worth mentioning, remember that teenage brains are not famous for their forethought in these matters. It is difficult to get teenagers to absorb what we know as truth about the life-changing consequences of online behavior. They are impulsive by nature. When teenagers get caught up in a moment, they can't resist sharing or venting, or they may feel a need to be included. Plenty of opportunities for discussion about specific examples of inappropriate online behavior will show up in the news, at your kids' schools, or in the community where you live. When you hear about a conflict between friends, in your children's school, or in another town that occurred because of a hurtful post or comment, ask your kids what they think about it: "How do you think you or your friends would handle this?" or "What would you say to support a friend in this situation?" or "What would have contributed to a different outcome?" Use these situations to help kids reflect and connect the dots over time.

These conversations give kids a chance to look at their online behavior through the lens of their parents' values, and may inspire them to reflect before they press send or post the next time. This approach requires energy and time, and will likely lead to some discomfort and possible disagreements, but if you avoid the tendency to become authoritative and controlling you will contribute to the long-term goal of helping your kids making healthier choices as they move forward. Demanding, yelling, and confiscating devices can feel like an immediate and impactful solution, but it almost always erodes respect and trust. Rein in your concerns about how your own image is impacted by your child's mistakes if you are alerted by the school or other parents to something your kid has posted. If we are genuinely interested in helping kids develop judgment and demonstrate the ability to reflect on their choices, we parents need to engage kids in calm, proactive conversations.

Let Them Find Their Way

The documentary film *The Race to Nowhere: The Dark Side of America's Achievement Culture*, which explores the relentless pressure on kids to "succeed," resonates with educators and parents across the country, yet the race goes on. According to the film's website, "Through the testimony of educators, parents and education experts, [the film] reveals an education system in which cheating has become commonplace; students have become disengaged; stress-related illness, depression and burnout are rampant; and young people arrive at college and the workplace unprepared and uninspired."[2] In addition to this film, there is a vast number of articles, books, blogs, and news stories about teenagers with anxiety, all of which point to the problem of kids feeling overwhelmed by expectations surrounding academic, social, and personal achievement.

The pressure for kids to succeed has driven parents to overbook their kids with multiple extracurricular activities. The compulsion to build résumés for college applications and work to increase kids' chances all around seem to have driven this generation of parents and kids to the extreme. Guidance counselors and therapists struggle to help parents find balance when they push to get their child into a prestigious school, sometimes

---

A High School Guidance Counselor's Perspective

Many well-meaning parents get themselves way too involved in their students' education, social life, and future path. Often, parents work hard to bail their kids out and minimize any consequences when their kids get caught making poor decisions such as cheating, drinking, or driving violations. How is that helpful to a child's development, if they learn that you shouldn't own up to your mistakes, and that there is a way out of consequences? That not only fails the individual, but also our society as a whole.

Parents say, "We do not care about our son getting straight As or going to a prestigious college, we just want him to be happy," but their actions and attitudes say something very different. It is hard to resist getting caught up in participating in multiple sports camps each summer, taking expensive enrichment trips, taking test prep courses, etc. Families feel that in order to be competitive they need to keep up with everyone else doing these things.

Schools might be partly to blame in this "overscheduled" world as well. The commitment required for kids to play a sport, participate in the school play, and be a member of the debate team, etc. is excessive. If a student makes a commitment to be a part of a school team/club/group, that often means sacrificing school vacation time (family vacations), weekends, and of course, afternoons and evenings spent together. Because schools want their teams/groups to be competitive with other schools, they need to increase practice time because that is what the other schools are doing, and the cycle feeds on itself.

overlooking red flag behaviors or states associated with anxiety and stress, such as cheating, disordered eating, cutting, depression, or suicidal tendencies. The intense pressure for kids to be exceptional has caused parents to lose perspective on what will help their children become happy, productive members of society. Having average kids is not enough for many parents, even though much of the research shows that people who are ordinary and well-rounded often lead happier lives than those who are driven to be exceptional.

Helicopter parents are one thing, but a good number have reached a level where they've become copilot parents. These parents aren't just hovering—now they are climbing into the cockpit with their kid, determined to help take off, fly, and land. They exercise increasing control over many aspects of their child's life: writing college application essays, finding their child a summer job, deciding what foods he should eat, choosing his clothing, and communicating with teachers and friends on behalf of the child.

These parents can't help themselves, despite the feedback they receive from their kids, teachers, friends, and articles about parents like them. From the perspective of parents who grew up before the Internet, the world seems overwhelming and difficult to navigate, a thought that can drive them to attempt to remove speed bumps for their children. These parents have good intentions, but their desire for short-term solutions could result in long-term disaster. Doing too much for kids interferes with their opportunity to learn from mistakes and thus diminishes their chances of become capable and responsible adults. Copilot parents go beyond enabling, to the point of disabling their children by taking over the controls and ensuring that their children avoid normal, healthy failures and challenges.

One glaring example of copilot parenting came from a coach at a boarding school and concerns a particular parent who tracks his child's phone from a thousand miles away. As the coach was driving a van full of athletes to a competition, a fifteen-year-old kid yelled from the back seat, "My dad just texted me to say you missed the exit for the shortcut, and you are driving ten miles per hour over the speed limit." Clearly, the kid didn't find this to be outside the norm for his dad. The same child told his coach that he'd once left his phone in his hotel room for a day, and his mom called his coaches because she thought he'd slept through his alarm, or worse... maybe he was no longer breathing.

Coaches and educators who hear this story shake their heads and smile

in recognition of what they have to deal with every day with overbear-
ing parents who are unable to let their children live their own lives and
solve their own problems. A parent who meddles at that level justifies the
texts and calls as concern for his child's safety and as reinforcement of the
importance of being punctual. But parents like this send the message that
their children are not capable or responsible. Without opportunities to figure things out on their own, it is no wonder we have a generation of kids
who are plagued with self-doubt, angst, and insecurity.

Vicki Hoefle, parent educator and author of *Duct Tape Parenting,* sums
up what is lost when parents become overinvested in their children's "success": "Life with kids is about accepting that kids and parents make mistakes, and mistakes make all of us look a bit messy around the edges. And
yes, it's true that showing up for life and all it has to offer can sometimes
expose our flaws to the world. It also offers parents a chance to teach their
kids about resilience, acceptance, and choosing family over an image."[3]

The Emotional Cost

A number of studies point to the fact that many teenagers are depressed,
overwhelmed, stressed out, and troubled by feelings of inadequacy. A common parental response is to fill their child's void with new stuff, such as the
latest phone or tablet, another pair of expensive boots, more video games,
or new clothes. Buying things for kids can seem like a quick fix; it's tempt-
ing to try to help kids avoid difficulty and ease their discomfort. But when
parents reward kids who seem stressed and overwhelmed with stuff, they
may inadvertently create a cycle that discourages kids from managing their
feelings of stress.

The buzz of new stuff is short-lived, but the burst of elation it brings
at first gives a false sense of happiness and can inspire cravings for more.
Filling voids with stuff does not build lasting connection or genuine happiness, however. Roko Belic, director of the documentary film *Happy,* spent
six years working on the film: "One of the leading researchers of happiness
in the world, Ed Diener, told me that a person's values are among the best
predictors of their happiness. People who value money, power, fame and
good looks are less likely to be happy."[4]

Overwhelming Choices

Grounding ourselves and tuning in to our inner compass requires that we pay attention to what distracts us. An array of choices is a luxury, but if we have too many options, life can be overwhelming. Exploring the Internet, for example, can consume hours of people's time as they look at their many options, such as resources for a project, TV shows and movies, airline tickets, ideas for ways to complete a task, and items to buy. Shopping online involves weighing a lot of factors before making a purchase, but shopping in a brick-and-mortar store can also be daunting. Think about the variety of apples available in stores these days. Back in the day, we could buy a McIntosh or a Red Delicious apple, with the occasional Granny Smith showing up for a few weeks a year. These days, grocery stores have a book in the produce department that guides customers in choosing and using the many varieties of apples available. Buying a pen in an office supply store can turn into a half-hour project, even if you went in aiming for a basic blue pen. When you finally narrow your choice down to one brand, the options within that brand add another layer of decision making: "Do I want the twenty-four-pack, the two-pack with the free compass, or the single pen that seems really expensive—but I'm too overwhelmed to do the math, and those sticky pads next to the pens look pretty cool." With all the decisions young people have to make about their academics, athletics, and extracurricular activities, deciding on what kind of apple or pen they want only adds to their subconscious clutter. The Internet has expanded the possibilities for everything we want, need, or think we need, but it also drains our energy, time, and brain space.

Acknowledging overwhelming choices ourselves and discussing this fact of modern life with our kids allows them to start developing the filters they need to sort through the many options. Encourage kids to make choices without exploring every option in stores and online; the search for products of any kind can become an endless comparison. Narrow the circle of options you present to them when they are young, and as they grow, remind them to practice narrowing to reasonable options on their own. Acknowledging the factors that clutter our lives helps kids identify the clutter in their own lives.

In a *Fresh Air* interview, Dr. Frances E. Jensen, a neurologist and expert on brain development, confirmed our need to examine the way we engage with information and input. Host Terry Gross asked Jensen to address the fact that people are overwhelmed by constant streams of information yet also crave it.[5] According to Jensen, medical education started taking a different approach to learning a few decades ago. Because there are too many facts to memorize during medical school, students are being taught efficient ways "to access information rather than absorbing, digesting, and ingraining that information . . . (doctors) cannot possibly stay up to date by memorizing everything. . . . Students are developing the skill of scanning and also validating information sources and knowing where to go when."[6]

Relaxation and Meditation

I was a student athlete in the 1970s and 1980s, so it was probably inevitable that I would have a hippie as a coach somewhere along the line. Yoga's current ubiquity makes this hard to believe, but it was not even close to commonplace at that time. I remember hearing from friends and parents who happened to drive by the field where the ski team worked out and spot our team doing yoga poses led by our coach. This was followed by some guided meditation. We mocked the yoga, cringed as horns of passing cars beeped at us, and shook our heads about what a waste of time it was to be doing yoga. Our coach was a man ahead of his time, as he had us stretch thoroughly, slowing down and paying attention to our bodies. As a college ski racer, I reached a point when it was necessary for me to incorporate mindfulness in order to stay focused, and I found myself conjuring up the exercises and wisdom from my old coach.

It likely won't be long before mindfulness and breath work are incorporated into family life and school curricula to help kids manage all the input and counter the stress they face. We know these practices are helpful, yet we continue hustling to keep up with life. When I taught first grade, I periodically led my students in guided relaxation and mindfulness exercises. Kids have open minds and enjoy trying new things. I incorporated exercises from a variety of sources, including my yoga instructor, a psychologist who helped me with my fear of the dark, Jon Kabat-Zinn's books, my father-in-law, who was a counselor, and my hippie high school ski coach. My students would always ask to do more "relaxation," and twenty minutes here and there helped recharge the students' focus as we moved through the day. If I taught now, I would do it every day. Sometimes I lead my own kids through some of these exercises at bedtime, and they love it. Ironically, our lives are so hectic we don't have time to do it often. But if we teach kids relaxation exercises and help them internalize the process, they will be able to use them on their own to relax for athletic competitions, academic challenges, sleep, and overwhelming situations.

Clinical social worker and therapist Lisa M. Schab, who has written books to help children, teens, and adults find healthy inner anchors, suggests incorporating mindfulness techniques and practices into everyday life because kids need help managing stress more than ever. She explains:

> While everyone experiences anxiety, some of us feel it more often, some more deeply, some less frequently, and some less intensely. Your own experience will depend on: Genetics—how your parents, grandparents, and ancestors experienced anxiety; Brain chemistry— the type, amount, and movement of the chemicals working in your brain; Life events—the situations you are faced with in your life; and personality—how you look at and interpret things that happen to you.[7]

Schab goes on to emphasize that your "personality, or the way you perceive and handle life events, is something you have a great deal of control over—probably more than you realize." With self-awareness about our own personalities, we can adjust and develop strategies to compensate for tendencies that create stress in our lives. As a high-strung, impulsive person, driving in traffic or bad weather causes me to be on edge and hyperreactive. Since my kids were little, I would turn the car radio off and ask them to quiet down for a bit until we got through traffic or I could get into a groove driving in the weather. Because I openly admitted that my personality limited me in certain situations, they responded with understanding and complied with my requests. They witnessed and now remind me of strategies that help me work around the common snags in my life, including deep breathing and relaxation. Over the years, they have become aware of their own traits and are developing strategies and relaxation techniques that work for them. Exposing kids to meditation and mindfulness exercises gives them more independence and techniques to manage stress and anxiety on their own. Meditation helps us understand ourselves better and lets us tap into our inner compass.

Social Courage

Practicing nonconformity is something we should all encourage in our kids, starting when they are young. Kids need to experience doing their own thing, being comfortable saying no when it is appropriate, contradicting the kids who use their social power in negative ways, and wearing clothes or colors that aren't considered cool. The sooner kids can liberate themselves from the expectations and pressures of others and follow their own inner compass, the more socially comfortable they will be in the long run.

Most of us learn to stop caring about the opinions of the crowd eventually, but until we make a conscious choice to disengage from peer pressure, it can feel like seventh grade never ends. Many people assume that peer pressure will ease when they leave middle school or that it will definitely stop when they become adults. If we want our kids to be strong, independent, and comfortable in their own skin, we need to start modeling independence for them when they are young.

These days, kids are constantly being reminded to avoid bystander apathy. Parents, educators, and coaches talk to them about how they should stand up to bullying, hazing, homophobia, racism, and cruelty. But it's unrealistic to expect most kids to immediately muster the strength and risk social rejection by calling peers out. They need practice speaking up on small issues (litter, disrespectful language, meanness, intimidation) in order to develop the courage to stand up when the stakes are higher (sexual assault, hazing, DUI). As parents, we can demonstrate social courage by establishing clear boundaries, showing we are comfortable being different, and speaking up when people are unkind.

Parents' Screen Time

It is also important for parents to regulate their own screen time. As the adults who provide for and organize the family, we may find it easy to justify our own screen time for work or our social lives, and for recreational distraction from our busy lives. We have all been in the position of telling our kids to close the laptop or put away their phones while sitting behind a screen of our own. The hypocrisy and mixed message is clear to kids of any age.

And when parents spend inordinate amounts of time looking at their smartphones or tablets, kids quickly get the idea that whatever is on that screen is more interesting and important than engaging with them. Parents claim their kids are busy with their own lives and aren't interested in talking to them anyway. They also complain endlessly about how sad they are that their kids spend so much time on devices, but somehow they feel that their own time spent on devices is important and appropriate. Sometimes we think our own busyness is more important than the busyness of others.

> "In order to be together as a family, we have to do things outside of home. Our kids are making their way into adulthood as productive workers, independent occupiers of their own time, and making their own choices—and no matter how we slice that, it is going to include the screen at times. It takes effort to balance screen time with family time."
> —Parent of three teenagers

Parents fall easily into the habit of letting their young children play with their phones and iPads. Kids stay still and quiet when playing with a device, and it is particularly easy to engage them with a device on which their parents are so dependent. They are curious about what is so interesting. I hear parents justify bonding with kids while using a phone as a way of preparing their kids for the digital age. Kids don't actually need training in this area. Their brains are still developing and they are wired to learn new things with ease. It is much more challenging for us as adults to learn to use apps, new devices, and updated programs than it is for kids. Some parents are delighted to see how quickly their kids pick up new technology, but even the most technologically deprived kid by today's standards can quickly adapt and learn how to use devices. As parents, rather than interacting with our kids by playing with technology together, we should practice turning devices off and working to build stronger connections by talking and playing face to face.

Our Family Balance

My husband, Bruce, and I made the rule that computers and phones stay downstairs and out of the kids' rooms. We don't take credit for their full acceptance of this non-negotiable rule—we assume they hear it as a recommendation by their school and see it as widely accepted by other parents. As more research comes out and guidelines are understood and accepted by parents, it is easier to engage kids and develop family technology rules that help everyone in the house find balance. Before his homework required computer time, one of our kids was always "checking the weather" on the computer. And he was, but that would lead to other links and related videos, and then to unrelated videos. Amazing how a nor'easter can lead to a sketchy video.

Screen time is unavoidable for most kids. Sometimes teachers assign YouTube video clips of instructions or educational documentaries. Homework that must be done on a computer means our kids can easily drift to the other interesting links that are dancing around the edge of what they have been assigned to watch. We could spend our whole evening monitoring what they watch, but that won't prepare them to regulate their own screen time when we aren't around. As a family, we agreed that thirty minutes of recreational computer time is acceptable for school nights, after homework and their cleaning contributions have been completed. There are times when they push the limit and take advantage of us being out or busy, but they don't resist or disagree when we have conversations about it. It is important to keep offering to take a walk together, play a game, or do a project. After you offer for seven days in a row, they may take you up on it.

"Both the social pull and more intense homework require Internet time. When we are all on our own island, I like to have an archipelago where I can see another island from my island; one couch to another couch. We quote Rudolph when he and Herbie [sic] meet up in the woods for the first time as being 'independent together.' Perhaps being together in one area helps us feel the closeness we crave. We balance the screen time with making bread together, talking over tea by the woodstove, or doing a project."

—Parent of two teenagers

You may be frustrated because the kids keep getting lured back into a show or "homework" on the computer despite ongoing conversations about screen time, but keep discussing the impact of screen time. What surprises me most is that clear expectations and boundaries seem to give kids comfort—they know that we are paying attention. They know what we value because they hear us talk about it. If we just shake our heads and seem irritated, they don't know what's going on—they can't read our minds. Keep talking about what you value and why. The payoff may not show up until the kids have moved out of the house, but keep talking.

We talk to our kids about balancing screen time with getting outside, reading a book, creating something, or interacting with others without a device. Because they are athletes, they generally get plenty of exercise and time outside. When our older kids first got phones, they were reading less than usual, but this eased once the novelty of the new phone wore off. They are allowed to watch online TV shows on weekends, and under special circumstances they can watch a show during the week. On a cold or rainy weekend afternoon or evening, the screen time can unravel into hours on the couch. Because we have kept the conversation going, they consider our input and usually respond in a somewhat reasonable way even if they disagree. We have a lot of discussions about balance. Visiting other homes and observing their friends' relationships with screens both helps and works against our efforts. They feel like they are deprived compared to almost all of their friends, but they also notice that a lot of their friends waste hours looking at screens.

I have noticed teenagers engaging on their phone as a default and space filler when they are sitting around with a group of friends, teammates, or classmates. Kids pull their phones out to check messages from parents, because they are bored, or because they want to avoid the appearance of not having friends. If one kid checks her phone, the others do too. Sometimes kids use the content of a text, video, or photo to start a conversation with the group of kids sitting around. They also use the phone to pull away but remain sitting with the group. Either way, most of the kids will take out their phones, which creates the paradox of being apart and together—a new norm for groups of kids and families. If a couple of kids in the group put their phones away, it is more likely that others will follow suit and reengage with the group. These patterns of phone use in groups seem to be accepted and occur with very little or no discussion.

Cornerstone Reputation

Kids often learn digital citizenship when they make mistakes or observe the mistakes of others. Educators and parents get frustrated with the way kids behave online, and with the fact that kids don't seem to absorb the message that everything they put out there in e-mails, posts, texts, or tweets could come back to haunt them. As the digital world has gotten more complex, the need to teach teens to be safer and smarter online has risen.

Educational company Cornerstone Reputation seeks to meet this need by offering individual services, educational presentations, and workshops at schools, colleges, and businesses about how to build a powerful online "digital trail." Cornerstone Reputation encourages people to be more positive and intentional with their online content and with the time they spend online. They provide several different services, including a report called the Comprehensive Online Readiness Assessment (CORA) score for high school, college, and graduate students, as well as for people switching careers. The results provide a quantified score of a person's online presence, enabling him to have a clear idea of how his online footprint could be viewed by admissions departments or potential employers.

In their presentations and workshops, the creators of Cornerstone Reputation share anecdotes about how online behavior impacted candidates for jobs, schools, and colleges, and gets students started on the process of cleaning up their online content while finding ways to be more authentic, positive, and intentional with their online activity. When describing the kinds of posts that have caused people to miss opportunities, they remind audience members that nothing is anonymous and that there is no such thing as "delete." Potential employers and admissions offices can often get full access to social media accounts to get a sense of applicants. Sarah Shea, vice president of educational development, explains, "Think of what you put out online as a tattoo. It is that permanent." The Cornerstone Reputation website provides links to extensive resources for parents, educators, and students of all ages.

Tips on Encouraging Digital Citizenship

By Sarah Shea, vice president of educational
development at Cornerstone Reputation

The technology that teens have access to is not only ubiquitous, it has utterly changed the way teens (and adults for that matter!) socialize. The majority of a teen's social life happens virtually; conversation points and inside jokes stem from who posted what, did what, and read or saw what online. Policing teens' online behavior and usage is not only futile, it can create backlash and tension in the house and a communication shutdown in the parent–child dynamic.

Now, that's not to say ground rules and expectations shouldn't be established for technology in the home, in school, in the car, etc.; they absolutely should! It also must be expected that teens will inevitably break some of these rules. In the way that we understand underage drinking happens, so too will bad online behavior. However, the wisest of parents understands that the best solution to manage something as scary as teen drinking is to educate children, empower them to make the best decisions in tough situations, and ensure they know what to do and who to turn to if they or their friends make a poor decision.

Teen technology use should be approached in the same manner. It is inevitable that a teenager will make some bad choices online. Rather than shame them and shut down conversation, equip them with the right information and motivation to enable them to minimize bad decisions, know what to do when mistakes are made or witnessed, and feel supported if and when hard conversations need to be had with an adult in their life.

Parents need to adjust the content of the conversations they have with their kids as technology advances and social media changes. Being proactive with guidelines and information while also allowing kids to make and learn from mistakes is a challenging balance that requires both our attention and our trust. Educating ourselves is a key part of this process. As you learn about what kids have access to online, you may feel overwhelmed and fearful. Becoming aware of what kids are doing and seeing online can inspire parents to want to move far away from anyplace that has Wi-Fi. Though it may be challenging to accept that your kids are exposed to so much you can't necessarily control, or even see, I am inviting you to get informed and get ready for conversations with your kids—these are ultimately your best weapons in preparing them for the complicated digital world they inhabit.

CHAPTER 3

Porn Culture

30% of all the data transferred across the Internet is porn. Internet porn sites get more visitors each month than Netflix, Amazon and Twitter combined.

—*The Huffington Post*, May 4, 2013

As a college speaker, I've learned that nearly all the guys I speak to have been viewing porn with some regularity since they were in middle school. In fact, it is so rare to find one who hasn't that those few fellas who don't look at porn gain underground fame among their guy friends. When I speak to all-male groups, some of the young men will occasionally brag about the one guy in the room who masturbates without porn. The guy is usually pretty open because he is already accustomed to being a human study of his male peers and relishes his countercultural role. In interviews with each of these guys, I usually learn that he is from a very rural part of the country where he had dial-up Internet until he was well into high school, and streaming issues kept him from developing the habit of looking at Internet porn. Once in a while I meet guys who just chose to not start looking at porn.

College guys describe the increase in their online porn habit as the result of dependable Internet access and time alone when their roommates are at class. When I first spoke to fraternities, teams, or all-male college groups about porn use, I was surprised by how open they were. My success in engaging these guys came because I stood outside the realm of their social, academic, and family lives, and I didn't scold or judge them. It turns out that young men will share almost all of their doubts, vulnerabilities, or questions about sex with a nonjudgmental, informative auntie-like figure who isn't fazed.

I was enlightened to a pattern of heavy porn use among guys who were lacking a lot of key sexual knowledge, despite having plenty of sexual experience. My conversations with them offered me an opportunity to relieve the angst of at least the heterosexual men by providing them with accurate information about what their female peers were saying they did and didn't enjoy about sex. While a much smaller percentage of young women view porn regularly, most are well aware of what their male peers are viewing and a good number of them believe they are expected to engage in the activities and behaviors found in porn.

Heterosexual guys express a lot of surprise and confusion about sexual acts that some female partners ask for, offer, and claim to enjoy. A good number of guys admit that they are just grateful for the opportunity to be naked with a willing partner, and they are therefore nowhere near as selective as they are often expected to be. One guy in a group said if he were asked to dress up as the Easter Bunny to get laid, he would do it. The rest of the guys laughed and nodded in agreement. Many of the stories I hear from young people indicate that some young women feel the need to compete with porn rather than follow their own desires. Some girls offer to perform sexual acts just because they think it is expected. Honest communication among partners about their expectations is not common, and the perception of what is "hot" drives a whole lot of sexual behavior that isn't necessarily satisfying for either partner.

"When porn becomes the only exposure you have to sex and sexuality from the time you are a prepubescent boy to when you have your first partner, it's going to really shape what you think about sex. There are a lot of unfair expectations associated with porn and some that are just simply unrealistic. My partner expected me to expect her to be a porn star, so at times I think she tried to act like it to fill the part. It was this cycle of acting on expectations."

—Male, age nineteen

Porn culture is not limited to online videos: pornographic images show up with regularity in advertisements, music videos, and video games. As a culture, we are desensitized by what we regularly consume passively and by choice. The connotations and underlying sexual messages that appear in a wide variety of contexts only become apparent and unsettling when presented in a way that commands the viewer to look and listen more closely. Communications professor Sut Jhally is the writer, narrator, and producer of the documentary series *Dreamworlds: Desire, Sex, and Power in Music Videos* which offers a powerful wake-up call for viewers. Video clips of familiar artists shown one after another provide a powerful example of just one medium through which porn culture infiltrates the lives of young people. Online porn represents a very concentrated dose of images that people are able to view privately without any demand for reflection on the messages conveyed in the videos. These days, almost all kids in the United States can access online porn.

Most guys about thirty-five and younger had full access to Internet porn when they became teenagers. While parents and educators have been busy respecting the private masturbation habits of boys, Internet porn has taken over as the primary source of their masturbation fuel and sexuality education. Internet porn is easily accessible and irresistible for many boys, who are more inclined than girls to respond to visual stimuli. The fact that we are living in a dichotomous age of hypersexualization and sexual repression has delayed honest conversations about the impact of online porn. Years ago, I approached several experts on boys to suggest that they broach the topic in articles or in a book, but I found that they were almost as naïve about the issue as most parents were at that time.

While a wide variety of lesbian porn is available, much of what is accessible is directed toward heterosexual men who want to see lesbian porn. There isn't enough demand for lesbian porn by gay women or enough gay women producing porn to shift the focus. Some gay women point to how the misleading aspects of porn can cause them to feel pressure to conform to heterosexual culture; for example, some report that they are frustrated that the culture of heterosexual porn has reinforced a trend toward shaving pubic hair, though others say they don't feel pressured either way.

Gay men are much less concerned, in general, about the impact of porn on relationships than gay women are. The casual shrugs and unself-conscious laughter in response to questions about porn use among gay men of all ages indicates a general acceptance of porn, but there is some frustration about stereotypes in porn.

"While porn has given me space to discover and identify my own sexuality by putting words to feelings, and terms to activities, the ways in which it was presented to me were problematic. Porn is presented to a gay male audience in a very heteronormative way (or maybe to a men-seeking-men audience, as there are many people who are interested in guys but refuse the label 'gay'). It is considered hotter if a gay guy hooks up with a straight guy rather than another gay guy. The idolization of the masculine straight man in gay porn makes the gay man inherently less masculine/more effeminate. For me, this creates tension between masculinity and sexuality. Most gay porn involves two young, white, masculine guys with large penises. If it's any sort of interracial or multiracial porn, it's labeled as black 'thugs' or Hispanic 'papis' etc. I see this intolerance as coming from *within* the gay community."

—Male, age twenty

Porn can be an obstacle that prevents kids from developing healthy ideas about sex for a number of reasons: while porn objectifies both men and women, most of what is viewed degrades women, reinforces role expectations, desensitizes the viewer to violent sexual behavior, creates expectations about how bodies appear and respond, and skews overall sexual expectations. Rather than trying to stop the porn industry, my aim is to inspire parents to have open conversations with their kids about porn. Given more information, kids may become more selective about what they watch, more willing to self-regulate their consumption of porn, and able to seek better sources for answers to their questions about sex.

From Stashing Magazines to "Doing Homework"

While masturbation is healthy and normal for men, women, boys, and girls, it is much accepted and encouraged among boys and men. Evolution requires boys and men to keep their sperm fresh, therefore masturbation is difficult to avoid. Masturbation fuel, however, has changed over the years. Some middle-aged heterosexual men react defensively against criticism of porn, assuming the critiques to be antisex and anti-masturbation; these men recall their own teen encounters with *Playboy, Penthouse,* and *Hustler* with feelings of guarded nostalgia. These days, *Hustler,* once considered raunchy, feels like a greeting card compared with what kids are viewing. Magazines are quite tame compared with Internet porn videos. Back in the day, boys had to work hard to acquire pornographic magazines. Getting access involved the risk of shaming by parents, older siblings, and other parents. Boys in neighborhoods worked together to gain access to stashes belonging to their brothers and dads. Groups of friends created caches of magazines in clubhouses or sheds, and borrowed from this underground lending library. But the endeavor required serious effort: hiking long distances, concealing the magazine in their backpacks, getting past family members, and hiding the contraband under their mattresses. When parents or siblings found the magazines, embarrassment ensued. Boys were temporarily deterred by the shame of teasing by siblings and serious talks with parents, but they inevitably returned with craftier plans to gain access. Girls were sneaking peeks at these magazines as well, but it was not common for girls to maintain a stash or to look at them regularly.

Reading erotic literature or looking at naked people in photographs required imagination; the viewer had to create a fantasy in his mind. Watching porn videos required less imagination and was a riskier and more public endeavor. Underage boys found ways to get into movie theaters that played late-night pornographic films. Despite the risk of running into adult men they knew, plenty made the effort. VCR tapes were a slightly more private viewing option for boys. A willing sibling who was of age, a fake ID, or an accomplice who could access a video from a dad with a stash were common ways of obtaining videos. Family video players were usually in a common space, which required boys to capitalize on their opportunities when adults were out of the house. The frequency with which tapes got stuck in the machines was a bit of a hitch for viewers. Disney videos seemed to always eject with ease, but *Debbie Does Dallas* was much more likely to get caught. Forks and crowbars were desperately used to force tapes to eject. If that didn't work, desperate boys would take the machine apart to remove the evidence with the minutes before parents returned home ticking away. Because accessing porn required so much effort, kids' exposure was limited. Sexual fantasies were fueled by one's imagination, exposure to minimal pornographic images, and memories of actual experiences rather than fueled by graphic porn that mainly shows sexual acts without intimacy.

Fast-Forward to a New Era of Porn

Critics of the Internet porn industry misfire when they blame high-speed Internet and the advancement of technology for so many boys having access to porn. It is the porn industry that has driven the advancement of computer technology and Internet speed.[1] The industry makes money by charging people to access websites, but that is challenging for young guys who rely on parents' credit cards. Free online porn videos have replaced magazines, and this fare is titillating enough, though tame compared to what is advertised for a fee next to the free videos. Unlike drug users, who need *more* of a drug over time, porn viewers need *different* material to keep engaged and aroused. The porn industry offers a boundless supply of material to keep up with this demand for variety.

Most current studies report that the average age at which a boy first views porn is, in the United States, eleven.[2] I have heard many parents claim that they are certain their teenage sons don't look at porn because when they ask directly, their sons claim they do not. Almost all the boys and young men I have interviewed count on their parents' naiveté. Guys share humorous stories about parents bragging to other parents about how much time their sons spend studying in their rooms. The common feeling among young men is that their parents don't really want to know what they are up to, and they tell their parents what the parents want to hear. They also claim that the chances are low that mom and dad would figure out what they're really doing, since the parents are technologically limited. They go on to say that parents would probably not bother trying to check their Internet history because they wouldn't know what to say or do if they found out the truth.

Internet porn didn't become a matter of public discourse until boys had become so saturated that its influence became glaring. During the stretch of time when there wasn't much reflection about porn, many parents felt it wasn't their business to embarrass boys with conversations about their masturbation habits and private lives. These days, kids are immersed in porn culture in many forms, with an onslaught of messaging reaching them through online porn, gaming, marketing, media, and music videos. Contrary to expectation, boys have a lot of questions about the content of and their relationship with porn. They are quite interested about what adults think about the prevalence of porn in their lives, and when parents, educators, and experts voice opinions about porn, kids are listening, even when they say they aren't. Even the rowdiest group of boys will listen with rapt attention to anyone who is willing to discuss the subject. In the U.K., ChildLine is a private and confidential support line young people can call about any problem they have. The number of calls from boys concerned about the impact of looking at porn has increased dramatically in recent years. According to Peter Liver, director of ChildLine, "Children of all ages today have easy access to a wide range of pornography. If we as a society shy away from talking about this issue, we are failing the thousands of young people it is affecting."[3]

Fantasy is what masturbation is all about. Online porn provides viewers high-impact video images they can watch conveniently and privately while avoiding emotional and physical vulnerability. The risk of rejection or shame is eliminated when one views porn in private and with the safety that comes with a device. Aside from the boundless supply of highly charged sexual videos, emotional safety is a contributing factor in so many boys and a smaller number of girls developing a regular habit of viewing porn.

Shifting Expectations

The number of sexual acts a boy views while watching porn could easily be in the thousands by the time he has his first sexual experience, or even his first kiss with a real-life partner. It is difficult for a boy or man to feel sexually adequate when his partner's body and responses don't match what he viewed for years before he had a partner. I have interviewed plenty of boys who saw online porn for the first time when they were in first grade. According to Alexandra Katehakis, founder and clinical director of the Center for Healthy Sex, "In today's digital world, most adolescents turn to porn for answers—and pleasure—and when porn becomes an adolescent boy's primary mode of sexual education, it can potentially be harmful to his brain's sexual development."[4]

In addition to using porn as a main information source and guide, many young heterosexual men rely on other "experienced" guy friends for information about female orgasms and "what women like." The specific ideas I have heard from the recipients of this guidance are almost always alarming and in direct contrast to what groups of women report that they would like to experience with a partner. Popular women's magazines with scantily clad women on the cover and articles that promise all kinds of answers, advice, and sexual adventure are commonly used as resources for heterosexual guys. In most cases, these sources prove to be unreliable, but the alternative of a guy admitting what he doesn't know and asking his partner brings the risk of ridicule, shame, and rejection. When a boy or man ejaculates regularly while looking at porn, he internalizes an association between that source and sexual pleasure. When he experiences the dopamine rush of orgasm, he reinforces his habit of seeking sexual pleasure associated with that specific image, experience, or situation.

The porn industry is bigger than the NFL, the NBA, and MLB combined,[5] and represents a $97 billion business worldwide and a $13 billion industry in the United States.[6] Keep in mind that these statistics could change as production costs come down, and anyone with a handheld camera and a computer can make and distribute porn, though the demand for porn will likely remain steady. My focus on porn use among boys and young men stems from a pattern of concerns I hear directly from boys and young men about their viewing habits. Porn and sex addiction can certainly be an issue for some boys and men, but the frequency among most guys in their teens and early twenties categorizes their viewing as habit. When guys sense hysteria and fear around porn addiction from a parent or teacher, they are not likely to engage in a discussion about the topic.

With so many younger guys masturbating using online porn, we need to encourage them to be more reflective about the messages they are internalizing. Most regular users are curious about the misleading aspects of porn and how their habit may be impacting their relationships and potential relationships. The idea that porn skews expectations of how bodies look and respond resonates with many guys, who report that it can be a challenge to reconcile the differences between what they see in porn and the sex they have with a partner, since very little converts to a real-life encounter, particularly around female pleasure. In heterosexual porn, augmented breasts, surgically altered labia, and exaggerated responses of pleasure are initially understood as fantasy. Over time and with repetition, however, viewers' expectations are shaped. According to Katehakis, "Between the ages of twelve and approximately twenty-five to thirty years old, the human brain undergoes a period of great neuroplasticity. The brain is in a malleable phase during which billions of new synaptic connections are made. This leaves us vulnerable to the influence of our surroundings and leads our brains to be 'wired' around the experiences and information that we receive during that time period."[7] This is a great reason to discuss with boys the messages that are out there before they stumble onto or actively seek online porn. Be very clear with kids about how porn misleads viewers with surgically altered performers, exaggerated sexual responses, and a high volume of degradation, objectification, and violence against women. Unfortunately, it will feel too early to talk with young boys about any of this, but explaining the effects of what they have seen after the fact is much harder.

Research by Donna Freitas, author of *The End of Sex: How Hookup Culture Is Leaving a Generation Unhappy, Sexually Unfulfilled, and Confused About Intimacy* confirms what I have been hearing about sex and masturbation from young people in the trenches of the hookup scene.[8] Once the porn habit is in full swing, it is difficult to put the genie back in the bottle; most guys, however, are willing to consider detoxing from porn for a three-week trial, using their imagination (aka "the spank bank") to masturbate. Most agree that their fantasies would shift if they were not consuming the visual images found in porn for a stretch of time.

My interviews and surveys of young men show an increase in the number of guys who can't get off without porn, a result of easy access, improved Internet speed, cultural acceptance, and/or habit developed with repetition. Guys who take breaks from looking at porn report a shift in the content and tone of their fantasies. Those who give up viewing porn for months and rely on imagination or "old-school porn" such as magazines and erotic literature report major shifts in the images in their mind. Many young men readily admit that porn clutters their minds with distracting images, and when they choose time away from porn, healthier images replace them. Since handheld devices and phones have become more available for kids in all socioeconomic classes, porn access is more widespread. *San Francisco Chronicle* reporter Regan McMahon summarizes why porn meets multiple levels of need: "If people want to escape feelings of low self-esteem, shame, isolation, or the pressures of life, work, or relationships, pornography is a place to get lost and feel wanted, imagining the perfect partners who always desires them—and whom they can always satisfy."[9]

Inspiration for Conversations

Simon Louis Lajeunesse, associate professor at the School of Social Work at the University of Montreal, led a research group looking to compare men in their twenties who had never consumed sexually explicit material with those who had, however the project had to be reworked when he failed to find any young men who hadn't viewed porn. The fact that researchers couldn't find any guys who don't look at porn matches reports I get from college guys themselves. High school boys are more reticent to admit, discuss, or ask questions about porn unless they are sure they won't be scolded or judged. However, they listen intently when someone is talking about it.

By the time guys get to college age, they quickly become aware of widespread porn consumption, and they feel less guilty. Very few parents and educators are talking to their sons about porn, despite the fact that it plays a large role in their lives. According to Professor Lajeunesse, "Pornography hasn't changed [men's] perception of women or their relationships, which they all want to be as harmonious and fulfilling as possible."[10] I agree with Lajeunesse that young men want their relationships to be as harmonious and fulfilling as possible, however, I hear from many men who are concerned about how their porn use has impacted and is currently impacting their sexual relationships.

Before I started conducting research and interviews about porn use, I assumed that Internet porn represented a harmless improvement over print porn, and that young men were getting all the answers they needed online. After the first few Q&A sessions with groups of college students, it became apparent that porn not only provides fantasy fuel but also serves as a sexual guide for many, which is causing confusion rather than clarifying what sex looks like and how bodies respond. Reconciling the images they see in porn with the experiences they have with a partner is challenging for young men. It is clear that we are living in the misinformation age rather than the information age; those seeking information about sex through porn actually know less about true pleasure than previous generations did.

> "Porn played a big role in influencing my ideas and expectations about sex. I thought girls liked going from slow to fast (aka the jack-rabbit). Watching porn made me think anything could be a hint that a girl wanted to have sex. I also thought that every girl had a bleached asshole and shaved pubic hair. This was not the case. I have learned to always ask if it's okay with your partner before trying new things. Porn doesn't teach about how to get consent."
>
> —Male, age twenty

Distorted images and misinformation are inhibiting healthy sexual relationships. Young men readily admit they seek in their sexual encounters confirmation and clarification about what they see in porn. Without much prompting, they share their frustrations, warped expectations, feelings of being misled, fear of partners faking orgasms without them knowing, and general confusion about sex and relationships. Porn seems to be magnifying feelings of inadequacy. According to Katehakis, "When an adolescent boy compulsively views pornography, his brain chemistry can become shaped around the attitudes and situations that he is watching. Sadly, pornography paints an unrealistic picture of sexuality and relationships that can create an expectation for real-life experiences that will never be fulfilled."[11]

When men get in the habit of using porn when they are young, they often hope (even assume) that masturbation and porn won't be necessary once they start "having sex all the time." Not many young men plan for a life of porn use. Instead, they optimistically view porn as a temporary gig to get them through to the promised land of regular sex with a partner. In one of my earliest interviews, a college guy naively said he would stop looking at porn and masturbating once he found a girlfriend or a wife. The poor kid got some unsettling news when I told him, "Take it from a mother of three with two jobs, one of which is doing research on middle-aged people and their sex lives: you will not have sex on tap. In fact, there are some serious dry spells after you have kids and for other reasons. Keep up the skills." He looked crestfallen, but I felt good about sending him toward adult life with his eyes open to realistic sexual expectations. I consider that talk a gift to his future long-term partner, even though it sounds like I shattered his dreams. Masturbation should be a lifelong practice for men and women. It contributes to maintaining sexual health, getting through dry spells, and augmenting a healthy sex life with a partner.

Taking a Porn Break

Male college students e-mail me privately about erectile dysfunction (ED) concerns more than anything else. The fact that 5 percent of men in their twenties report having ED indicates that it is more of an issue for younger men than many people think.[12] Angst around getting an erection, fumbling with a condom, antidepressant medication, obesity, drugs, and alcohol all contribute to ED in younger men.[13] While there are still some articles and research that claim there is no link between porn and ED, anecdotal evidence and more extensive studies are changing the perspectives of many medical professionals.

Personal reports from his clients as well as accounts found on dozens of websites and message boards convinced Washington, D.C. psychologist Dr. Tyger Latham that ED is the result of a complicated combination of physiological and psychological factors.[14] I have found in my own interviews with college men that taking a break from porn helped them get back to normal sexual function. The reports that porn is not addictive or an issue for young men are not particularly convincing. The feedback I get through interviews and discussions with many habitual porn consumers is that taking a break from porn helped them get back on track when they struggled with a variety of sexual anxiety including ED. The results from a study of twenty-eight thousand Italian men align with what I hear from a number of college men; researchers found "gradual but devastating" effects of repeated exposure to pornography over long period of time.[15] The head of the study, Carlos Forsta, reports that the problem "starts with lower reactions to porn sites, then there is a general drop in libido and in the end it becomes impossible to get an erection."[16]

"My 'figuring out' was done by trial and error and looking online. When I was thirteen, I was very self-conscious about my penis size and hesitant to receive a hand job. I thought girls expected a penis to be around six inches long. On a good day, I was pushing three and a half inches at the time. Worrying about my penis size during a sexual encounter in high school led to anxiety about getting an erection."

—Male, age twenty-two

When I first suggested to a group of college guys that they *consider* what might change if they didn't look at porn for three weeks, I didn't expect any of them to actually try it. But the suggestion that their imagination highlight reel might shift when they didn't have images created for them resonated with two of the guys. Six months later, one of them told me he was still not looking at porn, and the other had abstained for two months and had been choosing to use his imagination more regularly since then. Both reported having greater focus, more energy, more connected sexual encounters, and better erections, and said they were relying less on porn-driven images while masturbating *and* while having sex.

Whether porn is viewed directly or whether pornographic images have simply influenced widespread beliefs about sex, porn has created unrealistic expectations about what female pleasure looks like and how easily it can be achieved. It takes time with a communicative partner to sort out realistic sexual expectations and to get to know one another's bodies. Because so many young people engage in the hookup scene, often with partners who are not very familiar, sexual experiences often don't live up to their hopes and expectations. Many teenage girls and young women report that their male partners ask them why they aren't "like most girls," who remove their pubic hair, scream with pleasure, like anal sex, have small labia, and ejaculate across the room. Young men typically formulate these standards of women's bodies and behaviors after seeing a vast number of women in porn rather than seeing partners of their own.

When the appearance and responses of multiple partners are not consistent with what guys expect, they may begin to question their own bodies, penis size, and sexual skills. Taking a break from porn has helped some guys work out some of these issues and concerns. According to a new study published in the *Archives of Sexual Behavior,* "The more pornography a man watches, the more likely he was to use it during sex, request particular pornographic sex acts of his partner, deliberately conjure images of pornography during sex to maintain arousal, and have concerns over his own sexual performance and body image. Further, higher pornography use was negatively associated with enjoying sexually intimate behaviors with a partner."[17]

The Creators of Porn

The absence of tenderness, respectful interactions, and consent seems to be a theme in heterosexual porn. According to Enough Is Enough's "Internet Safety 101" page, "Of the 304 (porn) scenes analyzed, 88.2% contained physical aggression, principally spanking, gagging, and slapping, while 48.7% of scenes contained verbal aggression, primarily name-calling. Perpetrators of aggression were usually male, whereas targets of aggression were overwhelmingly female."[18] Not many years ago, ejaculating on a woman's face (aka the "money shot") was considered an extreme form of degradation. As Gail Dines, author of *Pornland: How Porn Has Hijacked Our Sexuality,* describes, "The ejaculate also marks the woman as used goods, as owned by the man or men who just penetrated her."[19] In her book, Dines quotes porn actor and producer Bill Margold, who explains the money shot in this way: "I'd like to really show what I believe the men want to see: violence against women. I firmly believe that we serve a purpose by showing that. The most violent we can get is the cum shot in the face. Men get off behind that, because they get even with the women they can't have. We try to inundate the world with orgasms in the face."[20]

When viewpoints like this are shared with groups of guys, most of them recoil in anger and irritation. Very few young men I have interviewed intentionally or consciously started out using porn because they felt anger, resentment, or violence toward women. Comments like these made by creators of porn seem to reflect their own lingering bitterness toward women, and they use their medium to reinforce their own views. It is worth disengaging from porn, if mainly to decrease the profits of a billion-dollar industry that is manipulating boys who have a strong tendency to seek visual images of sex. According to San Francisco psychotherapist Gregory Rowe, "For 90% of men, images are a big source of stimulation."[21] The porn industry knows this and is actually in a position to shape the tastes of viewers—in fact, the porn industry has the population of heterosexual and homosexual boys and young men by the balls.

Genital Image

In the United States, the trend of girls and women removing their pubic hair has moved into the population of high school girls and even middle school girls. Because it is illegal for producers of porn to put underage girls in their videos, they make women appear more childlike by waxing the performers from anus to navel and surgically altering their labia. These surgeries are now offered in clinics and hospitals all across the country, and are gaining in popularity.

Surgically altered labia may even seem common, because we see advertisements for "vaginal rejuvenation," "vaginal reconstruction," "labiaplasty," "vaginoplasty," or "vaginal cosmetic surgery" plastered across websites and the backs of magazines aimed at women consumers. The marketing alone can contribute to girls' and women's feelings self-conscious about their vulvas, and seeing or even hearing what women in porn look like reinforces concern about labia size and vulva appearance. According to a study by *BJOG: An International Journal of Obstetrics and Gynaecology*, "Women vary widely in genital dimensions. This information should be made available to women when considering surgical procedures on the genitals, decisions for which must be carefully considered between surgeon and women."[22]

> "When I was sixteen, my boyfriend told me I should get rid of my pubic hair. He said, 'All women wax their pubic hair off.' I believed him and shaved it off. I regretted it. Then he told me I was too flappy. Soon after, I figured out that 'all women' were the women he saw in porn."
>
> —Female, age twenty-one

Jamie McCartney is an artist in the U.K. who is responsible for *The Great Wall of Vagina,* a nine-meter-long polyptych that features four hundred 3D sculptures of vulvas made from molds of a broad range of real women ages eighteen to seventy-six. According to McCartney, "For many women, their genital appearance is a source of anxiety and I was in the unique position to do something about it."[23] Surgical solutions may be appropriate for a woman who has abnormally large labia that cause serious pain or discomfort, but those conditions are much rarer than marketing for labia surgeries would indicate. Most recipients of these surgeries choose to go forward because they believe they are not normal, a result of feedback from sexual partners or a lack of information about how normal female vulvas appear.

Pressure to meet genital image standards is difficult for young people to manage. Feelings of inadequacy about their genitals are an issue for many young men and boys, so much so that when a guy asks anything relating to penis size or adequacy, other guys in the room break into laughter with gratitude and eagerness for an answer. Male performers in porn are known for their oversized, anaconda-like penises. Says sex therapist Katehakis, "Pornography can be exciting for an adolescent boy to watch, but it can also be intimidating. It is important to note that the average size of a man's erect penis is approximately 5.8 inches long, while the average size of a male porn star's erect penis is approximately 8 inches long."[24] It is worth mentioning that the average depth of any orifice that a penis would penetrate is about four inches. Most guys have more than enough for a variety of satisfying activities. Somehow, though, enough boys and men fall for the penis enhancement scams that the industry is thriving.

Whose Needs Are Truly Being Met?

The way the men in hetero porn ravage their partners both vaginally and anally is misleading. A number of gay men have approached me after my college presentations, concerned about their heterosexual peers who are engaging in casual anal sex in a hookup scenario. Many of these young men are worried that their heterosexual male friends assume that all women enjoy anal sex based on what they see in porn. They are equally worried that their heterosexual female friends assume they will be expected to have anal sex if they want to be thought of as hot. Anal sex in heterosexual hookup scenarios has indeed become more common, whether the female partner enjoys it or not. While anal sex is pleasurable for some, there are plenty who report pain, bleeding, and tearing. Some girls and women say they do it because they think that is what guys want.

The general message from gay men is that heterosexual porn misleads by making anal sex out to be a common heterosexual activity that is "easy and comfortable" and went on to say that a good number of gay men don't enjoy anal sex because they find it painful. There was unanimous agreement in one particular group of gay men when one of the men explained, "Anal sex is a 'process' that can be enjoyable with a well-known partner, however it requires preparation, pacing, communication, and a good supply of water-based lube, which won't break down a condom."

Soon after I got used to the idea that casual anal sex is a thing among college-age men and women, despite the fact that it is not universally enjoyed, I discovered that casual anal sex is becoming a more common practice among high school students as well. The specific questions I get from students indicate that in many of these cases, the choice is not necessarily out of desire. It seems that boys and girls are curious because they hear a lot about it and think it may provide the pleasure that has been elusive for them so far. A good number of young people assume their partners really want to have anal sex and are willing. National sex surveys report that in 1992 16 percent of women age eighteen to twenty-four had tried anal sex. That number jumped to 40 percent in 2010.[25] There are certainly women who genuinely enjoy anal sex, but it seems clear that what is viewed in porn is impacting the number of people who assume it is what they want and give it a go.

Between porn culture and social media, perception about what kind of sex others are having and enjoying is massively skewed, and is inspiring people to jump into behaviors they aren't particularly interested in and don't find remotely pleasurable. When someone, really anyone who has a significant number of followers, retweets #analweek on Twitter, young people scramble to feel like they are part of the club. Generally, porn culture has created false ideas about sex for many high school and college students, with behaviors such as anal sex, violence, and restraint becoming normalized as part of the hookup scene.

Communication Required

According to Alexandra Katehakis, of the Center for Healthy Sex, "While masturbating to porn, the adolescent brain is being shaped around a sexual experience that is isolating, visceral, and completely void of any love or compassion."[26] Yet, Internet porn has become the primary sexuality educator for boys. Emulating porn is not only very common for young men, it is an easier path than admitting what they don't know or asking for guidance. But it also has an indirect impact on young women, as it inspires some of them to engage in sexual activities in which they aren't genuinely interested or that they find unfulfilling.

Some heterosexual guys don't make the connection between the pervasive influence of porn culture and some girls' and women's feelings that they have to compete with porn by "performing" like a porn star. Even though vast numbers of guys are not turned on by hitting or ejaculating on their female partner, they may oblige, taking such requests at face value. Some guys admit that such requests from girls give them bragging rights among their male friends, even though it doesn't feel quite right or satisfy them personally. The lingering worry for some of these young men is that something must be wrong with them if they are not into that kind of sexual activity, and they need to step up their game.

Some guys dream about a partner who acts like an insatiable porn star, while others wonder if women think guys expect that, indicating that a solid number of girls and women objectify themselves to please their partners. Women who perceive male partners as expecting or hoping for pornlike experiences and who try to perform to those expectations are more likely to make male pleasure, rather than mutual pleasure, a priority. While communication could clear up these misunderstandings, it continues to be the most avoided sexual practice.

Fifty Shades of Confusion

Healthy sex is about pleasure being given and received by both partners. Many high school and college students think that the sex they hear about, see in porn, or read about in novels like *Fifty Shades of Grey* must be what is missing in their sex lives. If sex is consensual, full of communication, and both parties are finding pleasure, partners should be as sexually adventurous as both agree to be. Unfortunately, I rarely hear about amazing, communicative sex from young people, who often experiment with partners they barely know in a hookup situation. People's fantasies run across a wide spectrum, and they have every right to follow their desires. Some psychologists argue that critics of porn and *Fifty Shades of Grey* are forgetting that these are about fantasy, and don't depict scenes that most people want to play out. *Fifty Shades of Grey* has temporarily jump-started a lot of adventurous sex for people of all ages. I have heard from many high school students who look to the Fifty Shades books for inspiring ideas. Unfortunately, the series has left many heterosexual girls and women feeling inadequate, either for not embracing sexual adventure or for being too willing to take part in sexual acts that are not pleasurable for them. After reading these books, heterosexual boys and men are left confused about what turns women on. On a number of occasions, boys who have read *Fifty Shades of Grey* have asked me if it is true that all women fantasize about being raped and roughly restrained during sex. The influence of this book series, as well as Internet porn and mass media depictions, contribute to young people's misunderstanding about consensual sex.

I have discussed the Fifty Shades series with a number of people in the communities known as kink and BDSM (a combination of bondage and discipline and sadism and masochism), as well as with people who express variations on these interests. I had wrongly assumed that members of these groups would consider the books a step toward more mainstream acceptance of their communities and sexual practices; it turns out that most members of the kink community, BDSM community, and their subgroups view consent as a key element in their sexual choices. As observed by a number of movie critics, reporters, and mental health professionals who reviewed the film harshly, lack of consent is a glaring feature of the relationship between the characters in the Fifty Shades series.

It isn't really clear how the passion for the books and movie is influencing the sex lives of the people who sing its praises. Almost everyone I interview claims the books were terribly written but interesting nonetheless. Some women admit that reading the novels jump-started their libido after years of sexual disinterest, but most said the fire waned quickly. Some women didn't enjoy reading the books but felt they might be missing out or that they would be considered prudish if they didn't. And a number of women who did enjoy reading the books said they wouldn't consider using nipple or genital clamps, much less ask their partner to whip their clitoris with a riding crop. A few innkeepers I know have noticed a trend of guests leaving behind riding crops and handcuffs at the end of a weekend, indicating that the Fifty Shades fantasy isn't all it is cracked up to be.

When girls and college women are trying to figure out orgasms, messages in the culture give the idea that rough sex may be the way to find true pleasure. College men often admit that they are not comfortable when they are asked to hit, choke, or tie women up, but they oblige because they have heard that women like it and fear they will be rejected if they don't go along. People have every right to push boundaries, but the rise of BDSM themes in the cultural zeitgeist, paired with a lack of communication between partners, has led to a lot of young people engaging in acts they think will be pleasurable for their partners, but which end up not fulfilling either partner. Sex should be mutually satisfying.

Those on the more sexually adventurous side may consider this perspective limiting and repressive of people's sexual inclinations, but figuring out how to meet one's own basic sexual needs and those of one's partner before engaging in threesomes, role playing, or rough sex empowers a person to find genuine satisfaction in his or her sexual experiences. Many young people assume they will feel satisfied by pushing their sexual boundaries in certain ways, yet end up feeling uncomfortable and unsatisfied. Many, particularly women, tend to just go along with what they think they are supposed to like, or believe that they will learn to like a particular act. They assume that they will catch on with practice, or when they become more comfortable speaking up to their partners. But going along without speaking up about one's needs despite not being satisfied can become one's practice. Not knowing what you like or not being able to tell your partner what you like is a clear sign that you should slow down and figure it out.

It is almost impossible to control kids' exposure to porn culture, especially now that more kids have access to the Internet and to digital devices; awareness of and direct exposure to online porn is almost inevitable for most kids. Even parents and educators have even become desensitized to the images and tone in videos and advertisements, which can lead us to be passive about discussing the impact of porn culture with children. Countering the influences of porn culture with honest conversations will increase our chances to guide our kids toward more realistic sexual expectations and to help them recognize that they are in a position to decide what sexual choices they make rather than follow what seems like the norm. Having open conversations with kids about the differences between healthy sexuality and what they see in porn can help expand their capacity for communication, which is key to making healthy sexual choices as they grow up.

CHAPTER 4

Sexuality Education for Younger Kids

Creating meaning and context around sexuality is the real challenge. Accomplishing that will take dozens and dozens of talks.
—Deborah Roffman, *Talk to Me First: Everything You Need to Know to Become Your Kids' "Go-To" Person about Sex*

Talking to kids about sex is something most parents anticipate with a level of dread. Conversations about sexuality are awkward—but they get easier with practice. There are any number of reasons parents avoid or delay taking on the role of primary sexuality educator for their kids—discomfort, denial, and confusion are just a few. Parents feel overwhelmed by media, marketing, and online influences. Many are waiting for the "right time" or for their kids to ask questions. Some hope their kids will take in the necessary information through osmosis. Others muster their courage to start, but even the slightest hint of kids' resistance breaks down their resolve. Because it is ultimately the parents' job to teach their children about sex, it is best for both kids and parents if they dive in early and often.

Anticipating a conversation about sex in an adult context is enough to rattle even the bravest of parents. But sex ed doesn't start with penises and vaginas: pace yourself. Let go of the idea of having "the talk"—teaching kids about healthy sexuality and relationships isn't a one-time deal, but rather a series of conversations that progresses over time. Starting as early as the toddler years, sexual education evolves throughout many talks, beginning with simply naming the body parts and advancing, eventually, to explaining the physical mechanics and the emotional implications of sex. Try to think of each conversation along the way as an investment in making future conversations easier. As Deborah Roffman says, "Talking to your kids about sexuality is talking to them about life."[1]

Encourage children to notice and discuss gender messaging and sexual tone in advertisements, movies, books, and programming. Their observations can lay the groundwork for conversations about values, respect, gender roles, stereotypes, and broader ideas about life and relationships. If you've laid the foundation, by the time your child is between the ages of five and seven, you'll find it much easier to explain the mechanics of sex. If you have been talking about relationships of all kinds up until that point, the physical details will not be a big deal. Sex is not just about genitals. Much of it is about relationships and loving connection, which may or may not lead to sex involving genitals. According to Dr. Justin Richardson, author of *Everything You Never Wanted Your Kids to Know About Sex (But Were Afraid They'd Ask),* "People have been told by experts that there's a right age to learn about intercourse. If you're talking about how babies are made, there's no age at which it is harmful to learn that the penis goes into the vagina. Yes, it's true that exposing a child to sexual stimulation is harmful. But telling a kid how babies are made is very different."[2]

If you are proactive with sexuality education when your kids are young, you'll give them a better chance of developing healthy ideas about sex, and they'll be more comfortable having conversations about it. It is much easier to practice, stumble, and reboot your plans when kids are young, because younger kids are more forgiving and have shorter memories. Take full advantage of having merciful children with short attention spans who will give you a chance to practice and gain comfort in approaching the topic. I think of early sexuality education as training for the more complex conversations that will have to happen when your child becomes a teenager. Once kids start having relationships or witness peers in relationships that are sexual in nature, they tend to be less receptive to your attempts to broach the topic of sex. Get ahead of the curve.

It is worth boosting your knowledge base and your courage by staying attuned to the latest research on sexuality education. There are so many great resources available; books and articles, along with TED Talks on the topic, can give you the fuel you need to get the conversation going and keep it going. I've been reading sex ed books and articles since I was a teacher, before my kids were born, and I reread and refer to resources regularly to increase my understanding and gain new insight. Being informed reboots my confidence and conviction.

Parents have to figure out their own approach for talking to their kids about sex, factoring in the personality and disposition of each child. It can be helpful to patch together ideas from other knowledgeable parents who are using information from reliable, current sources to find what works for you. My husband and I benefited from input from friends whose kids were a little older than ours, and who therefore had the advantage of hindsight. Talking with friends who can share fresh examples of their successes and stumbles is always helpful. Comparing notes and sharing stories gave us more ideas and helped us build comfort and courage. The "village" is essential!

I refer to my team of friends and role models who advise me about all aspects of life as my "healthy crew." Within that crew, there are certain people who are go-to folks for specific areas, such as parenting. Watching other people raise their kids and listening to their philosophies as they went along provided Bruce and me with a broad selection of examples we could use to create our own approach. This system is less a prescriptive approach and more an à la carte parenting menu, from which you take what you need and incorporate it into your own style. When you admit you need help, great ideas and advice are available—but you have to ask.

First Grade Is Prime Time

Pediatricians recommend that sexuality education start years before kids begin to develop and years before they become sexually active with another person. The general recommendation is for parents to explain physical sex when kids are between five and seven years old. Some kids are ready in kindergarten, and some may be more ready in second grade, but aiming for first grade is a safe bet. Having conversations about bodies and sex when kids are toddlers creates comfort and familiarity with terms. Compared with our own experience as children, this sounds too early, but the digital age has made it necessary and urgent to reach kids early with the correct information.

As parents, we may feel daunted by and nervous about what could go wrong in a conversation about sex, but making mistakes is part of the experience. You may find yourself at a loss for words, or may discover that you fall back on the vague language your own parents used. If you get off course, it is perfectly fine to tell your kids you want to start over. No one can predict the reaction of a kid. Assuming your kids will react with resistance or discomfort is a sure way to talk yourself out of starting the conversation. Anticipating awkwardness makes jumping in more difficult. Instead, muster up a positive attitude, and believe that the long-term benefits of an open dialogue around sexuality will make the teen years less challenging for the whole family. After the first few chats, talking about sex will get only get easier. Sexuality educator and children's book author Robie H. Harris advises, "Parents can frame answers about sexuality from young kids in context of values, such as explaining sex as an act of love, but they never should create an atmosphere of shame about the subject. Sexuality is an inherent part of humans."[3]

Tips for Talking to Your Kids About Sex

Use the proper names for body parts.
Be matter-of-fact and use simple terms.
Give kids access to books about bodies and sex—leave the books in your child's room and around the house.
Talk about love and examples of healthy relationships.
Initiate conversations—have conversations early and often!
Become approachable.
Keep conversations open ended.
Ask questions.
Ask if they want to hear more.
Listen to their reactions and responses.
Repeat yourself and ask them to repeat what they understand.
Avoid too much information.
Avoid too little information.
Weave messages about sex into everyday conversations about other topics.
Keep a positive tone in the conversations.
Admit that you are nervous, uncomfortable, or need practice.

Body Language

If parents don't step fully into their role as sex educators, it may take a village to fill in kids' spotty sexuality education. Like most parents in the sixties and seventies, mine didn't talk openly to us about sex or bodies unless backed into a corner. Luckily, I had a village of five older sibs, their spouses, and a few of their friends who periodically pitched in to set me straight. Without them, I would have been lost.

When I was five and my sister was eight, my dad left his career in New York City to buy a funky old inn in New Hampshire. His job in the city had been stressful, and he wanted more time with his family. My parents ran the inn together, and my mom was glad to share the parenting duties. She promised that my dad would connect better with his family by waking up to make breakfast and pack lunches with us every morning and making sure my sister didn't drown me at bath time. My parents were coparenting long before it was a thing.

Bodies and sex were not discussed with our dad. He managed to advise us on body care at a safe distance, orchestrating bath time from the hallway or another room. As we grew up, we caught on to the humor of our dad's discomfort; our older siblings were amazed to see him embracing all aspects of hands-on parenting as well as he could. Our tradition of nude runs and games while the tub filled obliged him to read the newspaper and call out directions from the comfort of his bed. He would yell things like, "All right girls. It's getting late. Time to get in the tub, and don't forget to clean your *popo*." That was his word for vulva. Popo was likely passed down from German relatives who shared his lack of ease around body talk, and who also relied on vague words to talk about taboo topics. His approach was on par with many dads of that era. Avoidance of specific language and an undercurrent of shame were ingrained in my family early in my life. Thanks to the sexual revolution of the 1960s, my older siblings were awakened despite my parents' antiquated attitudes, and I benefited from years of conversations with my open and communicative siblings, who provided me with detailed and accurate information about sex. I was raised in a unique situation, with old-fashioned parents who often avoided uncomfortable topics and adult siblings who were invested in helping me develop healthy ideas about sexuality.

These days, using correct and accurate terms is expected, but phrases such as "down there" or "pee pee" continue to grace the bath-time routines in households across America on any given night. Experts agree that "standard" words for body parts—rather than euphemisms and colloquialisms—are important.[4] "Teaching children anatomically correct terms, age-appropriately," says Laura Palumbo, a prevention campaign specialist with the National Sexual Violence Resource Center, "promotes positive body image, self confidence, and parent–child communication; discourages perpetrators; and, in the event of abuse helps children and adults navigate the disclosure and forensic interview process."[5] Experts make it clear that adults impact the development of children's attitudes about and comfort with their bodies and the topic of sex.

Parents' choice to take their role as primary sexual educator seriously or avoid it sends a clear message to kids about how their parents feel about the topic, and influences their own comfort in discussing sexual matters. I happened to have a rare combination of historical timing and responsible adult siblings who were comfortable in the role of sexuality educator to help me land on my feet. If we care about our kids' future sexual health and well-being, we need to remember that it can be dangerous to entrust others with the role of sexuality educator for our kids. As parents, we need to take sexuality education seriously, even as we maintain an openness and a lightness that allows for the inevitable stumbles.

The Gift of Naked Courage

Talking about sexuality with our kids is a challenging endeavor that models courage and emotional vulnerability. It can start with body comfort. While you don't have to be naked in front of your kids, it is worth considering. There is a broad range of comfort levels around being naked. If you are on the less comfortable end of the spectrum, think about pushing yourself to be more relaxed with your kids when they are really young. Your own attitude sets a tone for your children. My father avoided being naked in our presence at all costs. Once, I walked in on him about to step into his boxers. As I was putting on the brakes and turning around, he panicked and attempted to do a two-foot leap into his underwear. As I did a quick about-face and scrambled back down the hall, I heard the crash of his tall, ungainly body hitting the floor. My mom was comfortable being naked in front of us despite our brutal feedback about her body, but her attitude influenced our own comfort and body acceptance over time.

When our children were toddlers, I was motivated to do everything I could to make them feel comfortable with their own bodies as well as to talk about body parts and sexuality. Bath time and naked family members inspired chats about body parts and differences. As parents, our first chance to model our own body comfort is when our kids are little. It is much easier to unveil our naked selves before they have been exposed to marketing and media, because they won't serve up the tough feedback—yet! It is worth preparing yourself for their honest, unfiltered viewpoints as they get older.

> "The open, comfortable naked dad idea got derailed for a while when my daughter asked me, 'Dad, what is that flappy bag behind your penis?'"
>
> —Father of two girls

When my husband and I had kids, they regularly saw our naked bodies from the time they were young, as we changed clothes or walked down the hall to the shower. There's no need to overdo it, but there are many situations where it is perfectly natural that a family is changing clothes in one another's presence. Embracing nudity can show kids that you are comfortable living in a regular person's body. If we don't show them average, normal bodies, where will they see them?

As a middle-aged, big-boned woman with a solid layer of frosting, I consider showing my naked body a way of countering media images. It provides my kids with a broader appreciation of what female bodies look like. By showing them that I live in my industrial-strength, regular body despite my imperfections, they may catch on and know it is all going to be all right. As our kids get older, they see us naked less often, but when it happens, I stand strong in my body despite their reactions as they claim to being scarred, horrified, and gag dramatically at the sight of me. I consider my naked conviction a public service to any of their future female partners, who will be grateful for the way they are appreciated. If we are invested in our kids getting behind their bodies and owning what nature gave them, we should do the same. If that requires some time in counseling, make an appointment and start the work.

Inevitable Genitals

Conversations, bickering, and observational ramblings at bath time inevitably lead to the topic of genitals. This is when parents get practice talking about respect for personal space and bodies. It can get pretty outrageous in the bath zone, but it is important to rise up with courage and stay calm. My husband and I kept straight faces as we responded to questions or explained things, but in private afterward, we cringed, gasped, or laughed while reflecting about what worked and what we clearly needed to say differently. Kids take a lot of baths, which creates a sharp learning curve for parents. Tired, naked kids in a small space with access to water and bath toys create a recipe for mayhem. The unfiltered questions and comments about their own bodies and their siblings' bodies seem to have extra charge during this nightly ritual. Modeling comfort requires keeping the pulse down and facial expressions even when responding to questions, situations, and conversations. Bath time can be an exhausting way to end a busy day for parents, so take deep breaths before you step into the arena.

When a child touches or grabs her sibling's genitals, or any body part, for that matter, calmly remind her to keep her hands to herself and to respect the personal space of others. When a child spends a little too much time touching his own genitals, gently remind him that it is perfectly fine to do that in private. The tone of your reaction is the key to keeping these situations from becoming a way for kids to get attention; it is a fine balance to acknowledge that touching one's own genitals is normal and healthy while also helping kids understand it is something people do in private.

These situations help parents build resilience. When you react strongly in any way, you show kids that they can unnerve or provoke you. Even the littlest kids can sense when they have nudged you beyond your threshold or found out how to push your buttons. Your reactions set the tone for what conversations will be like as you move forward. You can always shift the tone, but it is important to appear unfazed, even when you are feeling quite fazed. Our kids followed our lead. Over time, we all—parents and kids—grow more comfortable each time we have a chat about anything relating to body parts and sexuality.

Bodies and sex are serious topics, but it is worth keeping your sense of humor—it will help you recover when things get rough. Allowing yourself to be vulnerable and admitting what you don't know increases your chances of getting the support you need from friends and other resources, so you can adapt your approach.

Glitchy Sex Ed in the Seventies

All of the kids in my family growing up had an unspoken agreement that our ability to steer clear of conversations about sex would prolong our father's life. My mom was not one to initiate a conversation about sex, but if we asked, she unleashed, which was alarming at times. If you asked a question, you had to be prepared to get blowtorched with information. I think she used that approach to keep our questions to a dull roar or to buy herself time to think. It was a highly effective tactic. Needless to say, I did not learn what sex was all about from my parents. My team of siblings and their spouses helped me get on the right track.

The kids in my family got a lot of grief on the school bus for being "flatlanders" when we moved to rural New Hampshire from Connecticut. There were a few older ruffians who went so far as to call me a "rich bitch." It was confusing to me because my parents were cleaning toilets and making beds at our family inn. I felt I needed a feisty response because I was struggling to make sense of it all. I decided to give these big kids the finger and simultaneously yell, "Fuck you." They would roar with laughter hearing this from an extra-small first grader. I kept this response in my quiver right up until third grade. Whenever they asked me what it meant, I put up my finger and said it again. I knew I needed to find out what it really meant, but most of my reliable sibling sources were in college or were only around in the presence of my parents.

My sister Sarah had a new smugness about her when she was in the middle of a sex ed unit as a fifth grader. One day, she asked me if I knew what the word "fuck" meant. I told her I thought it involved fingers and vaginas. After shaking her head in the most condescending way, she went on to give me the fifth-grade scientific version of how the sperm travels out of the testicles, up through the penis, and into the vagina, where it meets the egg. I remember thinking she must have been mistaken, and I responded, "That makes no sense. If the sperm is in the testicles, why doesn't the man put those testicles inside the vagina?" She didn't have enough information to explain that so I was forced to ask my mom. Approaching my mom was risky because she preferred to avoid the topic of sex, but if we asked a direct question, she followed with an aggressively thorough explanation, designed, I believe, to discourage us from asking again anytime soon. This was an effective tactic because it caused us to wish for the usual uncomfortable silence surrounding sexuality.

There was enough awkward secrecy about sex at my house that I felt compelled to run newly learned information by friends at school. Awkward secrecy was standard issue for most families back in the day. As I went through elementary school, I became the informant with a handy collection of sisters who became my expert clarification team when they were home for vacation. Even though things have improved for this next generation, many parents today continue to make awkward secrecy a family tradition. Given what our children are exposed to in the media and online, it is too much of a risk to let kids be guided by siblings and peers.

Relationship Possibilities

Before our kids got to first grade, I both stumbled onto and created opportunities to explain how the egg and sperm come together to grow a baby in a woman's uterus. The conversations came up organically when the kids were young because they asked questions about animal and human babies. In these situations, it is natural to talk to our kids about the variety of parents. Our kids have friends with two dads, two moms, moms and dads, and single parents. If your kids don't personally know same-sex or single parents yet, it is still important to make them aware of all the possibilities, in preparation for a time when they do. Not only does this model respect and acceptance, it also lays groundwork that makes the inevitable conversations about relationships and where babies come from much easier—in all kinds of families.

Kids are not as fazed as adults think they are when it comes to adoption, sperm and egg donation, and surrogate parents. Some parents assume these concepts can wait because they are too advanced and complicated for kids. The real source of complication is parents who are vague and uncomfortable talking about something that is unfamiliar to them. We need to get familiar. Most kids will be relieved when you help them make sense of where and how the sperm and egg get together in all possible ways. Facts are comforting in a world with a lot of gray zones. A matter-of-fact approach without judgment helps kids become more accepting, tolerant people.

"My daughter was adopted from China as an infant. When she was a toddler, the difference between the words 'China' and 'vagina' wasn't quite clear to her yet and resulted in some interesting public moments."

—Parent of a teenage girl

Yin and Yang

As my kids were heading toward middle school, I had the good fortune to get a pep talk from registered nurse and sexuality educator Jane Esselstyn. In her presentations to middle and high school students, she emphasizes equality, respect, and accurate language. Throughout her presentations for students and adults, she points to a yin-yang symbol to reinforce the idea that sexuality is about balance and equality. She reminds parents to choose words that reflect that same equality and respect when talking with kids about any sort of sexual behavior. When talking to younger kids (ages five to seven) about sex, a parent can say, "Sexual intercourse is when people's genitals connect." Esselstyn credits Deborah Roffman with another way to phrase it: "Genitals fit together like a puzzle."

Most important to Esselstyn is the idea that a sexual encounter is a fifty–fifty deal. Both parties are actively involved. Thus, her emphasis is on avoiding the one-sided narrative—in which a man is the actor and a woman is the acted upon—that seems to be the cultural norm. It is not often that sex is described as a warm, loving, act respectfully shared between two people—a woman and a man, two men, or two women. Students often describe sex as a man putting, penetrating, thrusting, or humping his penis into the woman's vagina. That language makes it sound like the man is the subject—navigator of the action—and the woman is the object—the one to whom things are done.

With her own kids and students, Esselstyn is careful to explain that a woman can slide her vagina over the man's penis, just as the man can put his penis in her vagina. It is best to have kids understand that both people involved are having sex together. This way, from an early age they grasp that they have choice and are participating in the action. This is a subtle shift in language, but when you consider the message we hope to convey about consensual sex to older kids, it's an important one.

Julie Metzger is a Seattle-based sexuality educator who has written girl and boy versions of *Will Puberty Last My Whole Life?* and created Great Conversations, which offers sexuality education classes for teens and pre-teens, as well as for parents of preteens, in a straightforward and humorous way. Parents who have attended describe her as "legendary" and "a savior" because their kids were thoroughly engaged in learning about sex. While answering a kid's question about the enormity of sexual intercourse, Metzger manages to address a serious topic in a positive manner that resonates with kids and parents: "This [sex] seems to be one of the biggest human-being actions, so I have to put it together with some of the biggest human-being qualities—trust, respect, love, commitment. That's why some people say this action belongs only to grown-ups."[6]

Unpredictable Kids

Even though my husband and I were ready and willing to talk to our kids about sex, none of our first few explanations went smoothly. And it wasn't as if we were totally on our game by the time our third child was ready to hear it just because we had been through it before. Each of our kids responded differently to our first round of conversations about how they were made. My husband was grateful that I was willing and eager to initiate these conversations, and he was the one who encouraged me to bring the discussion to a close once I'd answered the questions the kid had asked. We have a nice balance in this parenting realm. Some of us need reminders to answer only the questions that are asked, while others need reminders to answer *at least* the questions that are asked. The hope is that, if you have the luxury of two involved parents, you can balance each other out. If you are handling the conversations solo, find a good sounding board to help you debrief every once in a while. Even with two involved parents, my husband and I depend heavily on a number of friends who are sexuality educators and we tap into the wisdom of our siblings who have been through this. Depend on the village to become the best sexuality educator you can be. The variety of responses from our kids could never have been predicted. With all our kids in their teens now, we are so thankful we had the courage to dive in when they were in first grade. One of our kids listened intently to my explanation of how most babies are made, pondered the idea for a long, silent stretch, then asked, "Could I go play in the sandbox now?"

Another of our kids said to me, "You told me that women have the egg and men have the sperm, but you didn't tell me *how* they got together." I explained that, in most cases, babies are made when a couple has sexual intercourse. The dad's penis fits into the mom's vagina, then the semen carries the sperm out of the penis, into the vagina, and up into the uterus, where the sperm and egg grow into a baby. This time, my kid laughed in my face and said, "That is absolutely ridiculous." I went on to explain that couples have sex to make babies and also because it feels really good and is a way couples connect. If my husband had been there, he would have been giving me the hook at this point, but the laughter caused me to panic and want to fill the space. I considered that a partial success and vowed to be more prepared for the next chat.

When our third kid asked how babies are made, I was quite surprised by the series of questions that followed my explanation. I almost managed to respond calmly through all the questions. I was comfortably rolling along with solid answers when he asked, "What gets the semen to come out?" I felt at ease while I described that friction feels good and causes the penis to become erect and ultimately leads to ejaculation. I could have stopped there. But I went on to say that different things create the friction: vaginal intercourse, oral sex, and masturbation, to name a few. The questions kept rolling. Maintaining the outer appearance of being at ease required effort. My husband was asleep next to us, so was not available to help me avoid turning into the blowtorch mom I was in danger of becoming.

I was still relatively calm when my son asked, "How often do people have sex?" This felt okay because I wasn't aware of the direction he was going. I told him it is healthy for adults to either have sex or masturbate at least once a week for the health of their genitals, with a side benefit of enhancing the connection with one's spouse. My husband was stirring out of his sleep, no doubt wondering who the recipient of my overeducation was. My voice had become a little high and squeaky, and I started babbling that some people don't take the time to have sex because they are busy, tired, or may be too irritated with their spouse to be interested in sex. Luckily, I was cut off by the big whopper question that stunned me: "When is the last time you and dad had sex?" I was completely flummoxed and uncharacteristically silent. My husband calmly jumped in with, "That is a very personal question. That is one of the few things your mom and I keep private." The reliable husband rescued me from myself.

Fear of Blabbing Kids

My husband and I kept communication lines clear and open with our kids, leading up to the first conversation about the mechanics of sexual intercourse. They were all comfortable asking questions about sex by this time. I followed up with each of them to explain that not all kids have parents who talk openly about sex and to respect other families' choices by not passing information along. My older two kids said that wouldn't be a problem because they were embarrassed that their parents discussed sex so openly, and they would not be inclined to pass any information along. One of them added that she was glad to know the truth. The third said it was useless to try to explain such a thing to friends who were sure that "babies came out of their mom's butts."

A big fear on the part of parents is that their kid will be blabbing at school once they share information about sexual intercourse with them. It is much more rare than people think, likely because most kids are embarrassed to have parents who talk openly about these topics, and also because the truth is kind of scientific. Conveying all that information to other kids while playing Legos or during snack time is a daunting challenge.

If parents are evasive, some kids may talk publicly about what has piqued their curiosity, because the explanation was incomplete. Possessing saucy, off-limits information is more fun for kids than knowing the truth about sex. This combination of uncomfortable parents and incomplete explanations inspires kids to test the reactions of other kids and adults outside the home. Parents and teachers are quick to engage in these situations, either with clear answers or attempts to deflect. Clear answers are the best hope for closure. Deflection causes kids to keep shopping for answers, understanding, and reactions. If your kids are the rare ones who tend to share at school, you can hope that their candor inspires other parents to respond appropriately.

Informed Kids

Well-informed kids who received accurate information and honest answers to questions about sex throughout their childhood stand a better chance of making healthy choices. When conversations about sexuality have been a part of your family life, the topics are no longer loaded with mystery and charge. In my family, we followed our pediatrician's advice to teach our kids in first grade. Our kids are teenagers now, and there is very little awkwardness when we talk about sex because they got a lot of information years before it had personal connection and meaning.

Don't be deterred by kids who resist your openness and honesty, or if they misunderstand something you explain. The research is clear that kids of all ages want to know what their parents think and value. Keep sharing what you believe and feel about sexuality and relationships. Resistance is how they test your threshold. Be resilient and stay on course. If you stumble or have a setback, seek out reliable sources to help you quickly adjust your approach, regroup, and get back in the game. Kids want to hear what you think and believe.

Expert Advice on Sexuality Education Guidelines

By Jane Esselstyn, RN, sexuality educator

Talking with your family about sexuality creates a connection and a lifeline of health and support for their whole lives. Do not hesitate to talk with your kids about anything! It is never too early. They are *not* behaving in sexually intimate ways until puberty strikes (or well beyond). But they *are* curious, thinking, problem-solving, pattern-seeking, decision-making beings their whole life long. If they are asking you questions about sex, it means they believe *you* are the best resource. As parents, we should hope to be their resources—like tail-lights in the fog driving ahead of them, guiding them along the way. They can see what is either coming up soon or may happen in the far future. And they are looking toward *you* to be reassured.

We all expect that our kids will drive someday. They watch us doing so for years. There are rules around driving set in place to keep yourself and other safe. It is risky, it can be dangerous, and it is something we hope all our children do. It takes adult modeling—sixteen-plus years of it! Similarly, we raise our kids with the expectations that they will be able to make a fire. We teach our kids how to safely be around fire. It is beautiful, warm, fun to share with others, and it is risky and can harm you.

If you don't answer their questions, where will they go? Likely to a friend or the Internet, or, as one student told me, "If my parents don't want to answer it, I will just go to Google video." Have you ever typed the words naked, boobies, sex, kissing, BJ, penis, vagina, or three-way into your browser? That should inspire us all to dive into the topics with our kids before they go elsewhere.

This caring, preparatory guidance should be available when it comes to the topic of sex, sexuality, sexual behavior, sexual feelings, and the like. The real shift into becoming a sexual being swoops in around puberty, when, according to nature, they are ready for this new dimension of themselves. We want our kids to confidently head into life already knowing they are wired to be sexual beings and to feel healthy and normal. Don't hesitate to talk about sexuality in your home. By doing so, your kids will learn that these topics are important to think about, learn about, and talk about.

People often learn to associate topics around sexuality with embarrassment, loss for words, and uncomfortable tones and postures. Take a breath, lean in, and find the strength to answer your child's questions. It will become the armor that defends them against engaging in misinformation, drama, and rumors in their peer group or even on the bus ride home. Most importantly, your willingness to answer questions will remind them that you are a reliable resource for fact-checking new terms or behaviors that come up in their day.

Grab the Chance

Many parents tell stories about being questioned on the spot when the wrong link opened on a computer screen while they were trying to find a kid-friendly movie. The links for sketchy websites and inappropriate products purposefully include common letters and words to get more traffic and gain curious customers. It can be difficult to explain the pornographic images that show up with one mistyped character. Porn sites intentionally use names that are close to common search topics, so that the site will be found easily.

If an inappropriate image pops up on the screen, it is important to respond calmly to avoid engaging kids' curiosity even more. Preschool-age children may not fully register what has flashed before their eyes and may move on quickly. Older kids, however, may have questions, laugh, or even be scared about what they saw. In these cases, give a short, clear answer in a calm manner, even though you are on the spot. Preparing for the possibility ahead of time and deciding what kind of explanation fits your parenting style and the age of your kids will make the moment much less stressful. You might take the opportunity to explain that these pornographic images are created and placed by people who are desperate to get more traffic to their sites. The possibility of this occurring should motivate parents to start discussing healthy sexuality to ensure that their viewpoints and values are always a reference point.

Another situation that forces the need for explanation is being caught having sex by your kids. It is an unforgettable experience for the parents and the kid, and some kind of explanation has to happen immediately. When caught in the act, parents get pretty clever with their responses, hoping to distract their kids from asking further questions. "We were wrestling" or "Mom is having a back spasm," they say. The impulse to blurt random responses is common to all parents when they are caught in the act. Kids may be deterred from mentioning anything that would evoke further comment or conversation, especially if they have not been part of any conversations about sex and bodies. Since the image will stick in their mind, however, it is worth rallying to address it in some manner.

Whenever my own mother alluded to my parents' relationship as a sexual one, we kids steered clear of anything that could possibly trigger any more of those comments. In the long run, it was healthy for us to know that our parents were connected and expressed their love, but we didn't want to know the details. Just because most kids in the United States are brought up without many explanations about sexuality doesn't mean the norm isn't worth challenging. It is possible to talk about healthy sexuality without discussing the personal details of your own sex life, even after getting caught in the act or stumbling with your child onto a pornographic image or video online.

One way or another, the topic of sex will land in front of your kids. It is worth grabbing an opportunity to talk to them when the chance arises. We all hope for a benign example that has distance from our personal life. The trouble is that it is never as benign or distant as we would like, so we keep waiting. If any chance shows up and isn't personal, grab it. As crazy as it sounds, dogs humping in public are a common first exposure to sex and a prime opportunity to talk about sexual intercourse. Addressing the situation is necessary because a public sighting of dogs humping creates a charge of adult reactions. The standard mix of people discouraging the dogs, smirking, and concealing laughter and firmly reprimanding or attempting to break the dogs apart creates magnetism for kids' attention. They will have questions. You may be thinking, why rush this conversation? Give strong consideration to the preemptive strike of diving into the sex conversation at the first sight of dogs humping in public. It really does make the best of a bad situation.

Don't Delay

Robie H. Harris, author of several children's books, including *It's Not About the Stork,* counsels parents to start talking with their kids about bodies and sex early on: "My feeling is that if we're not honest with our kids starting at a very young age, then we have no credibility. If they know that they can get answers to their questions, then they keep asking the questions, and they'll come to us."[7] The longer we delay talking to our kids about sexuality, the more alarming the questions can become.

When kids are left to their own devices to make sense of what they see or hear on the bus, at recess, and at friends' houses, they will seek answers online, which can confuse them even more. When they reach a point where they are desperate for clarification of some term or phrase, they drop the big question bomb at the dinner table or in the grocery store. As a parent, you feel unprepared, trapped, and unsure of how to respond. It is really challenging to respond to questions from a second grader about oral sex or threesomes while filling out a deposit slip in a bank lobby or in some other public place. Various factors inspire these nerve-wracking questions. Sometimes your child is moved to ask you because a person, song, or advertisement reminded her of the question. Sometimes your child wants to test just how sketchy the term or phrase is by watching your reaction in a public place. In these cases, it is perfectly acceptable to admit the topic is inappropriate for a public chat, but promise you will follow up when you get to the car or get home. No matter what, you must follow up.

This is why I strongly encourage you to consider the value of training in the shallow end of dicey questions while your kids are young or—if you've missed that opportunity—as soon as possible, to prepare for the inevitable big ones that famously throw parents off their game when they least expect it. I hear many stories from parents who have been confronted with very awkward questions about sexual terms and sexual acts fueled by urban myths. For this reason alone, starting sex ed early is worth it.

Answering one of these difficult questions without having talked to your child about healthy, loving sex is rattling. If, however, you deflect or avoid answering a question about some particular act, the next stop for your child will be the Urban Dictionary or, worse, Google, which will produce a long list of links to help define or demonstrate with a video. If you try to explain healthy, loving sex for the first time after your child has stumbled on disturbing or disrespectful sexual images or language while seeking answers, your child is likelier to retain that more graphic image. Answering questions about any term or act fueled by urban myth is significantly easier when you have already had conversations about and provided a strong definition of loving and respectful sex.

Deborah Roffman explains:

[Young children are] not ready or even interested in knowing about sex in an adult context. They aren't ready to go out and make a living, either, but they can understand the concept of money and some of the things you can do with it. In other words, they're ready for beginning concepts that later in life with help them become financially independent.

Children are intellectually or cognitively primed to learn basic concepts about sexuality—and more and more sophisticated ones later on—just as easily as any other subject. Too often adults project their emotionality about the subject and then can't step back far enough to realize that perhaps *they* are the ones who aren't ready emotionally.[8]

When planning a talk with their kids, most parents worry that they won't know what to say or how to say it. Each child's temperament and developmental stage, as well as particular situations or questions that may have arisen, calls for a different response. Practice at conversations about sexuality with your kids will help you define your values and build your portfolio of responses based on those values. Diving into sexuality education is a lot like training for a marathon: if you do weekly long runs as well as daily short runs for maintenance during the four months before the race, the last six miles of the marathon will be tolerable rather than a painful slog. When parents avoid being the primary sexuality educator in the early years of the parenting marathon, they face a more difficult slog during the "miles" of the teen years. Even if you didn't do the early training, though, it's important to dive in with courage and a positive attitude as your children grow.

CHAPTER 5

Sexuality Education for Older Kids and Teenagers

Teaching kids about sexuality is about giving them the skills, the framework, for putting themselves out there in the world with confidence. It's about valuing healthy bodies and healthy minds. It's about giving young people the tools to make healthy choices.

—Al Vernacchio, *For Goodness Sex: Changing the Way We Talk to Teens About Sexuality, Values, and Health*

According to the most recent studies, the average age at which a boy first looks at porn is, in the United States, eleven years.[1] Kids are exposed to porn and media online, or they hear a whole lot about what is available from friends who have had free access to the Internet from a young age. This is why it is key to start the conversations when they are young, or as soon as possible. Parents who delay these conversations in an effort to "protect the innocence" of their children have good intentions, but they are unintentionally leaving their children vulnerable to having information gaps filled by misguided peers and the Internet.

If you missed the window to teach your kids about sex when they were young, start now, no matter their age. Addressing sexuality and porn with kids and teenagers is difficult and unpleasant for many parents, but it is important to give kids accurate and healthier versions of sexual relationships than they are likely to encounter if parents don't intervene. If we avoid talking about sexuality with our kids, we risk making them more vulnerable to the vast array of influences they confront on their devices.

We need to break the cycle of kids growing up uninformed or misinformed; otherwise, our kids will make choices about sexual activity based on messages they internalize from other sources. We need to contribute to what our kids internalize, because we want them to feel empowered to follow their inner compass and make healthy choices. Sharing accurate information early and often is a great way to start. According to Robie H. Harris, "Children and teens can make responsible choices about sexual health only when they have a solid understanding of their bodies and sexuality. Isn't this what we all want for our kids and teens—for them to be able to make responsible choices?"[2]

Mustering the Courage: Conversations with Older Kids

Conviction is key. Arm yourself with information and reasoning to fall back on when your teens try to talk you out of having a conversation about sex. In his book *For Goodness Sex,* Al Vernacchio provides examples of conversations, phrasing, and reasoning that will help any parent or educator gain courage to dive in, even if they're worried they missed the window. Teenagers squirm a whole lot more when parents fumble and cringe their way through these conversations. Younger kids notice less and are more forgiving; therefore, you can think of talking to kids when they are young as a chance to practice and build skills that will help you be on your game when they get into their teens. Keep in mind that some kids don't squirm, and in fact are fearless about the topic. These kids seem to have a sixth sense about a parent's threshold, and know just what kind of zinger question will cause us to stumble.

Snags, surprises, and setbacks are all part of the process. Since my kids were little, I have been very comfortable and open, and have been prepared with lots of information and resources to back me up. I withstood many stumbles and zinger questions when they were young, but I picked myself up and kept at it. Now that they are teenagers, and even bolder with their questions, I am rarely fazed. Since the tone was set long ago and everyone in the family is used to the sexual language and details, these conversations barely cause a ripple. If you are starting when your kids are older, hold strong. Conversing with a teenager about sex is like giving a baby a new food. She will spit it out and reject it the first ten times you offer it, but if you keep offering, eventually she'll accept.

Advice About Sexuality Education

By Dr. Michael Lyons, MD, White River Family Practice, Family Practitioner and Father of Three

Conversations early in your child's life and all along make subsequent discussions about sex easier. At the onset of puberty, sexuality in media, songs, and advertisements provide good conversation starters: "Do you realize what those lyrics really mean?" If you missed the early window, start now with, "I thought I was protecting you by not talking about sex, but now I realize sexual messages are all around you." Even if they squirm, keep going. Talking in the car is a good strategy, because they can't sneak away. Some of what you say will get through, no matter how hard your child might try not to listen.

Books complement those conversations, and often provide the education that we couldn't deliver. Don't count on your pediatrician or the school for sex education. The yearly doctor's appointments are only for planting seeds for parents to follow up. Schools can't address sex in much detail because their hands are tied. If it is too awkward for you to talk about sex, recruit an aunt, uncle, or friend who has an open mind to approach topics with your child.

Seventh- and eighth-grade kids are either nearing or have already reached the time when they start some level of sexual expression: crushes, kissing, or fooling around. The window for parents influencing future choices around sex is closing. This is the age to reemphasize the values we parents hope they will adopt. It is also important to address topics like pornography, masturbation, and what "good sex" might look like. By the end of middle school, no topic you bring up will shock them. Middle school students will have heard it. Conversations can be harder at this age, but you can say, "Sex conversations are something you have to put up with because it is my job as a parent. Sex and relationships are supposed to be fun. Here are things you should think about to make sure you have healthy, positive experiences when you decide the time is right for you." Once they are older teenagers, they will be making decisions on their own, and hopefully will draw from your input over the years.

Surveys have shown that young adults in their twenties often regret their first sexual experience(s), especially if they became sexually active in the early teenage years. As much as we may want our kids to wait until they are older to have sex, we can't make those decisions for them. There are older teenagers who find the right partner and are excited about the choice to have sex. We can't make the choice for them, but we can provide the message that healthy relationships include trust, communication, consent, and respect. I suspect all parents would agree that we hope when our children are in their twenties, they will be content with the choices they made as teenagers. It is challenging to know what to say and choose the education that will help kids make the right choice for them. Talking early, regularly, and honestly about sex with our kids is our best chance to help them make good choices.

What's my role as parent of a son or daughter who is fifteen in a relationship? Be around all the time! Welcome your child's partner into your home and family life, but avoid leaving them in the house alone. By nature, teenagers can be impulsive. Leaving them alone might encourage sexual activity before they are truly ready. The teenagers who are clearly ready to become sexually active will figure out their private time and place.

When your daughter is heading out for the night with teammates, give her reminders, so you are one of the voices in her head when she faces a choice, "We are aware you and your teammates spend time up in your friend's cabin. We are glad you take your team code of conduct seriously."

The Balance for Schools and Teachers

Despite the fact that parents are the primary sexuality educators for their own kids, many parents delay, avoid, or hope their children get the information they need elsewhere. When parents of middle and high school kids become aware that their kids are looking at porn, having sex, sending sexually explicit texts, or sexually harassing other kids through social media, they commonly blame the schools or the pediatrician for not teaching the children better.

In the case of pediatricians, two factors limit the amount of sexual education they can communicate to kids: time and the comfort level of parents. According to pediatrician Dr. Michael Lyons, "During the annual checkup appointments, our job is to plant seeds as guides for conversations between parents and their kids." Pediatricians often have only about thirty minutes during a yearly appointment, and must cover many issues during that time in addition to addressing sexuality. This is only enough time to plant seeds; parents need to provide the specifics.

Similarly, public schools are limited in what they can teach. Sexuality education in both public and some private schools has become a polarizing topic. Science and health teachers find it challenging to balance teaching what they know is essential information for kids in the digital age while meeting a broad range of parental expectations. Parental feedback and complaints about sexuality education range from the curriculum not having enough information to the lessons giving too much information to the course not imparting the "right" information. Ultimately, the time and energy required to deal with varied input and expectations leads to a watered-down curriculum in many public schools. When my oldest son was in fifth grade, he asked me if the school had changed the name for sex ed to "puberty education" because the parents get nervous. I didn't really have an answer that would challenge the conclusion he came to on his own.

Students are fortunate if they have a sex ed teacher who has the gift of conveying information about sex comfortably and with honesty, and even a little humor to take the edge off. It is a challenge to find educators who are at ease presenting information about sexuality *and* who have the skill and confidence to field questions from demanding parents. Expecting teachers and schools to find just the right sex ed balance to satisfy all parents is a recipe for disappointment. Schools are limited. With such a large number of parents wanting to outsource sexuality education for their kids, various organizations provide alternatives to the conventional classroom format, an approach I'll discuss later in the chapter.

> "I teach fifth and sixth grade, and we are simply teaching the unit on 'your changing body.' I am a bit embarrassed that it isn't more than that, and feel like there is a huge hole in the sex ed continuum at the elementary school level. There is very little talk in our district about a sex ed 'continuum' for the younger grades and whether we are responsible for teaching sex ed in the schools."
> —Classroom teacher in a Vermont public school

Independent School Challenge

Policies and rules concerning sex and intimacy are not issues for parents alone to navigate. Administrators, dorm parents, and counselors at most independent schools strive to find a realistic balance by aligning policies with parents' values while maintaining clear boundaries that are neither too permissive nor impossibly restrictive. Administrators get plenty of calls from parents who think the school needs to be more restrictive with students. Sometimes these calls come from parents who not only turn a blind eye to what their kids are up to, but whose homes or second homes are venues for parties and who, often unknowingly, provide access to alcohol. It is a tricky situation for parents and for faculties of schools. Teenagers are going to find a way to have sex. The fact that copulating students and used condoms are regularly discovered in the dustiest, mustiest, coldest, and most uncomfortable crevices around campuses reflects the sheer determination and innovation of opportunistic kids. The bar is low for kids with limited options. Administrators are obligated to deter sexual behavior on their campuses, and conversations initiated by complaining students about better options won't get much consideration.

The Thacher School, an independent boarding school in Ojai, California, has managed to limit kids' options and inspire buy-in to the rules and school philosophy. Thacher has created an environment in which students have an opportunity to avoid the cultural pressures most teenagers are struggling to navigate. The outdoor camping program and the horse program are equalizers for the students, and set the tone for life at Thacher. Spending the week before the school year starts hiking together up to fourteen thousand feet gives kids the opportunity to work as a team, feel capable, gain an ecological perspective, and learn how to take care of themselves and others while living outdoors. As a first-year student at Thacher, each kid is given responsibility for a horse, which includes riding the horse and caring for it regularly, as a means of learning about himself by mastering the horse.

As a speaker who travels to a variety of schools and colleges, I find it refreshing to witness Thacher's success in decreasing sexual behavior and use of alcohol and drugs on campus in measurable ways. Thacher's strict alcohol and drug policy is supported by the latest research on the way these substances impact memory and brain development in teens. Thacher is not only right in line with the current research on brain development, but the school became aware of that research before it was part of public discourse. Thacher also has a policy that forbids sexual intimacy on campus. Behavior expectations are clear, and the significant consequences for breaking the honor code are understood and respected by parents and students. Consistent follow-through involves notifying parents and suspension or expulsion when appropriate. Seniors are obligated to report disciplinary incidents to the college they plan to attend, motivating kids to make healthier choices.

In the late nineties, administrators at Thacher made a decision to address alcohol and drug use and sexual behavior by shifting their approach to improve the culture of the school. Most notable in these efforts is the use of surveys to measure kids' satisfaction with various areas of school life (e.g., clubs, organizations, dorm life) and behaviors (e.g., sexual, social, cheating). The Thacher administration's commitment to a multifaceted change in their approach resulted in a high level of accountability and buy-in among students and parents. Our wider culture sends a message to kids that they can avoid taking full responsibility for their behaviors and choices, while accountability is part of Thacher students' daily lives.

Independent schools could learn from Thacher's success, and public schools could incorporate some aspects of their approach, such as clear policies and consistent follow-through. Because sexuality education in the digital age requires a more direct approach to sensitive topics, some schools and parents may find they need to supplement their method with outside programs. Some communities solve this by bringing a program to the school, church, or community to support their efforts. Proactive sexuality education is our best bet to help our children develop healthy attitudes that will guide them beyond high school.

Get Real: Comprehensive Sex Education

Get Real is a program implemented by Planned Parenthood of Massachusetts and taught in classrooms with parental/caring adult involvement. Because of its successes in getting kids to delay sex, the program appeals to parents with a broad spectrum of values. "This is a program for older elementary and early middle school students that helps young people to delay having sex," says Leslie Kantor, a vice president for education at Planned Parenthood. "So even states that stress abstinence...might be very interested in this type of program since it actually gets to these abstinence kind of outcomes."[3] Get Real not only encourages kids to put off having sex but also informs them about correct use of protection. According to the program's statement, "Get Real incorporates five Social and Emotional Learning skills: self awareness, self management, social awareness, relationship skills and decision making as key elements in learning how to negotiate relationships. If young people can negotiate relationships, they can better negotiate sexual relationships."[4]

After participating in the program in sixth through eighth grades, 15 percent fewer girls had sex and 16 percent fewer boys had sex, compared with those who did not participate. This is one of the first programs to have a clear, significant influence on students' sexual behavior. Each year, students in the program attend nine classes, totaling twenty-seven classes by the end of eighth grade. Homework involves follow-up activities to engage parents and family members in conversations. Parents have been highly responsive and seem more willing to engage in sexuality education with their kids with the support of resources and guidance provided by Get Real. The success rate of Get Real has placed it on the list of evidence-based sex ed programs that are eligible for purchase with federal funds.

Get Real values, supports, and respects adolescents' rights and abilities to make informed choices about their own health and safety by:

- Offering factual, medically accurate, age-appropriate information
- Communicating about the benefits of abstinence
- Teaching effective communication and negotiation skills to strengthen sexual health decision making throughout life
- Providing accurate information about safe and effective protection methods that prevent STIs and pregnancy
- Believing that young people have a fundamental right to honest, accurate, comprehensive sexuality education[5]

Our Whole Lives

Sexuality education programs taught outside the classroom solve many of the issues in communities where public schools are limited and parents are reluctant to take on the role of primary sexuality educator for their kids. Our Whole Lives (OWL) is a program that is typically taught outside the school environment and is intended to cover topics that public schools are unable to address.

In the 1990s, the United Church of Christ (UCC) and the Unitarian Universalist Association (UUA) joined forces to adapt and update the About Your Sexuality (AYS) program to become OWL, a series of sexuality education curricula for six age groups: children in kindergarten to first grade, grades four to six, grades seven to nine, and grades ten to twelve, young adults ages eighteen to thirty-five, and adults. People of all faiths are welcome to participate in the programs, and the curricula are available through the UCC and UUA websites. According to Sarah Gibb Millspaugh, a Unitarian Universalist minister who served as outreach coordinator for the development of OWL, "[Even] when used without faith materials, Our Whole Lives is one of the most acclaimed comprehensive sexuality education curricula used by schools, teen pregnancy prevention programs, and sexual health organizations today."[6]

Our Whole Lives helps participants make informed and responsible decisions about their sexual health and behavior. It equips participants with accurate, age-appropriate information in six subject areas: human development, relationships, personal skills, sexual behavior, sexual health, and society and culture. Grounded in a holistic view of sexuality, OWL provides facts about anatomy and human development, and it helps participants clarify their values, build interpersonal skills, and understand the spiritual, emotional, and social aspects of sexuality.[7]

Parents of participants report that they are grateful their kids are receiving accurate information that will help them develop more realistic expectations about sexual relationships. Teachers of the program get a lot of positive feedback that the OWL materials make it easier for parents to broach specific topics with kids who have gone through the OWL programs. Leslie MacGregor, OWL facilitator for the seventh- through ninth-grade level, says she receives a lot of positive comments from parents, who share: "I cannot say enough about how helpful OWL has been, especially with encouraging and easing conversations at home. OWL helps us all become so much more comfortable talking about sexuality. The facilitators send an update for parents on what material is being covered each week, so it feels very natural to continue conversations at home."

According to MacGregor, "Every exercise is designed to help them become people who base their actions (sexual or otherwise) on a clear set of values. There is a structure from which to begin their journey that counters the overwhelming messages from the greater culture about sex." MacGregor has been teaching the OWL program to seventh through ninth graders for ten years—because kids at this age are usually becoming decidedly more interested in deliberate, physical sexual experiences with other people, this is the flagship curriculum. MacGregor encourages parents to recognize that, as adults, we cannot see the world through the eyes of teenagers anymore: "That vision is gone. I can't take away the 'big picture' view that being middle-aged provides, just to get on their level. The solution I have discerned is to listen more and talk less." The OWL curriculum and training sessions help adults (parents and facilitators) put this ideal into practice.

MacGregor went on to say, "The beauty of a program like OWL is that it normalizes conversations about sex between younger and older people. In the church setting, where I have taught OWL, the kids learn that they are respected and cared for by their community as emerging sexual beings.

Their thoughts and opinions matter, and their questions are taken seriously. A common comment on the evaluation forms is how great it is to be able to talk about *anything*!"

Circles of Sexuality

Advocates for Youth is in its fourth decade of promoting adolescent reproductive and sexual health policy and programming.[8] The program provides resources and lesson plans that help parents and professionals augment their own teaching. The Our Whole Lives curriculum for grades seven to nine includes Circles of Sexuality, a broad definition of sexuality that serves as a basis for discussion and activities created by *Advocates for Youth*. Circles of Sexuality has five components: sensuality, sexual intimacy, sexual identity, reproduction and sexual health, and sexualization.

A good number of parents struggle to understand sexual identity, in particular, and need support to help them teach the concepts in a tolerant, respectful way to their children. It is worth tapping into multiple resources to educate yourself as well as to prepare yourself for questions from your kids.

Clarity on Sex, Gender, and Sexual Identity

By Jessica Pettitt, speaker and consultant,
GoodEnoughNow.com

Sex, in a physical sense, references one's biology, anatomy, chromosomes, hormones, fertility, menstruation, menopause, and the like, and is often labeled at or before birth based on external genitalia (or lack thereof). An individual with incongruent physical attributes would be intersex (replacing the term hermaphrodite). An individual who is congruent with current sex-based expectations would be female or male.

Gender identity encompasses one's roles, expressions, and identities and how this is perceived and/or validated by others. Society in any given culture dictates what is typical and atypical of gender expectations, and this may change over time, place, and community. An individual who doesn't personally identify with others' expectations may fall within the trans umbrella of non-gender-conforming identities versus a binary feminine and masculine spectrum that aligns with a female and male sex. Women and men, and those outside the binary, can express, identify, and fulfill lots of different expectations of gender.

Sexual orientation is used instead of "sexual preference" or "lifestyle choices," which are outdated terms, and sexual identity is an even more inclusive term for one's sense (or lack thereof) of attraction as connected to one's gender identity. Sexual orientation best describes a romantic or sexual relationship (or lack thereof) with others. Lesbian and gay often describe women and men who are in relationships with other women and men, respectively. Bisexual, pansexual, and omnisexual describe an individual woman or man who is sexually and/or romantically attracted to another person or other people without a physical or gender limitation. Asexual refers to someone who is not sexually or romantically attracted to another yet may still seek companionship and even intimacy.

Heterosexual describes what our culture assumes to be the most accepted relationship, a woman and a man. This assumption is heteronormative—making heterosexuality an identity and an expected behavior the privileged group. One's attractions and/or relationship desires (or lack there of) may not change when gender identity/expression changes. Sexual orientation may not change but gender transition changes one's sexual identity.

Relationships can vary in a number of ways, as can gender and sex. It is our responsibility to educate ourselves and listen to other people as they share their stories and ways of identifying. Whether another person's story is reflected in our own lives isn't the point. Being able to listen, perceive, and validate another's story is truly being an ally.

Tolerance

According to CDC Youth Risk Behavior Surveillance Surveys, LGBTQ (lesbian, gay, bisexual, transgender, queer) young people are two to five times more likely than their heterosexual peers to report skipping school because they have felt isolated or experienced violence. LGBTQ youth are more than four times as likely to have felt unsafe during the past month and to have made a serious suicide attempt in the past year. According to Lee Che Leong, director of the Teen Heath Initiative at the NYCLU, "Curricular inclusion, especially within health education models, is a necessary component of remedying the isolation of LGBTQ youth."[9]

Parents and educators have many battles to fight. We need to dig deeper and address hate language with our kids, including use of words that may not sound hateful to them. Kids' use of the words "gay" or "fag" is something we need to address directly and in the moment. Tolerating use of these words is like neglecting a plantar wart: if you don't take care of it, the roots keep growing even though you can't see them. I hear kids and adults say, "I would *never* say those words to someone who was gay!" as if this restraint reflects the ultimate act of inclusivity and respect. The ability to select your audience is evidence enough that you know better. Such language is disrespectful and unacceptable.

Particularly for older kids and teenagers, it is safe to say that a number of their peers are questioning or have not yet come out. By using disrespectful language, kids (and adults) send a message to people around them that they may not be supportive and accepting friends. Sometimes kids use homophobic language intentionally to convince peers that they are not gay or to cover the fact that they are gay or questioning. At other times, these words are used out of laziness or to make it clear that the teen is not comfortable having a gay friend. Kids start using "gay" and "fag" in elementary school. Call your kids out, encourage them to call each other out, and accept being called out if you utter these words.

Many parents of this generation are more open and comfortable supporting kids who are gay, transgender, bisexual, asexual, or questioning. We have come a long way; however, it can take years for kids to get up the courage to come out to their parents, for a multitude of reasons. If a parent has made derogatory comments about gay, transgender, or bisexual people, a child who is deciding whether to come out may delay the conversation or talk to someone else who is more supportive.

Out of a fear of injurious homophobic, transphobic, or biphobic actions being directed at their child, well-intentioned parents sometimes make unsupportive, ignorant comments to a child who decides to come out. After wrestling with their own assumptions and fears, some parents are able to give their unconditional love and support to their son or daughter. Cruelty and lack of acceptance in pockets of our society could make life challenging for their child, and this is a legitimate concern for parents. Parents who are not accepting may disown their kids or require them to undergo ineffective sexual orientation change effort (SOCE), therapies also known as "conversion therapy," "reparative therapy," and "reorientation therapy." These "therapies" push many people back into the closet rather than change their orientation. Greater tolerance and acceptance from family and friends, as well as in society, would eliminate the mental health challenges that so many young people suffer while trying to mask their sexual identity.

It is important to educate and prepare our kids to have open minds, even if topics and issues are challenging for us as parents. Adults who are not aware of, or have not been exposed to, anything beyond a heteronormative view need to consider that their children may identify differently and that they likely study, work, and/or live with people who identify differently.

Some parents find it difficult to digest how much society and relationships have changed since they were kids, and therefore choose to disengage from their kids' personal and social lives. Ultimately, though, it is to parents' and kids' benefit if parents face what is going on in and around their children's lives. Increasing your exposure to new information and paying attention to shifts in trends and teen behaviors will enable you to have meaningful conversations with your kids.

Changing Landscape—Pubic Hair

The trend of removing pubic hair is another example of a change that leads some parents to engage in discussions with kids and others to bury their head in the sand. When pressed for justification, some girls and young women claim that they wax or shave their pubic hair to give better access to their clitoris. On the heels of the sexual revolution in the seventies, my sisters-in-law and their friends, both female and male, were talking about female pleasure with an openness and healthy tone I have not witnessed since. This openness that was perceived as salacious but, in comparison to the hypersexualized culture of today, it now seems quaint and relatively enlightened.

Access to the clitoris is not usually hair related, since there is no hair on the clitoris *or* the clitoral hood. Back in the seventies, pride in a righteous bush of pubic hair, along with a lot of other hair, was all the rage and was part of the message of being unrestrained by cultural expectations and norms. It was also a time when many more young women had full knowledge of the clitoris and its capacity for pleasure, a concept that was part of the conversations of sexually active young people. Unfortunately, pleasure education has been absent from open conversations among young people for the last few decades. The presence of pubic hair, however, shouldn't be an obstacle to the clitoris.

The primary motivator for removing pubic hair in this day and age is appearance. Hair is simply considered unsightly by some. Most girls and women who remove their pubic hair are shaving rather than waxing it, because shaving costs less and doesn't require a salon visit. Waxing or shaving can cause skin irritation, rashes, ingrown hairs, and infections. As unsightly and uncomfortable as these common conditions are, many young women are willing to endure them. In fact, there is a growing trend of mothers who don't want their daughters to be bothered with pubic hair taking their middle school–age girls to get rid of hair follicles before the pubic hair grows.

Despite the feedback young women get from male partners whose ideas about pubic hair are influenced by culture, porn and peers, most heterosexual guys will not forego a sexual opportunity based on the presence of pubic hair. Several confident young women I know put that theory to the test and reported how quickly pubic hair became a nonfactor when they addressed the issue directly with their male partners. Most young people are just trying to fit in, and are surprisingly receptive to reeducation about what their culture has taught them.

Most of the gynecologists and midwives I've talked to over the years are getting used to the broad spectrum of pubic hair maintenance they see, ranging from bush pride to trimming to Brazilian wax or waxed bikini line to full removal. When the recent hair removal trend caught on, some medical professionals wondered how patients could possibly find an internal exam awkward when they spent energy and time removing all their pubic hair and decorating their vulvas and montes pubis with tattoos, piercings, and/or bejeweling. While gynecologists and midwives are less fazed by the trend of pubic hair removal, it continues to be a topic of debate.

According to Mindy Schorr, certified nurse midwife, "Aesthetics are determined by the times we live in. Recent hair removal trends seem to follow fashion trends. As bathing suit styles changed over the years, hair removal has reflected those styles. What defines beauty is driven by culture." Schorr refers to a lecture she heard by Judy Burke titled "Bear or Hair." An expert on Renaissance art, Burke discussed the trends, risks, and benefits of removing hair throughout history, using paintings of nudes for illustration. Looking at paintings from various periods in history, it is clear that pubic hair removal trends are not new. Some evidence suggests that the risk of "vermin," currently known as "crabs" or pubic lice, motivated women living in the sixteenth century to remove their pubic hair. Other evidence indicates historical attitudes that hair on women was a symbol of masculinity and that pubic hair made women smell bad.

Hair removal techniques were and continue to be a challenging endeavor. During her research, Burke discovered a "book of secrets" from 1532 that included a recipe for hair removal that included arsenic and quicklime and endorsed timely rinsing the depilatory with hot water "so the flesh doesn't come off."[10] This sounds like a risky business requiring impeccable timing. The way society views and portrays women in media today correlates to Burke's following observation, "The renaissance nude wasn't simply a celebration of humanity, or a homage to a lost antique past, but popularized—even fetishized—quite narrow notions of attractiveness in a society where, for women, beauty was a cultural currency and could determine their future prospects."[11] As we can see in our own time, "narrow notions of attractiveness" continue to drive some women to spend a lot of time, effort, and money trying to meet beauty standards based on cultural notions. It is possible to change cultural notions with open dialogue with young women.

Pubic hair is credited for distributing pheromones, and while removing pubic hair reduces risk for several STDs, it increases the chance of contracting others. Research psychologist Jesse Bering warns, "Before you go scheduling your next Brazilian wax, consider that pubic hair does appear to offer some degree of protection against even nastier bacterial and viral infections. Although the diagnosis of pubic lice has seemingly plummeted as a direct result of human vanity in both sexes, cases of gonorrhea and chlamydia have increased over the same period, a correlation that may not be merely coincidental."[12] Researchers conducted a study of roughly 1,100 American undergrads to better understand pubic hair removal/grooming practices. The results, published in the *Journal of Sexual Medicine,* indicate that 95 percent of the participants had removed their pubic hair on at least one occasion in the previous month, with shaving the method used by 82 percent of females and 49 percent of males.[13] Women reported their reasons as having a sexual partner, appearance, cleanliness, and social norms. Men aren't reporting reasons as clear as women's; however, in my interviews guys often laughingly admit that removing pubic hair makes their penis look bigger.

Australian psychologists Marika Tiggemann and Suzanna Hodgson report that 76 percent of 235 female undergrads interviewed removed their public hair. For young women, the removal of pubic hair is significantly correlated with having a sexual partner, something that Hodgson and Tiggemann find more than a little troubling. According to their report, "The complete removal of pubic hair is also removing a key marker of adult female sexuality. The result is a prepubescent-like body that is highly sexualized. Thus it is another practice that may contribute to the increasing objectification and sexualization of young girls."[14]

Watch the Pros

According to the survey results of the National Campaign to Prevent Teen and Unplanned Pregnancy, "Nearly 87% of adolescents agree that 'it would be easier for adolescents to postpone sexual activity and avoid adolescent pregnancy if they were able to have more open, honest conversations about these topics with their parents.'"[15] When kids get to be teenagers, parents are welcomed into the doctor's office for the beginning of the appointment. This is a time to learn from the doctor by listening to the way she approaches difficult topics. Pediatrician Dr. Mary Bender says, "I often talk about sex pretty frankly with parents *and* kids rather than ask-ing parents to leave early on in the visit. I want to model talking about sex." She went on to say that she is more inclined in today's climate "to be explicit in telling parents that it is their job to teach about sexuality and that it can't be outsourced to school, pediatricians, or anyone else. This is especially critical in single-parent families with opposite-gender parent/child situations, in which the parent *really* tends to abdicate."

Bender uses this definition as a guideline for her patients: "Healthy sex is between two similarly aged people who care deeply about each other and explore each other's bodies for pleasure. If all these are not in place, it is not a healthy sexual relationship." Her intention is to acknowledge that sex is intended to be pleasurable for *both* participants and should be inspired by a shared emotional connection. Her emphasis on "similarly aged" people is intended to remind patients that sex with someone out of their age range is not only inappropriate but could be considered abuse. If this triggers a concern for a patient or a parent, she hopes that the patient will bring it up in the appointment or soon after with a parent or another trusted adult who can follow up.

You can get guidance and new ideas for keeping conversations about sexuality going by paying attention to how your child's pediatrician inter-acts with him. Some doctors take on challenging topics with kids in a way that shows off an apparently natural skill, but remember that pediatricians have ample opportunities to practice phrasing questions and responses with lots of different kids over the course of each day. They offer a prime example of how ease can be achieved with practice and experience, includ-ing missteps. Unlike kids, we parents aren't necessarily comfortable with sharp learning curves and being off our game as we learn new things, but if we embrace that openness, conversations about sexuality will get easier.

CHAPTER 6

Worthy Girls

Strengthening your daughter's intrinsic girlhood appreciation of what makes her body feel good and how it is strong, capable, and uniquely beautiful supports her in resisting the glitzy million-dollar advertising campaigns that aim to make her insecure about her looks so she will buy more products.

—SuEllen Hamkins, MD, and Renée Schultz, MA,
*The Mother-Daughter Project: How Mothers and
Daughters Can Band Together, Beat the Odds,
and Thrive Through Adolescence*

In my own experiences and observations as a teacher and a mother, I find it interesting how we nurture our kids in one direction or another depending on their gender. Watching parents and teachers point out bulldozers to young boys and princesses to young girls are two clear examples of how we steer our kids using a "positive jolly voice" to light kids up and influence them, both consciously and subconsciously. Do we use the same tone, facial expression, and enthusiasm when we point out bulldozers to girls? Do we even point out princesses to boys? We have seen some awesomely funny viral videos of dads with their toddler daughters in the backseat rocking "Let It Go." It is progress that we accept dads engaging in their daughters' interests, but imagine the comments and feedback that would result if a dad posted a video singing the same song with his toddler son. We have made progress, but the boundaries around gender expectations are still more absolute than is healthy for developing kids.

When our older two kids were six months old and a little over two, my husband and I drove across the country. We made an adventure out of time off, a wedding in Colorado, and friends to visit along the way. Thanks to napping kids, a pacifier, and great music, it was a surprisingly enjoyable sightseeing experience. I did an experiment with our two-year-old, to see if I could get him interested in something random by working the positive jolly voice and animated facial expressions. I chose water towers because there are a lot of them between New Hampshire and Colorado, but the choice could have been anything, as long as I was engaging with him about it with enthusiasm. It took about four sightings with me getting my big, jolly voice going to say, "Look, fella, there's a water tower." When the fifth one came into view he craned to see and burst out with, "LOOOK MOMMY, DEEEHHHZ A WAUTAH TOWAHHHHHHH!" My husband and I would laugh and respond with delight.

We kept this routine up all the way out West and then back home to New Hampshire, where we occasionally pass a water tower in our travels. Until he was about six, my son would get so hopped up about that one water tower that his younger siblings caught on. We finally confessed how we created the water tower obsession. Now it is part of our family lore and a point of reference when anyone in the family witnesses other parents working the positive jolly voice to get their kids interested in or motivated to do or wear something.

Gender in the Toy Box

When expecting parents announce the gender of their child, the pink or blue gifts start rolling in. Room décor items, bedding, clothing, and toys are made and advertised more specifically for girls or boys than ever before. Comparisons between advertisements for toys from the seventies and the toys of today show the sharp gender divide clearly. Forty years ago, play strollers, kitchen sets, and playhouses were offered in neutral colors such as yellow, white, red, navy blue, and brown. Almost all current toy strollers and doll accessories are bubblegum pink. A group called Let Toys Be Toys found that 80 percent of strollers in current catalogues are pink and 88 percent of dollhouses are pink.[1]

Currently, toys intended for boys are uber-masculine, and reinforce our culture's idea of masculinity—most of these toys are muscular and violent action figures. Elizabeth Sweet, author of an *Atlantic* article titled "Toys Are More Divided by Gender Now Than They Were 50 Years Ago," describes the change that came about in the 1980s: "As the bright palette and diverse themes found among toys from the '70s demonstrates, decoupling them from gender actually widens the range of options available. It opens up the possibility that children can explore and develop their diverse interests and skills, unconstrained by the dictates of gender stereotypes."[2] Most parents claim to want this for their children.

The marketing of toys over the last twenty years has created a wide divide that makes it hard for kids to branch out of their assigned gender territory of toys. In the 1990s, there was a move away from marketing to girls as future homemakers and toward marketing to them as bubblegum princesses. These days, dolls, ponies, unicorns, mermaids, princesses, and even fairies have a vixen twist of cute innocence with big, seductive lips and doe eyes. Just when there are signs of positive changes, mainstream toy companies take it to the next level and are rewarded by demand from consumers. As parents become desensitized to the likes of hot ponies and saucy princesses, we can easily slide into accepting the relentless messaging from porn culture intended to make our girls feel like they need to improve themselves and to have more.

Planting Seeds Early

The enormous social pressure on girls in middle school is clear to parents, teachers, and coaches. A major aspect of girls' social currency is rooted in physical appearance, including clothing and accessories designed to enhance a certain look. Peers, marketing campaigns, social media, fashion magazines, and tabloid magazines fuel the pressure on girls by giving them constant reminders of what they could and should look like.

By virtue of being connected with more people online, kids may feel less connected with themselves, making it more challenging than ever to stay grounded and to find their authentic selves. At a time when depression, drug and alcohol use, self-mutilation, and eating disorders are prevalent among girls, we parents need to take seriously our role as the first influencers of our girls' view of themselves. Most parents agree that it is important for girls to be valued for their character, mind, and abilities rather than what they look like, so we need to be vigilant about contributing to their positive self-image.

Parents have a chance to curb some of the pressures girls experience by being proactive when they are young. Encouraging girls to be physically active helps minimize their focus on their appearance. According to the Women's Sports Foundation, "It's important that girls develop a lifelong love of being active. Women who are active in sports and recreational activities as girls feel greater confidence in their physical and social selves than those who were sedentary as kids."[3] Girls who are valued for what their bodies can do rather than what they look like usually stand a better chance of surviving the onslaught of pressures about how they look. Minimizing exposure to marketing and media for girls in preschool could also slow the indoctrination of appearance obsession.

Conscious Clothing Choices

There is no question that the choices for age-appropriate clothing are limited. When you walk into any children's clothing department, the gender divide is clear, and even from a distance it is easy to see the dominance of pink and purple in the girls' department. These are beautiful, energizing colors, but they have been limited to girl world by clothing designers and merchandisers, while the range of other colors available is needlessly narrow.

As you look closer at the clothing, you'll notice that the styles are very similar to women's and teen styles, with tight-fitting tops, carefully placed ruffles, and revealing features. These days, stores could have one department with the same clothes in sizes 0–3 months through adult women's sizes. Enough moms who like certain styles of clothing themselves can't resist a miniature version for their little ones. Though babies and toddlers don't spend much time in an outfit, they are looking pretty fashionable until they soil their sassy little ensemble. Even parents who express concern about their daughters' future body image and self-esteem seem to accept the shift in styles for wee ones as harmless and cute. We say we want our daughters to be active, but then we dress them in confining skinny jeans or frilly dresses that can impair their ability to climb and move around.

The boys' department is a mix of superheroes, sports themes, camouflage, and neutral colors. When my sons were little, I remember having a choice of blue, gray, and green, with a few red options for moms like me who weren't afraid to add some pop to a toddler boy's wardrobe. Most of the more gender-neutral clothes I found for my kids were on the sale rack, in secondhand stores, or passed down from families who shared my idea of not feeding the fashion flame too early and not confining my kids to unspoken gender rules. Al Vernacchio, author of *For Goodness Sex,* nails it: "The problem with gender roles comes when we forget that they are societal constructions and start to believe they are somehow immutable, and when they become so rigid that they stifle individuality."[24] A wave of new kids' clothing companies, started by parents who wanted more options, have embarked on a "gender stereotype-bashing mission;"[25] Jill and Jack Kids, Svaha, Girls Will Be, Handsome in Pink, and BuddingSTEM are just some of the companies offering clothes that celebrate the range of kids' interests.

Few would argue the role the fashion industry plays in oversexualizing girls. Parents who are conscious in the clothing choices they make for their young girls could help their daughters delay focusing on their appearance. There is a disconnect between some parents' willingness to buy excessively girlie clothing and toys for their toddlers and their hope and expectation that their girls will make "appropriate choices" once they get older. Of course girls can be pretty *and* smart *and* fashionable *and* strong. However, the primary focus of many mainstream products and marketing campaigns is on improving girls' appearance rather than encouraging girls to be strong and smart. As parents, we can be one influence that steers girls away from focusing on how they look.

Managing the Fashion Ramp-Up

I remember standing outside music and gymnastic classes listening to moms claim how much their baby girls just "loved shoes," demanded to wear dresses, and had to have princess costumes. These little girls could barely walk on their own two feet much less develop such particular shoe preferences. Some parents feel relieved when assured that their kids fit into the range of acceptance for gender norms. There is also a tendency for parents to project their own interests and styles onto their kids. Playgroups, nursery school, and daycare are all places where kids' preferences are influenced, but our influence as parents can be significant. We hear many claims that the "nature" of girls makes them interested in pink princess gear, fashion, and caring for babies and dolls. Even if a child doesn't watch regular TV shows, she will be influenced by popular movies, print ads, and toy stores that reinforce many of these stereotypes.

The fashion pace picks up when girls reach later elementary school and feel increasing pressure to wear certain styles. Some parents give in out of a fear of depriving their daughter or because she asks relentlessly for certain styles. Following the trends is the path of least resistance for parents shopping for clothes with their girls. Parents who resist catering to the trends may question the boundaries they have set with their daughters as they look around the playground. It is challenging to hold the line and respond when your kids accuse you of being uptight or old-fashioned. Remember that standing your ground or even finding a compromise will give strength to other parents who are looking for support.

Many parents claim it is "just clothing" and decide it isn't worth a fight or even a conversation. Some naively hold the belief that they will be able to get the clothing situation under control when it really counts. Parents who have yet to experience a middle school girl trying to keep up with the high-speed fashion train should visit their daughter's future school just to get the flavor of what is coming down the pike. Ideally, kids who are encouraged to wear clothes that function and feel comfortable when they are young will be less vulnerable in middle school's arms race of labels and styles.

Middle school is the time when clothes become a currency of status and popularity. Just one of the ways popular girls maintain status and wield power is by defining the social expectations of the group and trying to make others pay socially when they don't fit in. Girls need practice being outside the expectations starting when they enter nursery school or play-groups, and parental guidance along the way will help them debrief and keep perspective as the pressure heats up. It can be challenging to balance honoring your child's desire to be fashionable, her need to be accepted by her peer group, and her wish to feel comfortable in her clothes. As with sex ed, alcohol and drugs, and screen time, talking with your kids early and often about clothing and your values around appropriateness will set the tone and create a base for conversations when middle school peer pressure lands on your kids with amazing force.

I remember getting friendly jabs from other moms because I didn't dress my toddler daughter in stylish girlie clothes or a princess costume.

I was offered ample fashion suggestions for my "adorable daughter" from other moms and was given bags of toddler-sized hand-me-downs that "would be so cute on her," including pants with glittery writing across the backside where her crinkly diaper would be. I passed these on to Goodwill, along with the skimpy spaghetti-strap tops, high-heeled go-go boots, and the predecessor of booty shorts. The accepted belief that marketing-driven sexualization is negatively impacting the body image of girls and young women doesn't seem to convert to the clothing and toy choices some parents make without reflection. Parents claim they are unable to fight the trends, find suitable alternatives, or convince their kids to wear anything else. In some cases, parents give up when their child is five years old, an age when they still have a chance to establish guidelines. It is worth maintaining your boundaries around fashion for as long as possible, because the pressure will ramp up quickly as girls get older.

Fashion Battles

Some parents let go of clothing standards to minimize disagreements with their teenage daughters. Sometimes one parent is concerned about what his daughter is wearing to school while the other has already done battle to find a compromise for the outfit in question. It is normal to cringe when you see your teenager wearing tight, revealing clothing. Investing time in ongoing conversations will help you avoid battles with your daughter that could potentially damage your relationship. Finding a balance between being overly permissive and too rigid will be a work in progress for years. A clear idea of your boundaries before you have the conversations will help you endure the setbacks on the path of fashion negotiations. Educate yourself, so you can figure out where you want to take a strong stand and where you can reasonably ease up on standards. It can be helpful to consult trusted friends who share your values, to read articles about over-sexualized fashion for girls, and to look through popular websites to get a sense of the retail choices you will be working with.

Most importantly, these conversations should happen before you get in the car to go to a store, and certainly before you get into the dressing room zone, where most negotiations and full-on battles take place. If you have *not* gotten over the need to be a cool mom, you are most likely destined

for conflict. Convey your thoughts, perspective, and concern about clothing, and be open to discussion about her thoughts on style and choices.
Looking online together can help each of you get an idea of how your ideas
differ and where they overlap. Teen fashion is a can of worms. If you surrender fully to your daughter's whims and her desire to be trendy, it will
be very difficult to encourage her to bring her choices into alignment with
your comfort zone in the future. Be ready for compromise but don't be a
doormat. Ask questions all along the way to encourage your daughter to
put more thought into her choices and to develop her own radar and critical eye. Even if she snarls at you, she will absorb your concerns.

There tends to be lots of debate with teens about tight clothing. There
is a difference between a fitted style and garments that are too small. One
compromise could be to ask your daughter if she will agree to wear a looser-
fitting top with her leggings or skinny jeans. Some parents make it clear
they won't pay for clothing that is a size too small or too tight. Whatever
boundaries you ultimately decide on, educating yourself *before* you get to
the store will help you be more realistic.

> "I explain to my daughters that I understand that fitted clothing is
> the trend, but I will only pay for clothes that fit appropriately. If they
> are that committed to an outfit that is clearly a size or two too small,
> I will not buy it or lend them the money for it. They can either bring
> their own money to pay for it or come back another time after they
> have earned the money to pay for it."
>
> —Mother of five

Be consistent with your message about what you are prepared to endorse
by purchasing and what your daughter must figure out how to buy on her
own, if she is intent on owning a piece of clothing you won't buy. Lending your daughter the money can quickly turn into giving it to her, which
defeats the purpose of teaching her to consider choices carefully. When
kids have to earn the money they need, they put far more thought into
what they are buying and why they are buying it. Parent educator Vicki
Hoefle encourages parents to have their kids work to earn money and then
let their kids save, spend, or lose their money to learn the value of it. If your
teenage daughter wants to spend $150 *of her own money* on a pair of jeans

that are too tight, let her do it. Most likely, she will reconsider the purchase when she spends the day adjusting her jeans to feel more comfortable or splits them down the butt crack. Natural consequences streamline the work of parenting if we are courageous enough to let them happen.

Jump-Starting the Storm of Body Consciousness

Our culture does a bang-up job indoctrinating girls with the styles and standards promoted through marketing and media, so there is no need for us to jump-start the process for our own daughters. My husband and I knew that our kids would develop more independence if we let them choose their own clothing and get themselves dressed. Giving our feisty four-year-old daughter wardrobe choices made her more willing to respond to directives that were actually important, such as, "It is time to get in the car" or "It's time for dinner." We were also aware that we could contribute to her future positive self-image by not focusing on her appearance. She put together some funky but functional outfits that gave her room to run, jump, and climb. When she was four, an adult leading a group of kids said to her, "Tell your mom that she needs to match your clothes and brush your hair more often." Normally, we processed those kinds of things at home out of respect for the many different approaches of the adults who work with our kids in a variety of capacities, but I couldn't resist speaking up about this one.

There is absolutely no need to do a speck of hairstyle or fashion training with your girls. By the time most are twelve years old, they will be brushing their hair many times a day and will most likely have developed some level of clothing obsession influenced by peers or marketing. Keeping the bar low around clothing when your daughter is young can be handy, in that when she does take a step up, moderately fashionable clothes will feel super sassy to her.

It is important to teach hygiene by encouraging kids to take baths or showers, floss and brush teeth, and wear deodorant when they need it. Encouraging kids to preen and worry about their looks seems counterproductive to the goal many parents share: discouraging our kids from growing up too soon and being self-critical. Certainly we don't want to set them up to be victims of bullying, but encouraging kids to obsess about the way they look *and* trying to delay self-consciousness in them seems like a mixed message. Peer and cultural pressures will catch up to them, eventually. A teenager who is willing to set out for the day without brushing his or her hair? Go forth, brave soul. Random, odd outfits they choose themselves? Cheers to building courage. Acne? Forge on with gusto.

As parents, we need to keep our underlying motives in check. Being concerned about how your kid's appearance reflects upon you may indicate it is time to change your lens. Sometimes directing kids' choices and nagging them about how they look can give parents a false sense of being connected and involved. When we are bogged down with appearances, though, we can miss opportunities to have much more important conversations with kids about sex, alcohol, drugs, porn, and friendships. Letting go of greasy hair and odd fashion makes room for conversations that could help your kids tune in to their inner compass and develop self-skills. Consider the conversations as training wheels that will get you on pace to pedal through the later teen years, when the stakes get higher and drinking and driving are at the forefront of your kid's social scene.

None of us really has time or brain space to spend worrying about what other parents think. If a parent judges you over how your kid looks, that may be a signal to filter the inauthentic person out of your social circle. Another factor to consider is that kids sometimes depend subconsciously on their bad hair, odd outfits, and acne to serve as a form of protection and a way of keeping overwhelming aspects of navigating their teenage social lives to a dull roar. Natural repellents buy a kid time to get her footing.

Modeling and Messaging by Moms

Al Vernacchio wisely summarizes body image in this way: "The tricky thing about body image is that it's not really about how we look. It's all about how we *think* we look. The definition of body image is the mental image we have of our physical appearance. It's crucial that young people understand this definition, because improving body image is all about changing how we think about our bodies; it's not about actually changing our bodies."[6]

Moms find it challenging to feel adequate about their bodies under the scrutiny of the culture, particularly as aging women (that is, over twenty-one, these days). Fashion and tabloid magazines have become like an anorexic training camp for girls and women. The tone of most of these magazines is gossipy and critical, and when our daughters see us absorbed in and hear us comment on the stories and photos, we pass the baton of obsession with damaging comparison of women based on appearance. Despite widespread awareness that many celebrities restrict their food intake to stay unnaturally thin and that many photos are altered, the aspiration to look like hungry famous women is considered normal and acceptable.

Modeling healthy eating and positive body image for your daughter, as well as encouraging her to critically examine images and messages in the media, can help her develop a positive self-image and healthy relationship with food. A girl with a tendency to focus on her weight can shift to obsession with her appearance and disordered eating if early signs of body image issues are overlooked. The invisible online world of teenagers makes it hard to be fully aware of all the sources that are influencing our daughters. In extreme cases, girls engage in chats through websites designed by anorexic and bulimic girls to support and guide others who engage in extreme disordered eating and obsessive exercise habits. As terrifying as this sounds, it is worth being aware of what is out there.

> "What is habitual body monitoring? We think about the positioning of our legs, the positioning of our hair, where the light is falling, who's looking at us, who's not looking at us. . . . In fact, in the five minutes that I've been giving this talk, on average, the women in this audience have engaged in habitual body monitoring ten times. That is every thirty seconds. Eating disorders are much more prevalent with those who see themselves as sex objects as well as suffer from body shame and depressed cognitive functioning. If we're engaging in habitual body monitoring, it simply takes up more mental space that could be better used completing a math test, completing your homework. It just sucks our cognitive functioning."
>
> —Dr. Caroline Heldman, professor of politics
> at Occidental College

Be in Your Body with Conviction

I had the good fortune of a mother who lived in her body with conviction. My mom gave birth to nine children in sixteen years, bearing her last child at age thirty-eight, when most women of that era were long past having babies. She told my dad that if they were going to have all those kids, he needed to help. He was one of the few dads changing diapers and helping care for kids in the fifties and sixties. My mom was very comfortable with her body and appearance despite tough feedback from my sister and me when we were young. We would tell her that she should dye her hair because none of the other moms had gray hair. She laughed and said she liked her gray hair, giving it a confident tousle. When we saw her naked, we were brutal enough to tell her she was fat. She would give herself a pat, put her hands on her hips, smile, and say, "Well, I am comfortable, and by the way, your father likes me just the way I am." By not being fazed by our criticism, she helped my sister and me internalize positive body image.

What she knew, and passed along indirectly, is that most heterosexual men are not as selective as they are accused of being. More than a decade of interviews with heterosexual men has made it clear to me that most aren't looking for sexual partners who look and act like women in magazines or porn. "Hot" by most men's real-life standards is about a woman's genuine responsiveness and comfort in her body. Men repeatedly tell me they are grateful for the opportunity to be naked with a woman. A common turnoff for men, however, is when a woman focuses on what she doesn't like about her body during sex rather than enjoying the experience. Men are often less worried about any fat on their partner's thighs and more interested in getting between them (graphic, but true).

It is important for women and moms to avoid focusing on or talking about weight—both their own and that of others. Aside from the risk of influencing young girls and women to focus on their own bodies and weight, it also gives them permission to criticize the appearance of other girls and women. Break the habit. If you're a man, and particularly if you're a dad, avoid contributing to body images issues for the girls and women in your life by not commenting on their physical appearance and that of women you notice in videos or walking down the street. Commenting about a woman's intelligence, quick wit, creativity, or positive energy could encourage your daughter to focus on developing those qualities.

Body image issues and self-scrutiny are challenging to overcome, but women who commit to shifting their perspective can find a healthier balance and create brain space for more productive pursuits. Developing and maintaining realistic expectations about how your own body should look requires detoxing from retouched marketing and media images. Staying off the scale helps prevent girls and women from fixating on weight and encourages them to focus instead on health. It is proven that if you consciously focus on what you like about your body while looking in the mirror, you will build a more positive self-image. In her TED Talk, Caroline Heldman says, "Body monitoring during sex, aka 'spectatoring' during sex interferes with sexual pleasure!"[7] So, choose your own brand of "hot" by getting behind the body with which you were blessed.

Halloween Costumes and Vixen Training

A teacher at an independent school was chaperoning a Halloween dance. The teacher felt compelled to confront a student about her outfit: low-cut push-up bra, thong, and stilettos. The girls explained that she was costumed as a Victoria Secret model for Halloween. Eventually, the teacher was able to redirect her, but the girl's total conviction and lack of self-consciousness to the point of exhibitionism gave the teacher pause. Theme parties and Halloween seem to be a green light for girls and women to show a lot of skin and avoid scrutiny and judgment, with the costume aspect of the occasion offered as an excuse. A college party with a "CEOs and Office Hoes" theme is a classic example of an excuse and an expectation for women to wear minimal clothing.

In the kids' costume department, choices for boys are usually powerful or really scary, superheroes or monsters. Choices for girls are similar to the adult women's costumes—skimpy and hot versions of everything from nurses to witches to vampires to mermaids. Vixen training is in full force at costume stores around Halloween. There is no shortage of cat suits on moms with strollers around town every Halloween. My husband and I got a lot of feedback in our effort to avoid costume trends with our toddler daughter by dressing her as a pumpkin, a tiger, a lobster, and a skeleton. When she got old enough to choose for herself, she chose to dress as a devil, the Grim Reaper, and a super-scary skeleton. A costume that leads to a huge bag of candy at the end of the night is what many kids consider a great choice.

Authenticity

It is easy for parents to point to "nature" as the force that steers their child toward toys, games, or clothes that are assigned by marketers to a particular gender. When kids are babies and toddlers, however, it is easy to direct their focus and interest to a wide variety of objects, including one as random as water towers. When kids start going to playgroups or preschool, the continued development of their genuine interests depends on what the adults and the peers around them are reinforcing. If social connection is dependent on knowledge of princesses and dolls for girls and knowledge of trucks and superheroes for boys, a gender divide is fueled, particularly if it is not questioned or discussed.

In many Waldorf schools and other private schools like the Willow School (see chapter 8), adults consciously support all kids in pursuing interests without regard for gender expectation. My own son took a liking to the color pink early in his life. The grief and feedback he has received from peers over the years seemed to inspire him to wear pink more regularly. Almost every time he wears his pink socks to seventh grade, someone teases him. Despite the fact that he is not fazed by the feedback, his peers persist in their effort to keep everyone inside the male gender fence. Kids who have parents and teachers who support diverse interests tend to develop and hold onto a more balanced identity. Giving kids the chance to feel comfortable when their choices and way of being fall outside the norm contributes to their development as healthy, independent, and resilient adults.

"Be available to your daughters. Let them know that you love them and are there for them. Have those hard conversations, but also remember to have those mundane conversations that begin with things like, 'How was your day?' or 'What subject are you enjoying most in school?' Converse! Remember to listen, and not while multitasking; be fully present. Even if they don't reveal their deepest, darkest secrets to you, by checking in you're letting them know you care, which is huge!"

—Female, age twenty-seven

Most parents hope their kids develop and maintain wholeness and authenticity. It takes practice and support for a kid to figure out how to be true to herself and comfortable in her gender identity on her own terms, and each girl needs to work hard to sort out what she values rather than what her friends or the culture tell her to value. Women and girls need to be reminded to be kind to themselves and one another. By offering support, we can help loosen the grip of peer and cultural pressures on young girls, and give them more room to find their personal balance of how to navigate the pressures.

Gray Hair

We all have our priorities when it comes to authenticity. I am on the more extreme end. I made an early, conscious decision to spend as little time, energy, and brain space on preening. Luckily, I developed resilience early in my life. Letting my hair go gray requires resilience because people comment freely and regularly. I respect my three older sisters who dye their hair and who tease that I, the youngest sister, am blowing their cover with my gray hair. I was inspired by my mom, who got behind her gray hair with such conviction that everyone around her got behind it too. Some women tell me they think I should dye my hair because I am too young for gray hair. As a society, we have lost touch with how gray hair works. The women who give me this feedback are much too old *not* to have gray hair, but I would never mention that directly because it would be considered a crime against my gender.

I view my gray hair, lack of makeup, and low-maintenance style as my gifts to the women around me. By hanging around with me, my pals feel a little sassier and more put together. I am the woman at weddings who puts other women at ease if they have been obsessing about whether their outfit is dressy enough. I am happy to be a walking public service. When I was a kid, I made a decision that I didn't want to surprise any future boyfriends by looking different than I had when we first met. I remember the big-time makeup eighties ladies in my dorm, in my family, and on my teams who looked a certain way with their makeup on. When I bumped into them heading to the shower early in the morning looking like vampires, I'd wonder how their boyfriends handled the contrast. I decided then that I was committed to presenting myself each day as consistently as possible to avoid misleading anyone. Clearly, I am an extreme in this way and would not even suggest this to anyone else. Self-acceptance is just one of the results of not spending time in front of the mirror or worrying about my appearance. Each woman has to find her own level of engagement and stay aware of how each choice is impacting her self-acceptance.

The Dove Campaign Study: The Real Truth About Beauty, Revisited

- Only 4 percent of women around the world consider themselves beautiful (up from 2 percent in 2004).
- Only 11 percent of girls globally are comfortable describing themselves as "beautiful."
- Seventy-two percent of girls feel tremendous pressure to be beautiful.
- Eighty percent of women agree that every woman has something about her that is beautiful but do not see their own beauty.
- More than half (54 percent) of women globally agree that when it comes to how they look, they are their own worst beauty critic.[8]

As moms, we need to spend time and energy being present with and kind to ourselves so that we inspire our daughters to do the same. Worrying about outfits, weight, appearance, blemishes, or aging may cause us to miss sharing a sunset with our daughters. Raising our girls to feel worthy means we need to cultivate our own feelings of worth, which may require a variety of efforts. These will be different for every woman but may include: developing clear boundaries, taking on a new challenge, getting counseling or therapy, taking up a sport, leaning on our healthy crew, or finding our own identity and purpose outside our role as a mom. Finding a good balance between being emotionally available to our daughters and taking care of ourselves will enrich our lives and the time we have with our daughters while they are still with us. And it will inspire them to find balance when they are grown and on their own.

CHAPTER 7

Empowering Girls

Strong girls manage to hold on to their authentic selves despite the high winds of adolescence. Belonging to a community or ethnic group gives pride and focus. The sense of belonging preserves their identity as it's battered by adolescence. A strong place gives them roots.

—Mary Pipher, PhD, *Reviving Ophelia: Saving the Selves of Adolescent Girls*

Empowering girls by raising their awareness and providing them with tools to help make changes in our culture can affect their immediate world and contribute to the lives of girls around them. There are many organizations, media groups, and sources providing guidance to girls on how to respond to the relentless messages they get about how they *should* appear, dress, and be in the world. The examples I introduce in this chapter are just some of the resources that can inspire girls to make a difference in their own lives and wider communities.

One thing is clear, no matter how much a girl is deprived of computers, Internet, phones, and TV, she receives the messages loud and clear that she could be hotter and thinner with the help of certain products and clothes. Luckily, some inspiring women and organizations are enlightening girls and women through great programming and positive messaging.

The same devices that have the potential to make girls and women feel less adequate can reach them with a variety of empowering ideas. In her

TEDx Talk "The Sexy Lie," Caroline Heldman reminds us that kids ages eight to eighteen spend an average of eight hours a day on devices and they see about five thousand advertisements a day (compared with the five hundred ads a day kids viewed in the seventies).[1] Heldman says, "What do advertisers do? They cut through the clutter with increased emphasis on violence, hyperviolence, and hypersexualization."[2] Detoxing by staying away from the sources of degrading messaging is a great way to reduce their impact, but pressure will still reach most girls through peers who buy in to the images they're presented with and are not reflective about what they consume.

Schools, parents, and coaches have been addressing the issue of girls and body image for decades, but the intensity and volume of messages today makes it feel impossible for even the most aware, vigilant parents, educators, and coaches to keep ahead of them. In her 1994 book *Reviving Ophelia,* psychologist Mary Pipher described "girl-poisoning culture" in a way that struck a chord for many readers.[3] Pipher enlightened us to the concept of consumer culture's harmful influence on girls long before the Internet had gained purchase as a way to reach consumers. Pipher's wisdom is today more relevant than ever, as online influences have widened and social media enable people to maintain constant contact with all their friends and an endless number of acquaintances, with whom they freely share their comments, photos, and opinions in a detached way. The accepted thoughtlessness that flies around social media, texts, and online commenting is a key ingredient in the increased level of exclusion, bullying, and harassment. With the relentless influences of the Internet, marketing, media, and porn, "the girl-poisoning culture" has been magnified to the point of toxicity.

As long as consumers continue to buy what they're selling, marketers and media that objectify and degrade women will persist, and girls will continue to feel pressured to conform to a narrow standard of beauty. Girls and women who judge and pressure one another to keep scrambling to fit the accepted image of "hot" help tighten the grip that marketing and media have on our culture. Several companies, organizations, and movements are consciously challenging the usual flavor of marketing messages in ways that are engaging more girls and women, encouraging them to get involved and contribute to positive changes.

Amazing Like a Girl

As part of its campaign to champion girls' confidence, Procter & Gamble's feminine hygiene brand Always used social media to promote a wonderful video with the final message: "Let's make #like a girl mean amazing things." The video went viral in the spring of 2014. While Super Bowl Sunday is notorious for commercials that are sexual and sexist, the Always brand surprised viewers with a shorter version of the video aired as a commercial during Super Bowl XLIX. The ad starts with a couple of women, a boy, and a man showing what they think it means to "run like a girl" and "fight like a girl." Each demonstrates an awkward, nonathletic style. The words "When did doing something 'like a girl' become an insult?" flash on the screen. Then younger girls who are asked to run, fight, and swing like a girl, do so with strength, athleticism, and fierceness.

In the full-length video, the message is even more powerful, ending with one athlete giving advice to younger girls: "If you are still scoring, still getting to the ball on time, and still being first, you're doing it right, and it doesn't matter what they say. I mean, yes, I kick like a girl, and I swim like a girl, and I walk like a girl, and I wake up in the morning like a girl because I am a girl. And that is not something I should be ashamed of, so I am going to do it anyway. That's what they should do."[4]

Support with Inspiration

Megan Grassell of Jackson Hole, Wyoming, started a bra company called Yellowberry when she was seventeen years old. While shopping for bras, Megan and her younger sister Mary Margaret were unable to find any that didn't have padding, underwire, or push-up features intended to make a girl look bigger and feel older. Megan decided to start her own bra company for teenage girls with a mission "to provide comfortable, alternative bras for developing girls." She decided on the name of the company because a yellow berry is one that is not there yet and because you can't rush those stages.

Megan was overwhelmed by the interest and support for her idea—her

Kickstarter campaign raised the money for her goal in just four days. Her company has been so successful that her mom has joined as a partner, and they have hired several employees. The Yellowberry Company will remain Megan's first priority even while she is busy studying at college. She has gotten feedback from girls who are thrilled to have cute bras that fit their style and activity level and from moms who are glad to have bra options for their daughters that are appropriate for their age. Megan says, "We want to support girls to be themselves and not alter who they are."

Yellowberry's backbone philosophy was inspired by lessons Megan came to understand in the years after the tragic loss of another younger sister, Caroline. With this inspiring mantra, Yellowberry makes customers feel part of a positive, healthy movement for girls: "Water the flowers every day. Watch quietly and observe. Go barefoot. Love the outdoors and nature. Seek and find a hug when you need one. Campfires are rare; eat as many marshmallows as you can."[5]

Real Beauty

Stacy Nadeau is a highly successful college speaker. Her message for college students was brought to life after she participated in the Dove Campaign for Real Beauty as one of the real women who bravely stood with five others in her underwear in a series of ads during the summer of 2005. Nadeau is a dynamic, engaging speaker who inspires thousands of audience members each year with her program, "Embrace Real Beauty." She is relatable, knowledgeable, and has a great sense of humor. She laughs when recalling the humbling but empowering moment when she got out of a cab in New York and was faced with a giant picture of her own healthy, normal, underwear-clad body plastered on the side of a building next to an equally large Victoria's Secret ad featuring a model who looks nothing like most healthy women.

Nadeau's presentations help women feel normal, healthy, and inspired to embrace their own real bodies. I have personally watched hundreds of women and a good number of men leave her presentations with a shifted mind-set about how they view and treat their bodies. Nadeau is changing lives because she lives her message: "Ultimately, everyone wants to feel good about their bodies. People are naturally drawn to people who feel good. I am happy with my body and grateful for my body, therefore people wonder, 'What is she doing?' or 'Why does she feel so good?' It is not because I have the newest diet secret or fit the narrow standard of beauty in our culture, but I embody comfort. That rubs off on people around me."

Reaching young girls before they buy into harmful cultural messages is something Nadeau believes can make a huge difference for girls and young women. She encourages *demonstrating* a healthy relationship with one's body rather than *teaching* girls about it. In my interview with Nadeau, she told me:

The best gift a mom can give her kids is do whatever it takes to get herself mentally and emotionally healthy about her body. Too many moms have their kids and put the needs of everyone else in the family ahead of their own. Five years later, after being focused on taking care of everyone else, they realize they neglected their own needs and didn't take care of themselves. When they express feeling unhappy about their body, it rubs off on children, especially daughters.

Nadeau stresses the importance of moms modeling positive body language and behavior by changing what they show their kids and what they say about themselves. Moms who say they are committed to helping their daughters develop a healthy body image don't always realize the impact they have on their daughters when they complain about their own bodies, chatter about food restriction and weight, make comments about how clothes fit, or apologize for passing along their body type. According to the Dove: Legacy campaign summary, "Caring about the way we look is not something we are born with: we often learn it from the women around us. And chances are, you're a role model even if you haven't realized it. So, whether you're a mum, an aunt, a neighbor, coach or family friend, you have the opportunity to make a difference to her self-esteem. All it takes is some positivity."[6]

Encouraging viewers to consider their beauty legacy, the Dove team filmed a social experiment asking moms and daughters separately to list aspects of their appearance with which they were satisfied and dissatisfied. Most of the mothers assumed their daughters would have nothing to say about being dissatisfied with their bodies, and were surprised when a comparison of the mother and daughter lists showed them to be almost identical. One of the moms summarized what she learned about what she teaches her daughters: "Self-worth and beauty can be an echo from me to them, and them to others."[7]

Encouraging and Modeling Self-Worth

By Stacy Nadeau, speaker, consultant, and coach

- **It is unhealthy to have to earn a positive relationship with your body through exercise.** Saying you need to run three miles before you eat a piece of cake teaches kids that feeling good about their bodies must be earned. Food is fuel. Exercise is for health.
- **If you are on a health journey, talk to your kids about it openly and positively.** Keep the explanation health-based rather than weight-based. Explain that you want to be healthy and strong or that the doctor suggested losing some weight as part of your health journey. Emphasize getting more exercise and eating healthy foods. Don't focus on size, weight, and measurements.
- **Treat yourself as worthy now.** Your aim should be to treat your body well. What if you decided to eat well and exercise because you love your body rather than hope to change your body? It is a huge perspective shift to say, "I am exercising because I love my heart and want to be healthy and strong."
- **Break the gossip and judgment habit.** Talking negatively about other people is unkind. Talking about another person's body is cruel. Children quickly learn that if their mom steps on others to feel better about herself, then it must be okay. Comments about bodies are internalized by kids and affect their own body image.
- **Tread carefully when your kids start learning and asking about BMI (body mass index) and calories because they are learning about it in school.** If your kid is at risk of being focused on weight, find a doctor you love and trust to have a conversation with your kid about being healthy and strong.
- **If you have a child, loved one, or friend with extremely disordered eating behavior such as bulimia, anorexia, or overeating, address it directly in a supportive manner.** Tell her that you love her dearly. Strongly suggest that she get professional help or treatment. Promise you will be there for her as an ally through all the work and effort of the healing process as long

as she is getting professional help. Explain that your relationship will change if she chooses not to get professional help because you can't watch her do this to herself.

- **Know that you can't save somebody.** If you are worried about someone, you need to take the role as the person who can help connect her with the support she needs. Remember, it is her journey.

- **If your child is in the middle zone (not extreme but has some concern about body image), open, clear, and honest communication can make a big difference.** People in this zone don't engage in extreme behavior. Instead, they may skip a meal once in a while or do three-a-day workouts to lose weight for spring break. It is important to encourage change in the conversation with people in this zone. A good start would be to discourage self-bashing and fat talk.

- **A relatively small percentage of the men who attend my talks have body image issues themselves. The majority of men who attend my presentations are worried about a girlfriend, friend, daughter, or sister.** There is a lot of love in the world, and most people have at least one person who loves them and has their back. If those who struggle with body image could remember the people in their lives who love them, they could lean into that love and support to start healing.

- **A nightly ritual helps parents and kids connect.** When saying goodnight, ask your child to tell you one thing about her day that was good and one thing that was not so good. This teaches her that you are emotionally available for her and that life has some highs and lows. Give kids permission to feel their full capacity of emotions by talking about the difficult parts of life as well as the easier parts. These conversations give parents a read on what is going on in their child's life.

The Representation Project

The documentary film *Miss Representation* opens with a series of statistics, the last one being that the average American teenager consumes ten hours and forty-five minutes of media each week.[8] The Representation Project, founded in the wake of the documentary's success, is countering the intensity and speed with which media reaches viewers by using social media to make more people aware of the toxic messages in an equally efficient manner. According to the organization's mission statement, "Using film as a catalyst for cultural transformation, The Representation Project inspires individuals and communities to challenge and overcome limiting stereotypes so that everyone, regardless of gender, race, class, age, sexual orientation or circumstance can fulfill their human potential."[9] This organization supports people seeking to inspire change, and its newsletters, posts, and website serve as a hub of information about opportunities to participate in the causes we believe in.

A group of feminists from The Representation Project started the hashtag #NotBuyingIt in 2012 to empower Twitter users to call out companies and brands that objectify and degrade women. Because the effort was so successful, the team partnered with body image experts at Emerge to launch the #NotBuyingIt app right before the Super Bowl in January 2014. The app enabled users to post their opinions about and reactions to the notoriously sexist ads easily and efficiently. According to the Indiegogo campaign used to launch the #NotBuyingIt app, its mission is to call out sexist media, promote what is positive, organize activists, get the attention of companies, and spread media literacy.[10] Via the app, consumers rallied to successfully convince companies such as Coca-Cola, GoDaddy, and American Apparel to change their marketing approach.[11]

People of all ages, including teenagers, are starting effective awareness campaigns and challenging media to advertise responsibly, and The Representation Project highlights hopeful stories of people who are making a difference. Eighth grader Julia Bluhm, for example, used Change.org to create an online petition to get *Seventeen* magazine to stop airbrushing models. Eighty thousand people signed, and *Seventeen* changed its policy.

"Stay true to yourself. Don't change yourself in order to please others! Voice your opinion. It matters! You matter! Spend less time worrying about what others think of you and more time worrying about what you think of you. Be kind to yourself and love yourself. If I had listened to that advice, I would've enjoyed high school and college so much more."
—Female, age twenty-seven

Two other middle school girls were inspired by Bluhm's success and started a similar petition to take on *Teen Vogue*.[12]

MAKERS

When orientation and workshop leaders ask high school and college students if they believe that women and men deserve equal rights and opportunities, almost all of them raise their hands. When workshop leaders ask the same group of students if they consider themselves to be feminists, a significant number of students, including girls and women, do not raise their hands *even though* the definition of "feminist" is a person who believes women and men deserve equal rights and opportunities. While some young women fully identify with the term "feminist," in alignment with the many women who fought for the freedoms, choices, and opportunities we enjoy today, others associate the word with angry, men-hating women. Some young people don't know the definition of feminist or don't believe a man can be a feminist. Some argue that we need a new term.

After participating in panel discussions and debates with college students about the identity challenges associated with the word "feminist," I was almost convinced that we need a change by the strong resistance to the term. Thanks to Sheryl Sandberg's book *Lean In*, I am back on board, encouraging people to embrace both feminism itself and the term, which expresses the fairness and equality almost everyone claims to believe in.

MAKERS: Women Who Make America is a 2013 documentary film that inspires people to embrace a feminist identity. More than four million people viewed *MAKERS* on PBS when it first aired, captivated by the detailed and personal stories about one hundred American women. This three-part film, its subsequent shorter video stories, and the additional six-part PBS series about modern women who have made and are making a difference give viewers a chance to review history and celebrate the progress made by feminists who faced daunting obstacles and overcame harsh criticism. The film opens with the story of Kathrine Switzer, the first women to run the Boston Marathon as a numbered entry, despite a race official's attempt to physically push her off the course. Stories about politicians, activists, athletes, media figures, and other trailblazers remind us of the sacrifices, efforts, and resilience required to bring about change.

Girls Leadership

Odd Girl Out: The Hidden Culture of Aggression in Girls by Rachel Simmons explores invisible bullying and aggression among girls, outlines social navigation strategies, and provides specific guidance that helps parents support their daughters. After Simmons's book became a best seller, she ended up on what she describes as a never-ending book tour, which led her to teaching and to cofounding Girls Leadership, an organization that seeks to teach girls "the skills to know who they are, what they believe, and how to express it, empowering them to create change in their world. We work with girls, parents and caregivers, and educators to ensure lasting impact."[13]

Girls Leadership offers a variety of programs, as well as online advice and resources, for school-age girls, educators, and parents. Thanks to the work of Rachel Simmons, leadership workshops, camps, and seminars for girls are cropping up all over the country, and girls are fired up.

My daughter attended one such camp, Girls' Leadership Camp at Kimball Union Academy in Meriden, New Hampshire, several summers in a row. GLC is a week-long camp for girls entering grades six through nine. The campers are sad when they get too old to attend GLC, but they will take the mantras, messages, and wisdom with them through life. Brooklyn Raney, founder of GLC, brings together a staff of incredible women who facilitate activities and workshops. Raney spreads her inspiring philosophy through a broad spectrum of challenging and empowering activities for the girls. They do an overnight camping trip, work with power tools to build outdoor furniture, develop personal goals, do community service, participate in team-building activities, write guided reflections in journals, and work with nationally known speakers. The staff and campers are drawn to Raney's dynamic personality, confidence, and wisdom.

I Am Who I Am: Tips for Parenting Girls

By Brooklyn Raney, dean of students at Kimball Union
Academy and director of Girls' Leadership Camp

The issues challenging girls' self-esteem and causing them to question their self-worth are difficult to manage for many of them. Some girls learn important lessons about relationships, personal values, and future goals; others struggle and waste years consumed by social circumstances rather than focusing on biology homework and soccer practice. The stories I hear—about social media, hookup culture, perfectionism, and body image—might encourage parents and educators to panic and tighten the grip on their adolescents. In reality, the exact opposite is what will most benefit both girls and adults.

Creating a culture that inspires a young woman to be confident and to find her voice is not an easy task. It starts with modeling confidence and character strength. Providing a platform for discussions about healthy living requires that we adults pay attention; below are a few tips that will help you make a positive impact on the young women in your lives.

Hit the mark. Underestimating or overestimating the abilities of girls can be devastating. Setting goals and expectations too high can make girls feel that they have lost before they have begun. Setting expectations too low can cause them to underperform and believe themselves incapable. Every time you face a task, consider the following questions: Is this something I have to do alone? Could a student/child help? Could a student/child do this independently? It takes time and energy set up the task for someone else, but allowing a young woman to contribute and feel capable is a great gift. Allow your daughter to set her own goals and encourage her to reach them. Debrief whether the goals were too high, too low, or just right. Success should be her own priority, not yours.

Offer questions, not answers. Ask more questions than you answer. Instead of providing answers to your child's problems, say, "That's a tough one. I'm not sure what I would do in that situation. What do you think?" Allow your child to work through scenarios and situations. To prepare children for times when you aren't around, take time to work through challenges *with* them, not *for* them.

Touch, don't look. For any challenging conversation, sit side by side rather than face to face. Direct eye contact makes it feel like an interview or an investigation, but a hand on the back or a pat on the knee will go a long way when you are listening and asking questions during sensitive conversations.

Build confidence. "Just be confident" is one of the most abstract and confusing things we say to girls, and the statement implies it is easy to accomplish. It is like telling someone with a cold to "Be healthy." Confidence requires feelings of success that grow through experiences over time. Deeply exploring interests, hobbies, and passions gives girls opportunities to learn and practice grit, determination, and resilience. Having many "self-esteem buckets" (school, sports, arts, family, community service, etc.) means one might fill us up if another is empty.

Model "I am who I am." Modeling vulnerability and self-acceptance is another gift for your daughter. Acknowledging your own strengths and weaknesses as well as asking for help demonstrates that perfection is not expected or possible. There should always be a desire to improve in every aspect of life, from making a three-point shot to being a better friend. Prioritizing effort and focus to improve rather than being the best will lead to greater satisfaction. Average performance is both acceptable and healthy. If you and your daughter can look in the mirror and repeat the phrase, "I am who I am" with pride, then you are on the right track.

There is a whole world of inspiration and guidance that can help us light up the lives of our girls once we choose to engage. Joining the Representation Project e-mail list, for instance, links subscribers to other causes and movements they may be interested in. Even if we think we are well educated as feminists, we need to be reminded of the messages that align with our long-term goals as parents. The lens gets foggy when we are deep in parenting, so it is important to stay attuned to new studies and updated information that can improve our approach. There are many cultural factors undermining the self-worth of girls, but parents who are well informed about the pressures and choices kids face today and are attentive to the conflicting messages our culture conveys to young girls have a better chance of empowering their girls and helping them feel worthy.

CHAPTER 8

Worthy Boys

If we teach our sons to honor and value their emotional lives, if we can give boys an emotional vocabulary and the encouragement to use it, they will unclench their hearts.[1]
—Dan Kindlon, PhD, and Michael Thompson, PhD, authors
of *Raising Cain: Protecting the Emotional Life of Boys*

It is challenging for parents and educators to find the balance between honoring boys' need for active play and accepting what feels like violent behavior. Boys tend to be more physically active than girls, however, tolerating overly aggressive or violent behavior does boys a disservice. The influence of toy and game marketing and media messaging is so constant that many parents surrender, allowing their boys to buy in to society's idea of masculinity without encouraging reflection. The cultural pressures placed on boys are different, but the relentlessness rivals that of the pressures placed on girls.

Consumers aren't willing to examine the impact of cultural pressure on boys until the boys show signs of cracking. As long as their boys appear within the range of what is accepted as normal, some parents feel grateful and don't question subtle signs of distress. Fathers who were victims of or witnessed shaming, bullying, or teasing when they were kids may feel relief when their sons blend in, because they want their own boys to avoid the humiliation of being ridiculed for being different. Most parents hope to have children who are strong, independent individuals, but the next best thing is for their kids—particularly the boys—to give the outward appearance of being in the range of normal. What it takes to stay in that range can wear on a boy's emotional well-being.

We live in a hypermasculine culture fueled by marketing and media, but our boys need support rather than scolding when they hit their threshold and feel different, alone, shamed, or humiliated. When parents and educators don't examine the expectations and pressures boys are facing, they may default to an attitude of "boys will be boys." Enough research and real-life experiences with kids, however, indicate that a permissive environment backed by a "boys will be boys" attitude allows boys to "behave in cruel and thoughtless ways."[2] In fact, it can be scary for boys to be given too much freedom and social and physical power without accountability.

On the other hand, parents and educators can be overly fierce about squelching boys who are active and have a tendency to play in a manner that appears to be violent. Ideally, channeling boys' energy in positive ways and giving them more room to be their full emotional *and* physical selves increases their chances of feeling more at ease in the world. When a boy is able to express his full range of emotions without restraint, he will be less likely to act out, feel a need to prove his worth, or elevate himself at the expense of others. If we are genuinely interested in boys being able to express themselves, we need to acknowledge that they are experiencing more emotional complexity than may be outwardly evident.

> "It's also hard to deal with loss. When family members or friends pass away, tragically or otherwise, it's hard to express those emotions and engage with people in ways that help the healing. This is an area where parents are essential—they should never underestimate how important they are in the sad times."
>
> —Male, age twenty-one

In his book *Boys Adrift: The Five Factors Driving the Growing Epidemic of Unmotivated Boys and Underachieving Men*, Leonard Sax identifies changes in the school environment, overmedicating for ADHD, video games, toxins in the environment, and widespread delay in taking on responsibility as the biggest contributors to the decreased motivation parents and educators are seeing in boys and young men.[3] Sax explains that boys feel more unwelcome in the classroom, particularly in the last fifteen years, as educational trends have brought more demanding reading and writing skills and seatwork into kindergarten classrooms. Brain research shows that young boys would benefit from a balance between experiential learning and work that requires sitting for extended periods At a developmental stage when most girls are capable of seatwork, most boys are not quite ready, schools are asking them to contain themselves even more. As a result, boys are feeling unsuccessful even as their school careers are starting.

An additional factor that has decreased experiential learning is the movement toward more computers in schools, including nursery schools. According to Patricia M. Greenfield, senior author of a UCLA study, *Computers in Human Behavior*, "Decreased sensitivity to emotional cues is one of the costs—understanding the emotions of other people. The displacement of in-person social interaction by screen interaction seems to be reducing social skills."[4] Face-to-face interactions provide opportunities for kids to practice working through conflict. Because nursery school is a prime opportunity for kids to develop empathy and the ability to read social cues, there is a movement to remove or at least reduce the number of computers in nursery school classrooms.

Emotional Literacy

Having conversations with boys about how the culture defines masculinity increases their chances of developing emotional literacy. Our assumption that boys lead uncomplicated emotional lives contributes to limiting their self-expression. Rosalind Wiseman, author of *Masterminds and Wingmen,* explains that we don't give boys the language for talking about emotions that we give girls: "When we do notice boys, it's usually because they're somehow failing or they're acting out in ways that appear thoughtless, reckless, disrespectful, threatening, or frightening."[5] Wiseman adds, "Frankly, we find it really challenging to admit how much we contribute to boys' alienation. But make no mistake—under that detached façade, boys are desperate for meaning in their lives and for relationships they can count on for support and love."[6]

> "All through middle and high school, I worked hard to avoid being sensitive or emotional in front of my guy friends and teammates. I felt like I was being fake. It was such a relief to make just a couple guy friends in college who were okay talking about hurt feelings and rejection."
>
> —Male, age twenty-four

Boys need practice and guidance in talking about their emotions to help redefine the rules of what psychologist William Pollack calls "Boy Code." By the time boys reach first grade, they are already practiced at harboring feelings of rejection, shame, guilt, and hurt. The rules of Boy Code are in full swing for even the most emotionally courageous boys. In his book *Real Boys: Rescuing Our Sons from the Myths of Boyhood*, Pollack says:

> When I began my research into boys, I had assumed that since America was revising its ideas about girls and women, it must have also been reevaluating its traditional ideas about boys, men, and masculinity. But over the years my research findings have shown that as far as boys today are concerned, the old Boy Code—the outdated and constricting assumptions, models, and rules about boys that our society has used since the nineteenth century—is still operating in force.[7]

Social Power on the Playground

Parents and educators are quick to voice their assumptions about boys being emotionally uncomplicated and easier to raise and educate. That may be true in the short term, but stress, angst, and anger have a way of showing up over time. When young boys have permission to express themselves in a safe and supportive environment, they are surprisingly up front. Teachers, coaches, and parents can set up opportunities for boys to express how they feel about conflicts with friends.

During my six years as a first-grade teacher, I saw beyond the generalizations about boys and the danger of assuming that all boys lack social angst or deep emotions. When they are as young as six, boys are expected to keep their tears and emotions in check unless the situation is really extreme. If crisis strikes and tears are unavoidable, it is understood that the boy in crisis is on his own without support from even his best pals. Only a few very brave and confident boys don't suffer social consequences if they choose to reach out and support another guy who has been pushed over the emotional edge. Most boys and men are not fortunate enough to have one of those brave guys in their corner. These situations are the breeding ground of bystander behavior, proven to be a significant factor in bullying and hazing among boys and young men. The social risk for boys in seeking support is often too great, inspiring them to compartmentalize emotions.

Michael Thompson, PhD, and Dan Kindlon, PhD, authors of *Raising Cain* found patterns among middle school bullies during their interviews. When given the opportunity to be alone with one of the authors and away from the group, the bullies would break down in tears, overwhelmed by the responsibility and pressure of being in a position of power. In a later book, *Best Friends, Worst Enemies*, Thompson examines the trend of sophomore year in high school as a time when boys with social power let go of their positions, with relief. According to Thompson, around that age, most other kids realize that there is room for all kinds of people and no reason to clamor for acceptance by the bullies in charge.

Recess is where social situations unfold with intensity for many kids. Even though I longed for a moment to regroup while my students went out for recess, the time spent on recess duty was revealing. Because there was tension and an unwelcoming spirit among the boys playing soccer, I would referee. When a teacher was on the soccer field, an outgoing, athletic girl would sometimes join the game until one of the boys, desperate to hold his place in the hierarchy would use physical aggression to intimidate her.

Many teachers who watched recess games from a distance would comment on how easy boys are because they "just play without drama or conflict." When I entered games, I noticed immediately that one Guy in Charge was in control of the game and that everyone else was clamoring to stay in his favor because he had a lot of social power. Guy in Charge would rarely be one of the better players, but other boys yielded to his rules to avoid conflict.

While I am a believer in kids working things out on their own, the thin layer of "harmony" masked angst and a highly charged dynamic among the boys. As ref, I would give a strike to anyone who used physical or verbal aggression, and after three strikes, the player had to leave the game. Within five minutes, Guy in Charge would have three strikes but resist the "out" fiercely; his minions would squawk to back his case, but I knew in my gut they were grateful for the clear boundaries. When he finally stomped off the field, they would shift back into game mode, their scowls changing quickly to smiles.

With the game was back in flow, the peace and relief the other boys felt would be evident in the way they played without self-consciousness. A few of the fellas would thank me in a whisper or remark how much more fun it was. Even the fiercest defenders of the Guy in Charge seemed less burdened once he was gone, and some were almost intoxicated by the freedom. They would play the last seven minutes of soccer in the true spirit of the sport: with joy and abandon. Over time, the kids got used to my rules, resistance mellowed, and soon all of recess time was spent playing a fun game of soccer. Guy in Charge would come back to play; he could blame me for cramping his style but enjoy twenty minutes a day when he didn't have the responsibility of making decisions, choosing teams, or being the go-to guy.

Recess Chats

Parents, coaches, and teachers who make it a priority to have conversations with kids, particularly boys, about navigating cultural pressures will contribute to healthier social dynamics. My good friends and former mentors, Terri Ashley and Riley O'Connor are thoughtful and reflective educators. While collaborating in public school, both discovered that allowing kids to discuss, process, and work through recess conflicts made it possible for more focused learning for the rest of the day. Terri and Riley started their own school for twenty students in kindergarten through third grade. The Willow School in Wilder, Vermont, ran for eight years, until they retired in June of 2012. The core philosophy of the Willow School was that social and emotional development goes hand in hand with academics. The academic program was individualized so kids could be challenged and progress at their own pace, a necessary approach in a multi-age classroom. Terri and Riley found that their focus on the emotional well-being of students enabled them to build trust in the group and go into greater depth with the curriculum.

Talking to parents of Willow School students reveals how the social and academic experiences at Willow differ from those in most other classroom environments. Parents of boys, in particular, mention how beneficial it was for their sons to be free to be their full emotional selves in the safe, family-like environment of the Willow School. While it was difficult to transition to fourth grade in a public school for some boys, having had the opportunity to express their authentic selves and practice using emotional language for the four years of early elementary school gave them a healthy emotional base.

"Recess chats" (class meetings) at the Willow School gave kids an opportunity to resolve playground conflicts every day. Terri and Riley found that the shame, fear, and anger that often lead to bullying dissipate when kids have a chance to process their emotions. Recess chats were so successful that the class began having them every day after recess. "You can't say you can't play"—a key aspect of educator Vivian Paley's philosophy and the title of one her books—served as a rule base at the Willow School. Paley, in addition to being an author of several books on the educational lives of young children, was a MacArthur Fellowship recipient and a kindergarten teacher at the Lab Schools of the University of Chicago. According to Paley, exclusion is a huge problem in schools, and one that needs to be addressed head on. Sad children can't learn!

Terri explains that even though first-grade problems seem trivial, they are distracting for children. When teaching other educators about the benefits of recess chats, she tells them stories about how invested kids become in resolving conflicts and how much more academic progress they make in an emotionally healthy classroom community.

Riley was thrust into recess chats after a science experiment she had carefully planned derailed because lingering hurt feelings and bickering kept kids from being able to focus, She abandoned her lesson plan and gathered the class in the meeting circle to find out what was going on. The supportive, family-like classroom made it possible for the boy who felt left out to share his feelings, and the kids responded with empathy and understanding.

Both teachers feel that discussions were *always* better when one of the kids facilitated the recess chat. The students were patient, asked spot-on questions, and were invested in the outcome of the discussion. The teachers modeled facilitation early in the year, and were available for guidance and support once kids were comfortable in the leadership role. Behaviors changed when a student ran the meeting, and kids held their peers to a high standard of behavior; kids generated practical ways to make all kids feel welcome and safe during recess. Students got better at determining what problems were worth working through. Sometimes they didn't need a recess chat, and sometimes they spent forty-five minutes processing a problem. The social dynamic and the academic focus were dramatically improved for the rest of the afternoon.

Andi Diehn, in her piece "Recess Chats at the Willow School," makes a great point:

> We may worry more about bullying at the high school level, when pimples, income levels, and social systems can cause rifts between people who used to be friends and know just what buttons to press to cause devastating reactions. But the seeds for bullying behavior are planted in the elementary years. This is when children learn how to act, how to respond, how to talk, and how to value themselves. If all elementary schools had daily meetings to discuss behaviors and feelings, we might see fewer victims, perpetrators, and bystanders in the later grades.[8]

Active Guidance

Masculinities researcher Josiah Proietti aims to give clearer emotional direction to boys and young men and help them find gender-balanced routes throughout boyhood, their teen years, and into manhood. Proietti says:

> We focus a great deal on the messages that boys receive about how to deny their more vulnerable sides, while missing the contradictory messages we send them about taking their masculinity too far. Most boys and men feel a great tension between these contradictory messages. Don't be a pussy, but don't be an asshole. Nice guys finish last, but all women really want is a sensitive man. More and more men get lost between two undesirable choices. Man up and suffer the feminist critique of being too hard, or soften up and suffer the shame of being too feminine.

He describes his own experience at age five of catching sight of a man in leather driving a loud motorcycle. Just as he got excited and leaned forward to take in this classic example of masculine power, his mother sarcastically made fun of the man, expressing how deeply she disapproves of such displays of masculinity. He knows now that his mother wanted to help him avoid the pitfalls of one-dimensional masculinity, but failed to offer him a balanced alternative. All five-year-old Josiah understood was that, although he was drawn to the man on the motorcycle, he was not supposed to be like him. He was torn between his natural interest and the expectations of his mom.

As parents and educators, we should recognize this challenge and support boys by offering specific ideas to reconcile the pressures to toughen up and soften down, and balance their natural drive to be tough with their inherent vulnerability. Having relationships with older males who are willing to share personal stories about self-doubt and overcoming emotional setbacks helps reinforce that a full spectrum of emotions is healthy and normal. Proietti encourages adults to model and explicitly teach boys that vulnerability is an act of strength, and ingrain the message that "being vulnerable is believing that we are lovable even with our flaws." Encouraging boys to name and discuss the phrases they hear that pressure them to act in certain stereotypical ways—such as "man up" and "be a man"—will help them sort through messages from adults in their lives. When boys watch movies, TV, ads, or videos, parents can guide them to identify the characters that fit stereotypes and those that are well rounded and emotionally healthy. Engaging in this way helps boys both define their values and align those values with actions that help them with their challenges, and gives them hope for surviving socially.

The Potential Impact of a Coach

Inspirational speaker, coach, and former NFL player Joe Ehrmann works to make societal change through the keynotes and workshops he offers through Coach for America. He and his wife, Paula, cofounded Building Men and Women for Others (BMWO). Ehrmann's message is that athletic teams can offer an ideal place to build boys into men who will have integrity, be successful in their relationships, and understand their responsibility to give back and make a difference.[9] In the documentary film *The Mask You Live In*, Erhmann reminds us, "The three most destructive words that every man receives when he is a boy is when he is told to 'be a man.'"[10] Boys who reach high school and college after years of feeling inadequate struggle to sort through the anger they harbor.

Many dads and male coaches endured experiences in their youth with bullying, shaming, homophobic banter, and harassment, though they may be reluctant to use those terms to describe their experiences. Older dads and coaches, in particular, often suggest that their athletes should just ignore or put up with hazing and abuse, claiming that they endured it when they were young and "turned out just fine." As a former athlete, former coach, wife and sister of coaches, and mother of athletes, I've observed male coaches for decades. Their own experiences, including their emotional scars, infiltrate the way they coach and the way they move through the world. Many coaches claim that, when an athlete is performing, whatever has aligned to make him perform shouldn't be messed with, even if it is anger, bitterness, and resentment. Some coaches claim that anger and feelings of inadequacy are what help a guy keep his edge in competition.

> "Not only do some coaches carry bitterness, many allow and even encourage shaming among their athletes. When a male coach calls an athlete a 'homo' or a 'pussy' when he performs poorly, it seems they want to appear cool by stooping to the athlete's level. It's more important that we show them that we are vulnerable, have flaws, and haven't excelled at everything. Boys need to know that it is okay to be a little quirky and have a little jank at times."
>
> —Sohier Perry, ski coach

Many coaches focus on short-term success, to get a kid qualified for a team, to get the athlete to another level of competition, to reflect their own coaching brilliance, or to achieve results that help them gain notoriety as coaches, which could result in more financial support for their athletic programs. Sometimes it is hard for coaches to keep the long-term goal for the individual athlete as a priority. Boys' angst and stress is often accepted, overlooked, tolerated, and even encouraged in some cases, to satisfy the agenda of a coach or parent. I believe that more athletes, particularly boys, would benefit if coaches and parents invested in helping them work through the emotional stress they carry. By sorting through the distracting stressors, they can create mental and emotional space that will likely convert to better results over time and make for longer careers.

Eric Barthold, coach, masculinity speaker, and creator of *Man Up and Open Up,* was inspired at a coaching clinic run by first-team coach for Manchester United, René Mulensteen. Barthold describes Mulensteen's philosophy as one that emphasizes "coaching for success." Mulensteen insists that coaches need to remember that their role is to coach kids and provide them with an atmosphere where they can succeed, have fun, and express their love of the sport. Mulensteen also described the difference between coach-centered coaching and athlete-centered coaching; when coaches focus solely on results, they put themselves on a pedestal where they become the first priority. Not only do the athletes lose out in terms of their sports training, they also miss many of the life lessons that sports can teach kids. There are many coaches who would benefit from a clinic with Mulensteen.

The Dual Lives of Boys

As a middle school girl, I was a righteous feminist trained by sisters-in-law and friends of our family who were at the heart of the women's movement in the seventies. I was the youngest of seven, and my parents supported my righteous whims. At age twelve I was a misguided feminist in many ways, and I took every chance to publicly sling some facts about how women and girls were discriminated against. In my mind, the one clear exception was that, as girls and women, we had more freedom to fully express our emotions. I was tough as nails and full of fire, but if I felt the need to cry, I could almost always let the tears roll without hesitation. I was well aware that boys were not afforded that luxury.

Playing baseball and tennis with boys in the summer and ski racing with boys in the winter meant I was neck deep in boys. I had earned enough trust from most of the boys on my teams and looked enough like a boy that I basically had dual citizenship, which enabled me—and continues to enable me—to talk freely with guys about even the most personal emotions. To this day, I am a trusted sisterly figure for many guys. I keep their secrets because I am well aware of what it can cost a guy to be vulnerable, despite the strides we have made as a culture. I affirm and encourage them to express emotions and tears, but I also respect their need for privacy.

My dual citizenship is epitomized by a situation that arose with one of my longtime ski racing and baseball pals when we were in high school. He and I spent a lot of downtime at baseball practice asking questions and informing each other about boy life and girl life, based on our own experiences and people we knew. We made the best of our time in the dugout with our gloves over our mouths, passing info while appearing engaged in excruciatingly boring games. This boy and I had some big laughs and shared an awesomely balanced, platonic friendship. One day at school, he and some pals were jockeying past me on the way to their lockers. One of the guys made a harsh, sexist comment in my direction, and the whole group piled on, laughing and mocking. I was hurt to see my good pal so easily influenced by his friends and to find myself the brunt of his uncharacteristic cruelty. Up until that point, I may have taken the familiar low road of reaching into my well-stocked quiver of mean comments to sling back at boys to give myself a false sense of power over them and to save face. In a rare moment of restraint and respect for my friend, I held my tongue and let them pass. I met his eyes for a moment and could see how conflicted he felt. He stormed on with his crew.

Later, I found a chance to talk to him alone. While no longer hurt or mad, I was curious about what was going through his head. What I didn't expect was the raw, deep truth that boys work so hard to disguise. He basically told me that he was sorry, hoped to not do it again, and that he was "just trying to survive." He spilled more thoughts about what it means to survive socially as a boy, but the specific phrase that changed my lens forever was the desperation in his admission that he was "just trying to survive." I could have let him have it or told him he was a weak conformist, but his honesty brought my deepest respect. I could tell how much courage it took for him to put that out there, and I was honored that he felt safe enough with me to describe what his world was really like. In that moment, our friendship reached a new level of trust, respect, and understanding, which hold to this day.

Men and boys freely admit that certain situations require them to live some level of a double life. Guys on teams, in groups, and in fraternities say that it is often easier to participate in the accepted banter—teasing, put-downs, degrading comments—than to call other guys out for their comments or just stay quiet. Groupthink can be a powerful force among boys. When they are given the chance to fly under the radar, protected by the safety of numbers, they may find it easy to compromise their values to fit in. Disrespectful language, sexist comments, homophobia, and thinly veiled racist comments flow from the mouths of many boys and men who know better. Our society almost encourages boys to develop a public and a private self by accepting that guys present themselves to teachers, female friends, parents, and others outside of their support network differently than they present themselves to teammates and close friends. When boys and young men are held accountable or at least questioned about the difference in the way they express themselves to different audiences, they can begin to reflect on the reasons, and surprising conversations can unfold.

When I was in high school and college, a number of my male friends talked privately about the hassle of maintaining an image around other guys. Adults spend a lot of time wagging fingers at and blaming young men for many issues in our culture, yet we don't really provide clear guidance or support them in picking a different road. Very few boys are asked, "What does it mean to be a man" or "What does it mean to be a boy?" As simple as these questions may seem, they can serve as a great platform for starting conversations with our sons or students, as early as the time they first walk down the "boy" section of the toy store: "What do you have to do to be seen as a boy?" And as kids get older, we can ask, "Do the values of being a man in the movies or on TV differ from what you want in a male role model?" and "What do boys have to do to become men? How does that happen?"

High school and college men often feel that they disappoint adults, and they feel collectively scolded for the exclusion, disrespect, bullying, harassment, and sexual violence going on at their schools. This contributes to their reluctance to get involved, attend events, or join efforts to make change. Unfortunately, some of the guys who stay strong and are upstanding in the way they treat others are overlooked. When boys and men are clumped in with whatever standing negative stereotypes holds for their group, their inspiration to do the right thing may wane. Some guys give up taking the high road and start behaving in ways that reinforce the stereotype.

Parents, coaches, and educators are in a position to model emotional courage for boys and young men and validate their full emotional capacity. Helping a boy become more self-aware and develop strong interpersonal skills benefits his emotional health over the long term. Giving boys and young men a chance to thrive emotionally, rather than just survive, could greatly improve the quality of their lives and their relationships.

CHAPTER 9

Setting Boys Free

Wholehearted people are those who are resilient to shame and believe in their worthiness. There are many tenets to Wholeheartedness, but at its very core is vulnerability and worthiness: facing uncertainty, exposure, and emotional risks, and knowing that I am enough.

—Brené Brown, *Daring Greatly*

Boys and young men need input from the adults in their lives to help them sift through the conflicting messages they receive about "being a man," and processing culturally defined expectations of manhood is a lifelong project. Adults who fully understand the emotional challenges boys face stand a much better chance of being able to help boys feel more whole as they enter manhood.

The transition to manhood for most American boys is an informal experience rather than one marked by a formal ritual, as occurs in certain religions and other cultures. Alcohol and hazing are the most common ways boys and young men welcome others into their social groups, teams, fraternities, or organizations. Basically, we leave it up to ill-equipped peers to guide, model, define, and escort their slightly younger peers into manhood. There is an unspoken promise that guys will feel "enough" once they have jumped through the hoops necessary to be a part of a group, no matter how humiliating the process.

"Suffer until worthy" is a prominent theme of the transition to manhood in our culture, even though worthiness remains elusive. Once boys and young men get through the hoops, they often realize they have more to prove, but they stay engaged because they assume that "enough" is right around the corner. Those who set up the requirements feel justified in putting others through the hoops they jumped through themselves. It can seem that revenge plays a role in the perpetuation of many accepted traditions, and alcohol plays a role in justifying bystander behavior. It turns out that our culture is set up to keep guys on the run, even if they made the team, gained seniority, became a member, got the job, achieved the status, or earned the salary. A feeling of adequacy isn't actually achievable until they make a conscious choice to stop running, disengage, and define "enough" on their own terms.

> "Boys have a hanging sense that men are supposed to know what they're doing with their life, which creates a need for boys to act like they know what they're doing and know how to get there. It's really hard when you feel like you can't ask for help. I've seen a lot of guys flounder in school, sports, or the social scene—or all three at once. They feel lost and can't ask for help."
>
> —Male, age nineteen

Admitting that you need help, feel vulnerable, or don't know the answer is discouraged in our culture, particularly for boys. Those who have the courage to ask for guidance from trusted role models find the transition to manhood smoother, but vulnerability is perceived as weakness. Brené Brown, a renowned scholar whose research topics include vulnerability, shame, and courage, is rattling this assumption with her books and with TED Talks that have had millions of views. Brown defines vulnerability as "our most accurate measure of courage." In her book *The Gift of Imperfection,* she describes the common traits of people who have "shame resilience" in "Ten Guideposts to Wholehearted Living." The guideposts that seem particularly important for boys and men include: authenticity (letting go of what other people think); intuition and trusting faith (letting go of the need for certainty); creativity (letting go of comparison); play and rest (letting go of exhaustion as a symbol of status), meaningful work (letting go of self-doubt); and laughter, song, and dance (letting go of being cool and in control).[1]

When given the opportunity, most boys and young men describe men they admire in a way that indicates that their role models are living wholeheartedly, free of the expectations placed on men. Somehow, boys and young men hold on to the idea that, in order to become anything like the men they admire, they need to suffer and endure the limitations of "gender straightjackets."[2] Strong connections with even a couple of men who have taken the straightjackets off can help younger guys let go of expectations.

> "Because I was constantly disappointed about how I looked in middle and high school (overweight, not muscular), I've subconsciously developed the twisted belief that physical appearance is the most important factor when it comes to overall success in life. My current bodybuilder-like physique and weightlifting habits are a result of that belief."
>
> —Male, age twenty

"Man Up" and Open Up

By Eric Barthold, masculinity speaker and presenter of "'Man Up' and Open Up," a program for middle school, high school, and college groups

For most of their lives, boys see "real men" as strong, powerful, in control, athletic, and yes, even middle school boys say that real men have sex with hot women. Boys who do not live up to that standard are sensitive, emotional, weak, shy, and wear skinny jeans, to name a few. When one boy exhibits these latter characteristics, his peers barrage him with verbal abuse: "Stop being such a pussy," "What are you, a fag?," "Don't throw like a girl," or "Man up." As a result of words like these and the messages they receive from media, adolescent boys feel constant anxiety that they aren't considered manly enough, or simply that they won't fit the concept of a guy. Proving they fit inside that narrow box of masculinity earns boys a sense of belonging and inclusion;

they put on their "gender straightjacket," don a façade of emotional internalization and detachment, and do their best to behave in ways that will make them seen as "a man." The problem is that it's impossible to remain in the box of masculinity all the time.

This "man box" becomes more immediate and entrenched in boys' lives when they transition to college, which in many ways and for many young men is a rite of passage to manhood. If a young man wears his Old Spice deodorant, drinks a lot, plays sports, and can impress the women around him, he is fine: he fits in the box of masculinity. But as soon as he becomes overly sensitive, cares too much about something (other than sports), or expresses any sort of vulnerability, he is called some variation of gay or womanly and pushed back into the box. And if the two worst things a guy can call another guy are a woman or a homosexual man, what does that tell us about the way our society views those groups of people?

In college, the evidence that justifies your membership in the man club centers mainly on how much you can drink, the crazy stunts you pull off when drunk, and how many girls you have sex with. It's such a heteronormatively charged atmosphere. Over Sunday lunch, some guys share—and embellish—stories of their weekend exploits. The craziest story sets the tone, until someone else advances a story more absurd or daring—suddenly, the initial storyteller finds himself back under the microscope. When boys see media images of college parties and hear their older peers' stories, they see sex as something that is expected of them and begin to question: "What's wrong with me if I hear all these stories, and yet I'm not having sex? Everyone else seems to be 'getting some.' "

Boys encounter this anxiety and self-doubt throughout their lives: "But I like playing house and I like reading…why can't I?"; "What's wrong with me if I'm too scared to go off that big jump, or if I don't want to try pot or alcohol?"; "What kind of man am I if I don't make the varsity team, or if I break down under the stress of school, or if am attracted to other guys?"

Many characteristics that "real men" exhibit are not inherently bad: it's healthy to be athletic, being responsible is a great thing, and there is nothing inherently wrong with driving a big truck. Rather, the problem with our concept of masculinity lies in the pressure that boys and men feel to be in that box all the time, because no guy can achieve that. And if we say that it's impossible to stay in that box, then we're saying it's impossible to live up to our society's idea of what it means to be a man. Boys will never feel "enough" in this context until they recognize the pressures of their gender and work to expand the "man box" by living both inside and outside our culture's impossibly narrow definition of a man.

Gather a Crew

Finding a "healthy crew"—a team of wise friends, relatives, and mentors who can be relied on for feedback and input—is a great step to creating a supportive network for anyone at any age. Maximizing the benefits of a healthy crew requires being vulnerable, which narrows the possibilities for most boys. A healthy crew of friends is not necessarily a boy's group of friends, teammates, or roommates. As a matter of fact, a boy's closest friends aren't necessarily all truly trusted friends. It is important for a guy to identify his most trustworthy friends in his own mind and to connect with them for advice. These friends are the ones who have his back, let him know when he posted something sketchy, and with whom he can cry; they're the ones to whom he can express himself fully without having to filter his thoughts. Having just one or two of these trustworthy friends can change a boy's life dramatically.

It is also important that a boy identify the reliable, supportive adults in his life, the grown-ups he respects and admires. These may include parents, though that's not necessarily the case. Advisors, instructors, teachers, coaches, and older relatives can also be dependable resources and play a role in a boy's healthy crew. To this day, I have special friends and relatives who guide me in different areas of my life: parenting, caring for an aging parent, speaking, marriage, and storytelling, to name a few. Some of my healthy crew are young enough to be my children, but their wisdom and expertise guide me in my work and life.

"I feel fortunate to have had a number of role models, namely my older siblings and a number of very close friends with whom I could share my emotions. I never got the message that showing emotion wasn't 'manly.' They earned my trust just by being outstanding friends."

—Male, age nineteen

Being Part of Change

Unless boys have grown up supported in the practice of talking about feelings and confining gender roles, it is difficult to engage them in workshops, presentations, and conversations about these topics. A common reaction is for guys to feel defensive. In many cases, the approach isn't welcoming and supportive enough to engage boys and men in this work. But before cultural attitudes can change, we need boys and men to take part in the conversations about ending sexual violence and creating a safe, healthy community for everyone.

Young men and boys tell me it frustrates them when it's assumed they fit a hypermasculine stereotype. When this stereotype is demonized, they feel defensive and conflicted about opening up. Many admit that it is easier to just lay low and hope to avoid being noticed. Boys are more willing to step into meaningful conversations about the one-dimensional stereotypes ascribed to boys and men if their most respected role models or teachers present them with related articles or stories. Boys almost always recognize themselves in the masculinities writings by Joe Erhmann, Jackson Katz, PhD, Michael Kimmel PhD, Dan Kindlon, PhD, William Pollack, MD, Michael Thompson, PhD, Leonard Sax, MD and PhD, and Rosalind Wiseman, to name a few.

It takes exceptional courage for boys to openly admit the emotional challenges they face, but they are surprisingly forthcoming when given a chance to share in a supportive environment. If conversations about gender expectations were a part of school, sports, and family life when boys were young, we could set a tone of comfort and openness that would encourage boys to explore the boundaries of gender expectation further as they get older.

Violence and Video Games

Video games are often the first stop for blame when we look at violence and male anger among young people. While there is some evidence that *violent* video games shift players' attitudes and behaviors, other games do not. According to multiple surveys, the average American eight to eighteen years of age plays video games for 13.2 hours per week.[3]

Regardless of where you stand on the matter of gaming or what kinds of games your kids play, it is important to discuss with them the influences of culture that are coming at them through a variety of media, including games. Keeping a positive, nonaccusatory tone when encouraging boys to reflect increases our chance of being heard. Boys are receptive to hearing what various adults in their lives value, and hearing others' opinions helps them figure out their own values. They are particularly receptive when adults ask for their input and perspective during these discussions. When kids feel seen, heard, and understood they are more likely to open their minds to other opinions. It may seem easier to succumb to pressure and allow kids free access to games because reflective conversations are challenging and create tension with kids, but the long-term benefits of keeping these conversations going could contribute to their healthier choices.

Parents tend to react strongly to the way boys play in groups or to their choice to play video games because they often assume that all the games are violent and will encourage their boys to become violent men. Michael Thompson, PhD, host of the documentary *Raising Cain* and coauthor of the book of the same title, clarifies, "No one wants their son to grow up to be violent. But interpreting play as an early indicator of violence is a misunderstanding both of the nature of boy activity and the real journey to violence that some boys undergo."[4]

Assumptions about the nature of violent boys have led to misguided zero tolerance policies in schools—such as not allowing aggressive language in written stories or rambunctious and competitive play at recess—despite the fact that there is no evidence that aggressive play or writing topics leads kids to become violent adults. In the case of writing topics, a prolonged pattern of writing about violent, dark topic could reflect deeper issues worth addressing, though not always. On the other hand, overreactions of teachers and parents can fuel some kids to seek more negative attention. Teachers with good sense usually understand how to balance supporting kids' self-expression with helping them expand their writing topics.

Finding balance around the manner of kids' play is something teachers and administrators work on every day in schools. A structured school environment with clear expectations and follow-through diffuses most violent, hurtful behavior in classrooms and at recess. It is possible for kids to stay physically and emotionally safe if they play competitive recess games and sports that involve some contact and physical challenge. There are certainly kids who need reminders about the difference between overly rough play and aggressive competitive play, but full restriction on any recess competition can backfire for kids who need a physical outlet after a lot of time doing seatwork. Conversations about being competitive and playing aggressively versus physically hurting and playing in a violent manner should begin when children are young.

According to Leonard Sax, we have learned a lot about boys who are most likely to bring a gun to school: "That boy is more likely than other boys to be an honor student; he's more likely to be shy, a loner; he is less likely than other boys to participate in aggressive sports such as football. We now understand that aggressive play, such as dodge ball, does not increase the risk of truly violent activities such as a school shooting."[5] Sax, along with many other experts, does believe, however, that violent video games and too much time playing them contribute to violent behavior and attitudes.

Helping our boys find balance and gain awareness of how gaming impacts their lives requires ongoing conversations. While some parents would prefer that their kids not play video games at all, it is unrealistic to expect that boys, in particular, will not have opportunities to play at friends' houses or on friends' devices. If you choose not to allow video games in your own home, explain your reasoning rather than lecturing your kids. Sharing and discussing perspectives and values about gaming could be enlightening for you both. My husband and I have chosen not to have games in our house because the number of screens already dominating our kids' academic and social lives feels unhealthy. We expected resistance and were surprised that there was close to none.

In my family, we have a goal to keep the bar low on gear, technology, and void-filling opportunities. The kids are agreeable. We accept that they occasionally play games on their phones, but these are usually trivia-related or other nonviolent games. We accept that they will play a variety of games at friends' houses, including violent games. It has surprised us when they express gratitude for *not* having video games in our house. Conversations about balance of screen time and the effects of gaming are being internalized over time. Having friends with various levels of game access and obsession helped our kids develop their own opinions about video games. Sometime they indulge fully and other times they are annoyed by their friends' obsession. Finding what works for your family will be much easier if you are willing to listen to your children's perspectives and to articulate your own.

Viewpoints from Gamers

I had the good fortune to expand my understanding of the gaming world, thanks to two young men who had the courage to enlighten me after I presented at each of their schools. They challenged me to see more of the layers in the gaming world rather than make sweeping assumptions about gaming and gamers. Both these young men are avid gamers, and they reflect about the negative effects of gaming as well as the positive ones. Both have plenty of peers who are addicted to gaming and who struggle to self-regulate the time they spend playing.

While the views of these two young men did not change my decision to disallow games in my house, I learned that there are many games that are educational and help players develop specific skills. Many of us judge gaming based on what we see in the marketing of popular violent games such as *Grand Theft Auto*, *Call of Duty*, and *Assassin's Creed*. One of my consultants admitted that he enjoyed some of these popular games in moderation, but he also described many nonviolent games I didn't know existed.

As someone concerned about violence in video games as well as the way women are degraded and sexualized in them, I'm encouraged to hear that women are becoming involved in the development of games and shifting the market. I was surprised to learn that as of 2014, 48 percent of gamers are female,[6] and, according to the International Game Developers Association (IGDA), the number of female game developers is on the rise. A 2009 study showed that 11.5 percent of game developers were women; today, women make up 22 percent of game developers, while 76 percent are men and 2 percent describe themselves as transgender or androgynous.[7]

The uptick in the number of female developers is inspired by greater demand for and interest in a wider style and tone of games. It is refreshing to hear about games created by women that are engaging and challenging for both male and female players. Some game developers aim to increase the participation of underrepresented groups in media, including sponsoring opportunities for women in the gaming industry. Like porn, gaming is only growing, so it is important to educate viewers and encourage broader representation in the industry to create more educational options.

One of my young consultants paces his gaming by making it a reward for completing his workouts and homework. He believes some kids whose parents restrict their game time at home struggle with self-control once they are away from their parents at boarding school or college. He was able to develop restraint without parental restriction. "The negative effects of gaming are from binging and getting addicted to gaming. You will fail if you just play video games all the time and don't do your work. Some people binge and forget to eat, sleep, or take care of other necessities of life. Most things are okay in moderation, and gaming is no different," he says. Clearly, free access or restriction to games will have different effects on different kids. He went on to say, "The major benefit of gaming is learning a new-age art form. Films can be art, and games are just another way of expressing creativity, except in an interactive way."

Roland Downey, an eighteen-year-old senior at a small Vermont boarding school, shared gaming research he used for a paper on the topic. I expected him to justify the violence, as he is an enthusiastic gamer. Downey plays a wide variety of games and was very clear about the negative impact of violent games. In his paper, he described, "three main types of video games: puzzle video games (which are usually nonviolent), violent video games (which are obviously violent), and educational video games (which are usually nonviolent)." Puzzle games require players to solve a series of intellectually stimulating puzzles to advance to the next level. Violent video games are based around killing enemies to get to the next level. Educational games are designed to teach students any number of subjects. Downey explained, "Video games teach in a different manner than the traditional educational model by teaching 'actively.' . . . [Video games] provide immediate feedback on any action a player takes."[8]

Downey found recent research on the value of educational games, referencing The Quest to Learn School in New York City, which has a highly engaging curriculum that balances the use of computer games with opportunities to develop strong interpersonal skills. The school collaborates with the Institute of Play to provide an academic experience designed to engage kids who had lost interest in school. Based on state standards, the core curriculum maintains a focus on twenty-first-century skills, including collaboration, problem solving, model-based learning, and empathy. Lessons are taught through video games and game development, but there is also a heavy emphasis on collaborating to solve problems and completing quests without computers. Katie Salen, executive director of the Institute of Play, describes their aim: "We wanted to design an experience that really cared about engagement—not engagement just for engagement's sake—but engagement that really was in the service of learning."[9]

Privilege and Entitlement

The behavior or reputation of a few individual boys or men can inspire outsiders to generalize about the whole group by calling them "assholes." In reality, most groups of boys or men have only a small number of truly mean-spirited assholes. Most groups also have a small number of courageous guys who have set themselves free from gender expectations and genuinely do not care what others think of them. These guys are immune to the pressures of Guy Code. The majority of guys choose to fly under the radar, hoping to avoid being noticed and to avoid taking responsibility by not noticing. Many lay low as much as possible to survive or they align with some of the asshole behavior in the hope of being given a role in the hierarchy under the "mastermind," as Rosalind Wiseman describes in *Masterminds and Wingmen*.

Whenever a guy steps out from under the radar, other guys are quick to call him "gay" or a "pussy," two words that send most scurrying back under the radar. Some young people think "pussy" means wimp, unaware that it is a derogatory word for vagina. Guys often taunt and belittle each other with "pussy," equating it with women or weakness. "Gay" and "fag" are considered hate language when used in a degrading way, yet these words remain acceptable to many who know better. Claiming to be respectful and aware enough not to direct these words toward their gay friends, but using them to degrade their heterosexual guy friends, is ignorant. As with pussy, this use of words implies the friend is weaker and more feminine, like a stereotypical gay man. If you are a parent, teacher, or coach, making it clear that you won't tolerate the use of homophobic language reminds kids to reconsider, even if you are the only adult in their lives picking this battle.

Most boys and men display homophobia because it has long been an accepted way to elevate themselves and put someone else down, to stave off accusations that they are gay, or to feel more masculine than their target. Homophobia is not only hurtful and disrespectful, it creates an unsupportive environment for anyone who is considering coming out. Sometimes the intention of outwardly homophobic people is in fact to create an unsupportive environment and make their fear, discomfort, and beliefs clear enough to discourage anyone who may confide in them.

As parents, educators, and coaches, we must call kids out and enforce consequences for all types of disrespectful language. Michael Kimmel, author of *Guyland: The Perilous World Where Boys Become Men,* describes the way guys keep one another under the radar, "Our peers are a kind of 'gender police,' always waiting for us to screw up so they can give us a ticket for crossing the well-drawn boundaries of manhood. As young men, we become relentless cowboys, riding the fences, checking the boundary line between masculinity and femininity, making sure that nothing slips over. The possibilities of being unmasked are everywhere."[10]

A lot of guys want to align with jerks who have social power, hoping to soak up some of their social capital. While there is a lot of talk about holding these obnoxious guys accountable, not many adults do it. Speaking to boys and men about privilege and entitlement makes them defensive. Beginning about ten years ago, I started talking with a group of guys about my "asshole ticket theory." I remember the first group of men looking up at me with wide eyes and knowing smiles, seemingly shocked that I was naming the unspoken hierarchy. Some guys in the group elbowed friends and exchanged glances. After that talk, several guys came up to tell me that my asshole ticket theory was spot on regarding the social hierarchy among boys and men. They went on to express their frustration at having a roommate, teammate, or good friend be the biggest asshole ticket holder and be unaware of how those tickets give him power. In her recent book, *Masterminds and Wingmen,* Rosalind Wiseman referred to the same concept as "asshole passes." It is not surprising that people refer to privilege with the word "asshole," and that it resonates with boys and men.

The figurative asshole tickets are the accepted currency we grant special people in our culture, particularly men who rely on their privilege and take advantage of the slack they may be given. If a guy is handsome, athletic, smart, and rich, he is granted a large stack of asshole tickets; the number of tickets correlates with how special he is perceived to be. Girls, women, parents, other kids' parents, teachers, other guys, and coaches seem to accept the currency of asshole tickets. A guy can be rude, sexist, homophobic, racist, obnoxious, or cruel, but peers and some adults rarely hold him accountable because he has the free pass of his asshole tickets. We often hear people excuse boys because they are young and will "grow out of" their bad behavior. Half the time, a guy who continues to find these tickets accepted is surprised he is cut such slack. It is scary for anyone to have unclear boundaries or a fence that moves, but our culture makes taking advantage of privilege hard to resist. When a guy runs out of asshole tickets, if he is special enough in a couple or all of those categories, he will get a fresh, new stack of tickets.

"The most popular and resident jerk in my school was a tall, stocky guy. He was wealthy and had an air of entitlement around him. He was in your face, which made it hard to disagree with him. Nobody wanted to argue with or challenge him in a public space since we were intimidated by his money and short temper. He couldn't have done anything to any of us, but that didn't stop us from being afraid of him."

—Male, age nineteen

Nowhere is this slack more visible than in professional sports. I happen to be a football fan and also find the sport a useful tool for teaching our kids about choices and consequences, privilege, entitlement, and attitudes. Players experience extreme highs and lows—in their personal lives, managing fame, and within the game itself. Talented players are granted truckloads of asshole tickets. Some players seem to avoid using their tickets, despite their good looks, intelligence, exceptional skills, and wealth. Perhaps in some cases they overcompensate for the expectation that they will behave like entitled people and abuse their power.

Some athletes forego opportunities to use their power and take the high road despite the fact that many teammates, owners, coaches, and fans would tolerate their misbehavior. My hope is that more boys and young men recognize these players as role models and emulate the way they handle status, athletic prowess, and available slack. If we are truly serious about having fewer assholes in the world, we need to face the fact that as a culture we are still accepting asshole tickets and still expecting guys to behave like assholes.

Privilege and Entitlement

By Josiah Proietti, masculinities researcher

When working with boys and men, we too often confuse "entitlement" with "privilege." It is true that men are granted special social goodies (higher pay for the same work, more credence for their leadership abilities, less criticism for sexual activity, and so on) for no other virtue than their manhood; this is *privilege*. Not all men, however, internalize this privilege into an expectation that they deserve these social rights, which is *entitlement*. In fact, most men grapple with male privilege the same way many white people grapple with race privilege. Once people understand that they are propped up unfairly at the expense of others, most just feel awful about the problem. Becoming aware of male privilege and the benefits that accrue from it is just one step in a developmental process toward becoming a balanced man and activist in the world of gender inequality.

When we speak about entitlement and the role it plays in men's lives, an internal shame bell goes off, and therefore a defense mechanism brews in many men's hearts. We need to understand that every man must go through the process of understanding his privilege, facing the emotions it brings up, and turning those emotions into a healthy understanding of how to be a part of the change toward a more egalitarian and free society. If we fail to distinguish the difference between entitlement and privilege, many men will get stuck in the defense part of the process. Many men already feel subjectively powerless, even though they are granted special powers that others are not granted. If all they hear is us accusing them of being overentitled, no progress will be possible.

A Call for Guidance

Michael Kimmel, author of *Guyland,* says, "As a society, we must be active, engaged, and interventionist, helping America's guys find a path of emotional authenticity, moral integrity, and physical efficacy, and thereby cast themselves more readily into an adulthood in which they can truly stand tall. We can—and must—empower boys to be more than complicit bystanders. We can help just *guys* to become *just* guys."[11] To make a difference in the lives of boys and young men, we need to intervene by encouraging boys to critically examine the culture they live in and to detox from sources that feed unhealthy messages that drive the culture. Men and boys commonly respond to shame with anger or by completely turning off. They see men in media reinforce that it is appropriate to lash out violently or retreat into a shell where all emotions are hidden, internalized, and left to stew. Some boys remain inside that shell until those suppressed anxieties, uncertainties, and frustrations build to the point where the emotions become too much to handle. Feeling inadequate or out of control can lead them to lash out in an attempt to gain some sort of control over who they are as a man.

Raising Cain by Dan Kindlon and Michael Thompson remains an influential book on boy culture, though it was written almost twenty years ago. I read it when I was an elementary school teacher, read it again when my boys were little, and continue to pull it out as a helpful reference. Kindlon and Thompson outline the role of nurture and nature in the lives of boys. The research and the interviews reinforce that parents, teachers, and coaches are in a position to nurture and support boys in a way that could liberate them from the cultural expectations of what it means to be a man.

Peer pressures and cultural expectations for boys make it challenging for them to feel adequate. The stakes are even higher as they reach an age when sexual relationships and substance use are added to the mix. It can make a big difference in a boy's life if his parents engage him in supportive educational experiences, emotional training, and opportunities to reflect; expose him to strong role models; and guide him to pay attention to his inner self, starting when he is young. These positive influences can build confidence and increase his chances of making healthier choices in social situations.

CHAPTER 10

A Hookup Culture Fueled by Alcohol

The argument that "boys will be boys" actually carries the profoundly anti-male implication that we should expect bad behavior from boys and men. The assumption is that they are somehow not capable of acting appropriately or treating girls and women with respect.

—Jackson Katz, educator, author, lecturer, and social critic

The combination of sex and alcohol is nothing new for teenagers and college-age kids. The desire for sex and a desire to be part of the hookup scene lead to reliance on alcohol to ease social awkwardness. Drinking alcohol to excess lowers inhibitions, and the hookup scene flourishes under these conditions—very intentionally. There is an unspoken social contract that many people at parties are open to engaging in heavy drinking and/or casual sex. Social media and word of mouth help normalize the behaviors and feed the widespread perception that "everyone is doing it." Getting drunk and hooking up is considered a rite of passage that young people laugh off.

"Hooking up" may mean simply kissing or it may refer to some combination or variation of oral sex, intercourse, or anal sex. "Hooking up" is a conveniently vague term that allows young people to be a part of the scene at some level and maintain privacy at the same time. It can ensure avoidance of scrutiny and pressure if you and your chosen partner didn't really do much more than cuddle or make out. If two people had intercourse, saying they hooked up can keep judgment at bay by avoiding details. There is often an imbalance of expectations and motivations for each of the people hooking up. Sometimes the imbalance inspires one of them to share details with other people as a form of social currency, a way to gain status among friends, or to publicly shame the other. When someone feels regret, shame, or embarrassment, it is acceptable in the hookup scene to claim being really drunk as an excuse for the behavior.

> "I rely heavily on alcohol and social events involving alcohol to get the confidence to start relationships and facilitate hookups. In high school, I didn't really hook up with people until I started drinking and was never in a serious relationship. Alcohol lowers inhibitions. I feel more confident and less nervous when I drink."
>
> —Female, age nineteen

Parents Setting the Tone

The messages kids internalize about sex, alcohol, and drugs when they are young and throughout middle and high school will shape their attitudes and influence their decisions when they are on their own. While kids are still living at home, parents are in a position to guide them toward developing a strong inner compass that will help them work through difficult decisions later. Heading to college, to work, or on a gap year is a dramatic shift to a much more independent existence away from the rules and consequences enforced by adults at home or at boarding school. Stumbles, failures, problems, and setbacks are to be expected—these experiences provide great learning opportunities, and build resilience. Kids who land on a college campus unprepared can easily get swept up into the social scene because it is the first time they have experienced freedom. Conversations with your kids can help them anticipate how they will respond to social pressures. The transition to life away from parents will be smoother for kids who have been given tools to find their way on their own terms.

Parents don't have much say about choices kids make once they graduate from high school. I've included stories, quotes, and information about college students and college life in this chapter to help motivate parents to be proactive in talking to kids about what they will face in college or out in the world. Once kids graduate from high school, plenty of parents surrender to an "out of sight, out of mind" philosophy, taking a light attitude about the social lives and conduct of college students. It is certainly the path of least resistance, and does work out for many families.

Getting kids safely to graduation can feel like a triumph for parents who have kept their kids from exposure to parties, sex, alcohol, and drugs throughout middle and high school. Experts agree that delaying use of drugs and alcohol through the teen years is beneficial for developing brains. According to neuroscientist Dr. Frances E. Jensen, it is important for teenagers to know that addiction works more efficiently in the adolescent brain, just as it's easier for teens to learn a new fact.[1] Because we can't predict how each kid will engage in various social situations, our best bet is to develop a strong connection with our kids—with that in place, we can set ourselves up to be their sounding board when they have questions or when the social seas get rough. Our conversations need to include accurate information about what kids will face, without lectures or fear tactics to dissuade them from engaging. Well-informed parents who approach the conversations with calm conviction will at least be heard and may make a more lasting impact with their message.

Advice About Teen Drinking

By Chris Seibel, LCMHC, MLDAC, student assistance counselor at Hanover High School in Hanover, New Hampshire

- Never be comforted by the data, because your kid may not fit the norm. Pay attention to your own kid's behavior. Data gives us an idea of the norm to use as a base for your approach.
- If your kid is engaging in risky behaviors (violence, sex, drugs) at fourteen, pay attention. Kids who smoke pot or drink at or before age fourteen have a much greater chance of lifelong addiction issues compared with those who start at eighteen. Kids who

engage in risky behaviors at seventeen or eighteen years old are less likely to develop lifelong issues.

- Encourage your kids to delay using alcohol or drugs at least until they are out of high school. Because the brain is still developing, adolescents are prime for addiction. Toddlerhood and teen years are "windows of sensitivity" for the brain. Encourage your child to delay engaging in sex, gaming, drugs, alcohol, and porn.

- If your kid can't delay because the peer group accepts/requires substance use, have conversations about values, consequences, and brain development. This is like swimming upstream because kids are away from parents for eight to ten hours a day, during which they are exposed to more messages from peers. Talk to your kid about why you won't allow him or her to hang with peers who make poor or risky choices.

- The majority of kids who experiment in high school end up making it through safely. Pay attention to how your kid is using: your kid coming home smelling of alcohol or marijuana once is one thing; you finding a pipe and a bag of weed in his room, which indicates regular use, is quite different.

- You get good at what you practice. "Good" doesn't mean you can handle drugs and alcohol better. It means being comfortable getting drunk, throwing up, and blacking out. Alcohol starts out as a stimulant and quickly turns into a depressant. Teens often drink too much too fast, and their bodies shut down or black out.

- Drinking in high school is not how kids learn to drink socially or moderately. Kids in high school drink to get drunk. Peers reinforce and normalize inappropriate behaviors such as drinking until they throw up, having drunk sex, or funneling beer.

- It is not realistic for parents to teach kids to drink socially at home. The "set" (state of mind of the person) and the "setting" (the environment) are two factors that influence choices. A glass of wine with family at Thanksgiving dinner is a setting that would not encourage a teenager to drink excessively, particularly when everything in her life is going well (the set). When the set changes— she had a breakup, didn't get playtime in the game, feels socially awkward, got a low grade—and the setting changes—she's in a charged environment with peers who are drinking, loud music, party atmosphere—the choices will usually be different than they would be at Thanksgiving dinner. Thinking your kid will drink in the same way with friends that she does at home is naïve.

- Build supports among parents. If your kid has friends whose parents endorse, support, or enable drinking, you are in a tight situation. Practice pulling your kids out of situations and have more conversations about why. It is easier when you share values with other parents in your kid's circle of friends. When you don't, you can explain that what other families practice doesn't work for your family. This is similar to explaining to a kid why your family is not taking a trip to the Caribbean like his friend.

- Parent hosts of parties often say they won't let kids drive (but kids will), they won't let kids drink a lot (kids will find a way to drink more), and they will make them stay over (some kids won't). These parents are usually naïve. Some parents think they are the exception, with a kid who will follow their rules. Kids can't control their friends. It is challenging when your own child has close friends whose parents endorse teenage drinking in their house and ignore underage drinking elsewhere. Parents who look the other way with regard to kids' drinking need to expect more from their children and more from themselves by looking in the mirror and figuring out why they feel the need to go along with this behavior.

Marijuana

People insist that marijuana is natural and "much better" than alcohol. Even where it is legal, it is against the law for people under twenty-one years of age, but that is not slowing down kids who want to get high. Most teenagers are not smoking or ingesting pot, because marijuana is not considered a rite of passage for teenagers the way drinking is. Current brain research confirms that developing brains are much more vulnerable to addiction. Kids who start using marijuana before fourteen years of age are four times more likely to become addicted,[2] and kids whose parents have a positive attitude toward marijuana are five times more likely to use it by eighth grade.[3]

Parents who claim they were not harmed by marijuana when they smoked it thirty years ago need to look more closely at the recent research before they relax about their kids smoking or ingesting marijuana. According to the University of Mississippi's Potency Monitoring program, "The average potency of marijuana has jumped from 3.4 percent THC in 1993 to 12.3 percent THC in 2012. Scientists at the lab say they've seen samples as high as 36 percent."[4] Smoking or vaporizing marijuana is a quick way to get high, however smoking marijuana exposes people to more toxins and tars that cause respiratory problems.

Ingesting marijuana means that effects may not be felt for forty-five to ninety minutes, because the substance must be digested. The effects last longer, but they take time. This has proven problematic for inexperienced and impatient users, who ingest too much because they expect to feel the effects sooner.

Generally, people who use marijuana show a decrease in motivation, interest, and focus. Pilot studies using simulators show acute impairment for two to six hours after use and carryover effects for up to twenty-four hours.[5] It is estimated that 9 percent of people who use marijuana will become dependent on it. The number goes up to about 17 percent in those who start using when they are young (in their teens), and to 25 to 50 percent among daily users.[6]

The Elusive Nature of Social Comfort

College party culture should inspire parents to get informed and engage their high school students in conversations about what they will encounter when they leave home. Four out of five college students drink alcohol, and about half of college students binge drink.[7] I've traveled to a wide variety of campuses over the past decade, and it is evident that kids who head to college uninformed and unaware of the social pressures surrounding alcohol use find it challenging to navigate the social scene. Drinking in moderation is not common in college. According to the office of the vice provost for university life at the University of Pennsylvania (VPUL), "The average college student spends $900 a year on alcohol and $450 a year on books!"[8] Current college students report that they see a few students attending parties and choosing *not* to drink alcohol, but excessive drinking is quite common.

Middle-aged people who challenge the idea that college students today drink to greater excess than students of the past usually start with a story about how much they and their friends drank at a party, and then go on with a lot of details. My first response is usually that it is sad to hear a middle-aged person bragging about how much he partied. Then I point out that he remembers the specific details of parties, which is often not the case with current college students, who hear about their party experience from observers who were somewhat more sober. Current students who endure stories from alums bragging about their party days don't usually think the old guys are cool or interesting. Some take note of what to avoid when they get old and attend their reunion.

Young people assume that, by the time they are finished with college, they will have it all figured out sexually and socially. What no one admits or talks about with them is that finding sexual and social comfort is a lifelong process. Depending on alcohol to feel more comfortable in conversations with potential sexual partners is more likely to become a habit than lead to social ease. Repetition and practice ingrain behaviors. The tendency to use alcohol to keep feelings of awkwardness at bay doesn't magically disappear after you've been doing it for years. Practicing sober courage in social and sexual situations is more likely to lead to genuine comfort and confidence.

> "I wish I had known more about how to interact with girls. It takes a while to truly understand that you don't have to be macho or mean, that most people don't hook up with tons of girls, that relationships are really mutual, and that everyone is flawed and nervous."
> —Male, age twenty-one

Feeling stressed or under pressure puts people at risk for using alcohol, drugs, or sex to check out, disconnect, or numb themselves. Alcohol use and binge drinking are common problems for high school and college students, and are not only accepted but encouraged in many environments. Binge drinkers will find plenty of company in a party scene. Committed nondrinkers, surprisingly, find it much easier to hold their ground than drinkers who try to drink moderately. With heavy drinking as the norm, partygoers tend to nudge people who aren't drinking much to keep drinking. People who aimed to drink moderately either get tired of resisting or lose track of their consumption. Sometimes moderate drinkers find being around really drunk friends annoying, so they join in. It takes discipline to drink moderately at most high school and college parties.

Being a Nondrinker

Growing up in an inn observing the drinking habits of guests and family, including older siblings and extended family, had a big impact on me. I decided to be a nondrinker early in my life, even though my siblings insisted I would eventually drink because "all teenagers drink." As a contrary, stubborn kid, I was defiant about my choice. During middle and early high school, I was harshly judgmental of people who drank and did drugs. A friend who was already done drinking and using drugs by tenth grade taught me to accept other people's choices yet stay true to my own conviction to not engage in drugs and alcohol. Because there was no doubt for me, it got easier to enjoy parties and explain my choice if anyone pressured or judged me. By the time I got to college, it didn't even take any thought to navigate a serious party culture as a nondrinker.

A clear pattern became apparent to me as an adult: in every drinking environment, with all age groups, having a drink in hand puts people at ease, whether it is a first or a tenth drink. In fact, just holding a drink changes people's dispositions: even before they take a sip, they feel more at ease and interact more openly. Today, as a nondrinking innkeeper, I find the tension among guests who arrive early almost unbearable as they try to find ease before the alcohol has arrived at the party. Alcohol is a social lubricant on which many people of all ages depend.

> "In my first year of college, alcohol was involved in finding sexual partners. The more causal factor, I believe, is the party atmosphere, which offers a casual place for classmates and people of similar ages and interests to come together and mingle. The presence of alcohol merely provided me an excuse to be outgoing."
>
> —Female, age twenty-one

Handy Examples

Most people have one or two members of their family or extended family who struggle with alcohol or drug abuse. Even if family members are not affected, there is always some family friend or acquaintance with issues that are apparent. While there are certainly patterns of behavior for alcoholics and drug addicts, there is a wide variety of ways the issues manifest in individuals. Some drinkers get silly while others get mean. Some get quieter while others get chattier. Some drinkers slur sloppily and some don't change at all until they are suddenly asleep. Functional alcoholics can go along unnoticed, and functional alcoholism is possibly the most dangerous type, as far as risks for health and safety are concerned.

Rather than shielding kids from the impact alcohol has on those we know and love, allowing them full exposure can give them a realistic idea of what drug and alcohol use looks like beyond the buzz. Witnessing only the fun, buzzed, charming person is not as impactful as seeing the full cycle, including the backside of a big evening. Compassion is required when processing observations with your kids, but an unvarnished view can be the best form of education. Raising our kids in an inn is like living in a petri dish; our family has the advantage of an ongoing study of human nature.

Pacing the Panic

There are many stories in the news that cause widespread panic among parents who have kids entering their teen years. Parents tend to freak out when they hear reports about lipstick/rainbow parties (guess which girl gave you a blowjob in the dark by the lipstick she is wearing) or Skittles parties (choosing random pills in a pile collected from medicine cabinets), assuming they are sweeping the nation. In fact, they are usually isolated incidents, yet the reports create the myth that these kinds of parties are happening everywhere and heading our way like a tornado. According to one high school counselor:

A report of an incident makes parents go nuts in the desire to keep their kids from choosing to participate in these parties or pacts.

Most kids would have no problem avoiding these situations, and they laugh when we warn them about lipstick parties. I wonder if clinging to these reports helps parents feel like they are doing something by focusing on avoiding these situations. Or does it reassure parents when they know their kids aren't involved in this and that gives them reasons to relax.

Some statistics are worth paying attention to, but kids would benefit and listen more if parents channeled their panic into productive conversations. High school parties hosted by parents who condone alcohol contribute to its acceptance as part of a social scene that involves heavy drinking and hooking up. Freshmen college students who began drinking and/or reported being drunk before they were sixteen years of age were more likely than other freshmen to binge drink in college.[9] The restrictions imposed by college administrators can reach only so far on most campuses, where alcohol and drugs are readily available and the hookup scene is widely accepted. Pregaming (drinking before a party) is very popular for underage drinkers and for those who fear they will not have access to enough alcohol once they get to a party or bar. Pregaming leads to more drinking, high-risk behaviors, and unfavorable consequences such as blackouts, hangovers, unplanned substance abuse, or unprotected sex.[10]

When parents hear about sexual assaults, binge drinking, and incidents of students being intubated at the hospital after blacking out from alcohol consumed on campus, they tend to use fear in their last-minute attempts to prepare their kids for college. Generally, these last-ditch efforts are ineffective. Young men receive harsh warnings from their parents that their lives will be ruined if they commit sexual assault. However, young men may have difficulty reconciling those messages with the realities of the college party scene, where heavy drinking and capitalizing on hookup opportunities are part of the accepted culture.

For decades, we have warned young women that they can avoid being raped if they don't drink too much, stay with friends at parties, and avoid dressing seductively. Aside from blaming the victims for the way they dress and how much they drink, the guidelines have not impacted the choices young women make or improved the statistics directly. The fact that one in five women will be sexually assaulted on campus indicates that teens would benefit from earlier and more comprehensive alcohol and sexuality education to help them navigate what lies ahead. It is unfair to expect that kids who have been raised in a restrictive environment will suddenly develop self-restraint once they are on their own. If we want our kids to make healthy choices when they leave our homes, we need to give them many opportunities to make choices, face consequences, and take on responsibilities when they are young. These experiences prepare kids for their adult lives as they practice listening to their own inner compass to guide them in their decisions.

Sexual Assault

Most sexual assaults are committed by a man against a woman, Assaults committed by women against men and in same-sex scenarios certainly occur and are underreported, but the statistics of women being assaulted by men remain higher. By describing rapists as "monsters," we risk keeping the many people who have or may commit a sexual assault from recognizing their crime or recognizing that their sexual practices would be defined as sexual assault. It is naïve to assume that "such a good guy would never do that." Good people make bad decisions under the influence of alcohol, particularly when consequences can be avoided. Some rapists don't understand that what they have done is rape. According to the United States Department of Justice, "Sexual assault is any type of sexual contact or behavior that occurs without the explicit consent of the recipient. Falling under the definition of sexual assault are sexual activities as forced sexual intercourse, forcible sodomy, child molestation, incest, fondling, and attempted rape."[11]

Most sexual assaults on college campuses occur in a hookup situation and involve alcohol. The website for the vice provost for university life at the University of Pennsylvania (VPUL) states, "Alcohol use is frequently associated with acquaintance rape. One study found that 70% of women and 80% of men had been drinking when a sexual assault occurred. Alcohol impairs judgment and lowers inhibitions making it easier to force sex on an unwilling partner."[12] Clear communication and requests for consent continue to be considered "too awkward" for hookup participants. This must change!

Many sexual assaults are not reported because the victim doesn't want to endure the process and doesn't think she will be believed, especially if she was drinking. It is still common for defense lawyers to blame victims for what they wore and how much they drank. Just a few years ago, I participated in an event that ended with a panel of lawyers talking about sexual assault. The defense lawyer mocked my use of the term "enthusiastic consent" and finished his presentation by telling the female college students in the audience, "Don't ruin a young man's life by getting him sent to my office." This well-educated yet ignorant man seemed to have no consideration for or awareness of the emotional pain victims endure. The Rape, Abuse, and Incest National Network notes that sexual assault victims are "three times more likely to suffer from depression, six times more likely to suffer from post-traumatic stress disorder, thirteen times more likely to abuse alcohol, twenty-six times more likely to abuse drugs, and four times more likely to contemplate suicide."[13] The percentage of false reports is small, and is equal to that of false reports of other crimes. While a small number of men commit sexual assault, there is a strong likelihood that a man who has assaulted someone will repeat the crime if he has not paid consequences.

"If we can give people the tools to speak up and get to a place where men who act out in sexist and harassing ways will lose status, we will see a radical diminution in gender violence."[14]
—Jackson Katz, PhD, educator, author, lecturer, and social critic

Addressing sexual assault has been a huge priority on most campuses, but meaningful progress is slow. It is encouraging to see colleges revamping their policies and investigative processes to meet the requirement of Title IX and the Clery Act. Even students admit that alcohol and sex are not a healthy combination, but the already widespread acceptance of a hookup culture involving alcohol perpetuates the problem. Student organizations across the country are working to make changes, driving some inspiring efforts to end sexual violence on their campuses. One of the more effective efforts I have seen was at Colby College, where MAV (Mules Against Violence—the school mascot is a mule) and an offshoot organization called Party with Consent are both raising awareness and inspiring changes within the party environment. Eric Barthold and Jonathan Kalin were respective leaders of these two organizations, and have continued with the work since graduating. What stood out for me was the strong participation of men, which helped reach a wider spectrum of students.

Colby is where I first heard students being encouraged to seek enthusiastic consent—verbal consent that is clearly communicated—from their sexual partners. Most young people know that "No means no" and that physically restraining someone against her (or his) will would be considered rape, however people continue to be sexually assaulted even when they say "No!" repeatedly and clearly.

Being under the influence of alcohol contributes to attackers convincing themselves that they can use coercion to turn a no into a yes. Yes is the only word that means yes. In her "Girls Fight Back" workshops, Gina Kirkland encourages participants to make the requirement be a "Hell yeah."[15] Sexuality educator Al Vernacchio suggests we aim for "active positive consent." These two terms and others, such as "affirmative consent," are gaining acceptance by many students, even those who initially thought they'd find using them awkward. Middle-aged people often find these terms to be "too much" or "not romantic." Extra effort and less romance seem like an easy price to pay to avoid sexual assault. Young people are making the shift and are opening up to the idea of saying, "Can I...?" "Do you like...?" or "Would you be interested in...?" A number of schools have launched campaigns with the motto "Consent is sexy!" Let's help this idea catch on.

Finding Hope

I feel hopeful in the midst of the accelerated awareness and more open dialogue, particularly on college campuses, thanks to the public outcry and the threat of withheld funding. Brave victims who are willing to share their stories, names, and faces in news reports are forcing widespread awareness. Columbia student Emma Sulkowicz reports being a victim of sexual assault in her own dorm room on the first day of her sophomore year. A visual arts major, she titled her 2014 senior thesis "Mattress Performance," or "Carry That Weight." To protest the university's response to her allegation—an inquiry found the accused attacker "not responsible"—Sulkowicz was determined to carry her mattress until her attacker left or was removed from campus. She wouldn't ask anyone to help her carry it, but she did accept help if someone offered it. Sulkowicz explains, "A mattress is the perfect size for me to just be able to carry it enough that I can continue with my day but also heavy enough that I have to continually struggle with it."[16]

Most men are not rapists. I meet many respectful and aware young men who are tired of being collectively blamed for sexual assaults and embarrassed by the reputation of their campuses. I speak to groups of Dartmouth College students on a fairly regular basis—Dartmouth has been the target for a lot of criticism for its insufficient investigative processes in sexual assault cases. Women have found it challenging to make change and raise awareness at Dartmouth for as long as female students have been enrolled. I have had the honor of knowing and working with many of the resilient women who speak out despite the challenges and setbacks they faced during their time at the school.

Traveling around the country, I have encountered student organizations on other campuses making impressive progress, including some that have limited resources, little support from administrators, and seemingly endless obstacles to navigate. I hoped Dartmouth students would look outside the Ivy League for ideas about how to make more significant change. The student activism around sexual assault at Colby College, for instance, could be a model for other schools. Small groups of men at Dartmouth have been making efforts to change the culture, but it has been hard for them to get purchase. What seemed like hollow efforts by the Dartmouth administration to engage in real change and an outsized interest in maintaining the school's reputation led me to put my speaking time and energy in other directions. Then two amazing young men changed my mind.

When I agreed to meet Connor Gibson and Robbie Tanner, I didn't expect to be inspired. During our one-hour discussion, my hope for Dartmouth was renewed. What caught my interest was that Robbie and Connor were genuinely invested in changing the culture of Dartmouth by enlightening their male peers about sexual assault. As fraternity brothers, they fully acknowledged that fraternities earn their reputations, but they also believed fraternity brothers could help solve issues surrounding alcohol, drugs, and sexual assault at the college. These fellas fit into what I call the bold 5 percent of men who are brave enough to step out from under the radar, where safety in numbers protects them from having to take responsibility. The courage that is bred in boys and men like Robbie and Connor can be infectious, and in the case of their peers, it has been. They are willing to put themselves out there, work hard, follow through, and do what is right. These young men are invested in making real change in the Dartmouth culture.

During their sophomore year, Robbie and Connor were inspired by a presentation given by seniors reflecting on gender and comfort in the Greek system. Encouraged by the positive response from the fraternity brothers who attended, Robbie and Connor committed to being part of the effort to change Dartmouth's culture despite the pressure of heavy workloads, ten-week terms, and some student apathy about sexual assault. They decided to host another event, called "Respect Works," which included a panel of students who would share their own sexual assault experiences, followed by three middle-aged women speakers. None of us could imagine how this idea would rally fraternity men to participate during their busy sophomore summer, but they were willing to try. One of the speakers was a member of the steering committee who would talk about moving Dartmouth forward, the second speaker was a dynamic lawyer who would address the legal nuances of consent, and the third speaker was me: I was asked to present my thoughts on hookup culture, porn, relationships, and sexual communication.

I was surprised that men were so attentive, responsive, and fully engaged in the presentations and activities. Some attended with the purpose of saving their fraternity, while many were clearly invested in being part of the change. After the event, I had conversations with several of the participants that made it clear that men who are nineteen or twenty years old are open to information and ideas about how to reframe expectations of their college social lives. Having had more education about sexual assault, consent, substance abuse, and bystander behavior than the seniors, this group of sophomores seemed more awake than men just a few years older. Most understand the factors that contribute to the tolerance of sexual assault. Dartmouth President Philip J. Hanlon showed his support by joining the group for a candlelight walk to the center of campus, where people shared their intentions and hopes for moving Dartmouth forward.

If I hadn't agreed to meet with Robbie and Connor, I would have lost an opportunity to participate in a step toward change, missed the chance to connect with a group of thoughtful participants in the event, and held onto my erroneous assumption that men at Dartmouth are apathetic. I am pleased to have been proven wrong. Robbie and Connor had the courage to put themselves out there and successfully rallied groups of men from almost every fraternity at Dartmouth to participate in making change. More conversations are taking place at Dartmouth as a result. When voices, opinions, and perspectives are heard, hope catches on.

CHAPTER 11

Moving Beyond Hookups: Finding Communication and Pleasure

The more students talk about hooking up, the clearer it becomes that it has less to do with excitement or even attraction than with checking a box off a long list of tasks, like homework or laundry. And while hookup sex is supposed to come with no strings attached, it nonetheless creates an enormous amount of stress and drama among participants.

—Donna Freitas, *The End of Sex: How Hookup Culture Is Leaving a Generation Unhappy, Sexually Unfulfilled, and Confused About Intimacy*

Sex can be fulfilling and pleasurable when the participants have a loving and respectful connection that enables them to communicate openly and clearly. Being comfortable *not* knowing and having the courage to seek information through reliable resources seem to be common traits among sexually knowledgeable and satisfied people. Most people are reluctant to admit what they don't know about sex because they assume they are the only ones who missed out on key information. Despite the Internet, or perhaps because of the Internet, many adult men and women know very little about sex and female pleasure. While helpful and accurate information is available in a variety of resources, most people choose the anonymity of online sites, and, unfortunately, searches require sorting through a lot of misleading, highly viewed pornographic material to find much-needed reliable information and guidance.

> "I hadn't expected that my first sexual experience would be awkward, wouldn't last long, and that neither of us would know what we were doing."
>
> —Male, age nineteen

Disconnected Connections

Some people think that they are not responsible for what they say or do while under the influence of alcohol or drugs. Hooking up with a random person requires some level of disconnection from one's healthy sexual self. Many people who hook up start their interactions via texting, which can create a false sense of "knowing" a person. Some people flirt their way toward a hookup through texts, so awkwardness is almost guaranteed when they ultimately reach the moment of truth and find themselves physically and emotionally naked together. No matter how a person frames a sexual encounter, it is, and should be, an emotionally and physically vulnerable experience. There is no app that can provide rescue from that situation. Being under the influence of alcohol (or, less commonly, a drug) is the most common way people attempt to make the encounter more comfortable. True courage requires that we open ourselves up to a connection with another person, to the risk of rejection, and to emotional vulnerability—and it requires that we ask for consent or guidance from our partner.

> "I am just tired of having a relationship based off sex. I want to be intimate with a person without sex. Hooking up makes me feel undervalued and not appreciated because the person only wants me for sex."
>
> —Female, age nineteen

No Shame

Independent school administrators are surprised by students' lack of embarrassment and remorse when they are called to the office for sending nude photos of themselves through Snapchat. One student didn't even understand that she was in trouble, because at her former school, girls commonly thanked boys for accepting their friend requests by sending a nudie. A lack of remorse and self-consciousness is also evident when kids are caught having sex in classrooms, on turf fields, or in the stairwell of schools. One head of school reported that, when he catches students having sex, they don't even hustle to get their clothes back on. Sexual acts and images are so commonplace that it seems like kids want to be a part of it.

Both public and independent high schools have growing issues with sexual harassment via texts, Yik Yak, Snapchat, and Facebook. Anonymous posting seems to inspire courage in people who would never be able to show such harassing behavior in person. Girls often ask about the best way to respond when they are harassed in this way. Not engaging seems like the most effective way to dissuade the sender, but reporting the incident is also important. Some boys use the negative approach to fish around for a potential hookup: many boys report that they consider being called an asshole in response to an inappropriate text a sign that there is a chance the girl could be convinced. In an article for the *Telegraph*, "Children and the Culture of Pornography," reporter Cole Moreton says, "Boys have always tried their luck but now they have the technological means to apply pressure on phones with cameras and messenger networks that no adult ever sees."[1]

Motivators to Hook Up

A participant in a high school discussion group of sophomore girls said, "If you hook up once, that means *one* of the people is interested. If you hook up twice, that means *both* are interested. If you hook up a third time, then it's 'a thing.'" All the girls nodded in agreement, as most high school and college students do when I repeat this statement. Reverse dating seems to be the way it goes for a generation that thinks "dating" is old fashioned. Recent research shows that many teenagers and college students—both male and female—are equally interested in relationships and privately hope that hooking up may lead to a relationship. The perception that everyone is hooking up creates a lot of pressure on teens and college students to be a part of the hookup "club." Even middle school and high school students who don't have access to alcohol feel some pressure to get on board with the hookup scene.

Young people choose to engage in, or stumble onto, the hookup culture for a variety of reasons. A primary factor is the perception among young people that they are missing out on having the amazing casual sex that everyone else is having. When you join in, fewer people bug you about why you are not hooking up. Meaningless, casual sexual encounters have become normalized.

Young people often treat hooking up as something to get through and check off a list, as if it were a necessary rite of passage. Wanting to feel hot and desired inspires some young people to engage. Many young high school girls hook up with older boys because they are honored to be chosen and to feel part of the scene. Kids who have restrictive parents may find that the freedom of boarding school or college inspires them to lose their virginity to "get it over with." Some people seek stress relief or sexual release. Many actually stumble into a hookup because they are too drunk to know what they really want. Others are not drunk but blame alcohol for the hookup to avoid judgment from peers. Because female orgasms are uncommon in a hookup scenario, it is apparent that the hookup isn't really about pleasure for many of the women. What I have learned from young men, and what has been confirmed by Freitas's research, is that even though most guys get off during a hookup, many report feeling unfulfilled by the experience.[2]

Many who think they will "gain experience" by hooking up a lot discover that mileage does not necessarily deepen sexual understanding and knowledge. Hooking up with a lot of partners can actually reinforce ineffective techniques, unless partners are willing to ask for and give feedback. The assumption that "experienced" partners know what they are doing deters some people from giving feedback. Listening to experienced men describe what they think "women love" is disconcerting. They often describe the very techniques and moves that women in groups complain about their partners using. Women I interview individually and in groups typically say they are reluctant to give a male partner feedback even if the sex is awful, and particularly if he is very experienced. The most common reason they give is that they don't want to hurt the guy's feelings. For years, I was aghast at women's willingness to forego their own satisfaction to please their male partners, and tried to rally them to own their pleasure by figuring out for themselves what they liked and then guiding their partners. When the involvement is a one-time or short-term thing, though, most don't think it is worth it.

Heterosexual boys and men long for input, guidance, and direction from their partners, but feel they are supposed to know what they are doing already, and therefore try to figure it out. Teammates, fraternity brothers, and friends depend on their sexually experienced peers to give them information. Unfortunately, unless the experienced friend has had a very comfortable and communicative partner, he is at risk of repeating what he has learned from porn and the experienced guys who guided him. Because most heterosexual men don't feel comfortable asking for guidance from their partners and most heterosexual women won't speak up, people are having a lot of below-average sex, which internalizes a low standard for what sex is supposed to be like. Despite the unfulfilling sex, people keep at it. Al Vernacchio suggests, "If you can't look a person in the eye and talk about it, you shouldn't be doing it."[3]

Unfulfilling Hookups

We all hope that our children will grow up to find life partners with whom they share a strong connection, respect, and open communication. Unhealthy choices and mistakes along the way are part of that process. Setbacks can also help young people recalibrate their standards and can inspire more appropriate choices as they move forward. Experts agree that practice and repetition of choices and behaviors can contribute to patterns; all the relationships people have impact their subsequent relationships. Kids who put up with abusive friends could end up choosing a partner who treats them in a similar way. Repeated casual sex without personal connection or honest communication with a partner can influence relationship expectations.

> "No matter what women say, it's hard to have a no-strings-attached hook up. I hope for more ownership of my body and confidence in my body. I am looking for more meaningful connections with potential for sustained happiness rather than random hookups that leave me feeling alone and empty."
>
> —Female, age twenty-seven

Hooking up with a stranger, acquaintance, or friend diminishes the chance of an emotionally or physically fulfilling experience. The "good in bed" myth perpetuates the idea that good sex is reserved for people who just know a lot, have had a lot of experience, or are conventionally hot, desirable people who look like celebrities and act like porn stars. In reality, every person of any age or sexual experience has the capacity to be an amazing and loving sexual partner for a person with whom he shares a strong connection, trust, and respect. These factors, however, are not part of the hookup equation, which is mostly about physical connection rather than intimacy. Al Vernacchio has wise advice for young people: "The best sexual activity doesn't come from a manual or a list of instructions. It comes from knowing your body, knowing your partner's body, and communicating about what brings both people pleasure. That's what we all should do when we engage in sexual activity."[4]

Many young women express frustration that boys and men are praised for hooking up with a lot of people while girls and women who do are called sluts. Some women decide to buck the double standard and approach hooking up as an empowering act that they can do the same way guys do. When asked how that feels over time, these women often say that it is unfulfilling and not what they had hoped for. During a presentation for college men and women, one of the women stood up to tell the whole group that women should do what they want and hook up with as many guys as they want. She was forceful and fiery in her statements. As she concluded her rage about the injustice, she started crying, admitted that it wasn't satisfying, and said she was just mad at guys who can do it without getting attached.

While there are guys who treat hooking up as a higher form of masturbation, that is not the case for most. The generalization that guys don't care about relationships and just want sex is actually not true. Recent research aligns with what I have heard from young men for years: during her research on college hookup culture, author Donna Freitas discovered, "There are many men out there at colleges and universities across America who are sad, ashamed, and/or ambivalent about hooking up and the sex they are having; who wish for long-term relationships, dating, love, and romance; and who feel that their sex lives are actually pretty unfulfilling, even bad and embarrassing. If they want to be regarded as 'real men' or 'guys,' however, they also feel they must go along with the hookup culture without complaints."[5]

Wrap It Up

Obviously, condoms do not protect people from the emotional risks surrounding sex, but they do decrease the chances of contracting a sexually transmitted infection (STI) or getting pregnant. While condoms are not 100 percent safe, they make sex *safer*. Using condoms correctly and consistently is not a common practice, however, despite the claims of some young people. When I speak with sober students, they say they use condoms "all the time," but the health services professionals on campuses where I speak report that they treat a high number of STIs and listen to students who regret a decision not to use a condom in the heat of the moment when they were drunk. Many young men claim that it can be hard to get it up or get off using a condom, particularly when they are drunk. Some young men brag that they must be too big for condoms because they break several during one hookup. I can usually get their attention by pointing out that condom breakage is unlikely to be a size issue, since most condoms fit over an adult forearm up to the elbow, and that possibly the issue is using a porn-inspired jackhammer style of penetration in an unaroused, dry vagina.

Teenage girls often claim menstrual cramps or irregular periods as a reason to use a birth control method like the NuvaRing (vaginal ring), which releases hormones known to reduce the side effects of menstruation. Parents often feel relieved to not have to think about being grandparents any time soon, and send their daughters off to college on the birth control pill, patch, shots, implant, or vaginal ring. These forms of birth control are effective in preventing pregnancy when used correctly, but many young women contract or pass along STIs when they choose to have sex without a condom. Condoms should be used regardless of what other method is in place, and I tell students to always carry condoms.

Seeking Pleasure

People will make their own decisions about what they enjoy and engage in sexually, but hopefully they get a chance to discover what they find pleasurable before they are swinging from a trapeze with a double-headed dildo and jumping into sex with multiple partners. Figuring out sexual pleasure with oneself before engaging in a sexual encounter with another person is both wise and the safest kind of sex. A fair number of young people are willing to engage in a threesome or a foursome *before* they have figured out how to communicate comfortably with one partner.

> "Some think that drinking alcohol will enhance the experience of physical intimacy when just the opposite is true. Alcohol decreases clitoral sensitivity and vaginal secretions in women and contributes to impotency in men."[6]
>
> —Office of the vice provost for university life
> at the University of Pennsylvania

It is fairly common for girls and young women to be game for adventurous sex, and many high school girls hook up with older boys at their schools. A teacher at an independent school described a conversation with her sophomore advisees, during which she learned that all six girls had extensive sexual experience—including oral sex, anal sex, vaginal intercourse, threesomes—in hookup scenarios rather than with a committed partner. When she asked them if they had ever had an orgasm, not one of them had or knew how to make that happen, and the girls claimed it would be awkward to talk to their partners about their pleasure. While there can be a wide variety of pleasurable sexual contact that does not involve female orgasms, it is clear that the sex many young people are having is not particularly pleasurable or emotionally fulfilling for either partner.

While most boys and men are getting off in a hookup, they also report that the encounters are emotionally unfulfilling. The fact that many guys are looking for connection is contrary to the generalizations we hear about guys and sex. I also hear from college men that unless they care about a person, masturbation can be "easier" than hooking up because it requires less energy than "dealing" with another person.

> "Sometimes I would rather just beat off to porn rather than hook up with a girl. It is kind of a hassle to have sex with a girl who comments about being self-conscious about her body. I would never notice if she didn't keep bringing it up."
>
> —Male, age twenty-two

The pattern of unfulfilling hookups for girls, boys, women, and men is evident in current research as well as in the personal stories I have heard over the years in interviews. Many complain that sex just isn't what they expected. Alexandra Katehakis summarizes the hookup culture and links the disappointment it engenders with the skewed view of sex presented by porn: "Pornography shows us a world where relationships mean nothing and immediate sexual gratification means everything."[7] The way sexual fulfillment is acted out by women in porn makes it seem easy, but in real life female pleasure is much more elusive.

Faking orgasms is common practice for teenage girls and young women because they assume they are incapable of orgasms or don't want to make their male partner feel sexually inadequate. Experts and sexologists agree, however, that with the right information, all females have the capacity for orgasm. The notion of women putting the sexual needs of male partners ahead of their own leads to dissatisfaction for both partners. While the intention behind faking an orgasm may be kind, partners who learn the truth feel tricked and hurt. In order to experience pleasure, most females need to figure out their own pleasure zones. In a group of women, one young woman asked why men "insist on having sex like a jackrabbit" even though it hurts for women. The rest of the women in the group cheered and laughed in agreement. When I suggested they tell their partners that it hurts, one woman said, "I don't tell him to stop because it hurts. Faking an orgasm gets him off. The sooner he is done and stops the better." More laughter ensued. The obvious answer is to communicate clearly, but women often feel discouraged from speaking up about their needs.

Most sexual dissatisfaction is rooted in a lack of communication. Despite the standard banter we hear about young men being selfish sexual partners, most

"A great sexual experience would be with a partner who is fully present, engaged, and taking his time. It often feels rushed with pressure to perform and to climax, which makes it a negative experience. Communicating about what we like or don't like greatly improves the experience. In the past, I would have negative hookup experiences because I wouldn't speak up; I would just bear through it because I didn't want to hurt the guy's feelings. I've learned that I can and should speak up."

—Female, age twenty-seven

heterosexual men are not only interested in but obsessed with how to please women sexually. Guys assume they are supposed to know how female pleasure works, and women assume men know. Speaking up and admitting what they don't know would help men provide a more fulfilling experience for their partners. Few women speak up when they are uncomfortable or dissatisfied—women should communicate their needs more clearly with specific guidance.

Some Facts About Female Pleasure

Many young women don't understand their own capacity for pleasure and wait for their partners to figure it out. Despite the complicated nature of female orgasms, few parents or sex ed programs are teaching kids anything about how female orgasms work.

> "If girls and women find masturbation more 'creepy' than sex with someone they barely know, that should inspire them to reconsider their choices."
> —Sexuality educator and counselor

When I talk to heterosexual men about female pleasure, most admit that their first impressions were formed by porn, which notoriously misleads viewers about what women enjoy sexually. If more people understood the following points about female pleasure, perhaps they would improve their sexual communication, find more pleasure in sex, and form healthier standards for choosing partners.

1. The sole purpose of the clitoris is pleasure. What makes the clitoris elusive is the fact that it lives under a hood, which is like a garage protecting the clitoris's eight thousand nerves (double the number found in the penis). The bulb of the clitoris is very sensitive. The shaft of the clitoris is slightly less sensitive and a good place to stimulate if the bulb of the clitoris is too sensitive at first. The clitoral legs extend into the walls of the vagina, adding some sensitivity, though sensation there is not as intense as it is in the area around the clitoris or the vulva, depending on the woman's individual anatomy. The

clitoral hood is actually a handy feature in that it protects the clitoris from stimulation from clothing when nonsexual tasks must be done.

2. It is estimated that 70-80 percent of women do not experience clitoral orgasms with penetration alone. This has led to many women thinking they are not capable of orgasms, though most women are, with additional stimulation from another source—touch, finger, or vibrator. A woman or her partner can lend a helping hand during penetration.

3. The average time men take to reach orgasm is usually much shorter than that required for women. This poses a timing issue for heterosexual couples unless there is good communication or use of foreplay to help both partners experience maximum pleasure. There is an assumption that two women can give each other orgasms easily, but every woman's pleasure zones are set up a bit differently and respond differently—what brings pleasure for one woman is not only different from other women, but it could change each day, each cycle, and as she ages. It is helpful for a woman to guide her partner verbally and clearly. I always say, "Be the GPS for your partner."

4. Erogenous zones vary from person to person, and they also shift. Communication is required to know if one's partner enjoys being caressed on her neck, earlobe, hip, feet, nipples, elbow, or wherever a zone may be. Remember, erogenous zones move camp; "reliable erogenous zone" is a contradiction in terms. Figuring out a partner's desires requires adaptation and communication every time.

5. Located two inches up the front wall of the vagina, the G-spot works differently for every woman. Stimulation of the G-spot can help arousal progress for some women. Some have a completely unresponsive G-spot, some have a G-spot that is responsive every time she is penetrated, and other women have a G-spot that is responsive some of the time. Some women develop a more responsive G-spot as they age. Stimulation of this area can lead to more intense arousal and cause a tensing of the vaginal walls. Some refer to this tightening as a "vaginal orgasm," not to be confused with the "clitoral orgasm." Vaginal orgasms are a wonderful sensation, but the clitoral orgasm is much more intense, resulting in a dopamine rush.

The Misguided Alpha Dog

Sometimes there is one guy in a group who has been the source for sex guidance and wisdom for all of his friends. A guy who has had a lot of female partners doesn't get much honest feedback (I have interviewed some who have had fifty or sixty partners by the time they are twenty-one). Perhaps his partners blame themselves for their lack of a good time and endure because they feel honored to have a sexual encounter with this particular guy. The "experienced" guys I have interviewed over the years tend to not have a lot of useful knowledge. I have listened to guys confidently claim a winning blender/boring-out approach to intercourse or a vigorous jackhammer style they are certain will "hit all the spots." Hooking up repeatedly without communication or feedback from partners reinforces a lot of distorted ideas about sex rather than leading to greater awareness.

One of my aims is to convey that mileage does not result in a good understanding of true sexual connection and pleasure. I caution guys to avoid espousing "expertise" to less experienced peers who hang on every word, as well as not to depend on what they hear from peers about women's sexual desires. My hope is that they will instead initiate more open communication about needs and expectations with their partners.

It doesn't take much for young people to lose track of realistic expectations and healthy ideas about sexuality. Unreliable resources are ubiquitous in the digital age. Most parents hope their children will delay having sex and grow up to have healthy and fulfilling sexual relationships. It is unfair and irresponsible to rely on teachers, doctors, and blind faith to inform and instill confidence in kids. Parents need to actively engage their own kids in conversations about bodies, relationships and sexuality, starting when kids are young. Parents who contribute to their kids' sexual knowledge base and guide them in developing their values increase the chances of their kids making healthy choices. By modeling open communication and genuine connections, parents help set a healthy, positive standard for their children's future relationships.

Conclusion

Our youth now love luxury. They have bad manners, contempt for authority; they show disrespect for their elders and love chatter in place of exercise; they no longer rise when elders enter the room; they contradict their parents, chatter before company; gobble up their food and tyrannize their teachers.

—Socrates, 470/469–399 BC

Even a couple millennia ago, elders as revered as Socrates were worrying about the poor manners and morals of the young. Socrates, people! Adults' observations of kids have not changed. The context in which kids grow up, however, changes radically with each generation. Parents and educators must give kids increasing independence and responsibilities while at the same time providing guidance and advice along the way. It's a dicey balance. The parenting adventure is filled with conflict, delight, overstepping of bounds, recalibrations, missed cues, getting off track, realignment, connection, miscommunication, and rebooting. The relationship between parent and child is ever changing, and requires an open heart and a willingness to invest in what matters.

The digital age has made teenage life much more complicated. Many interactions kids have are not visible to parents as the kids grow into teenagers, as devices have changed the ways kids interact and therefore have changed their relationships. In order to convince our kids to look for a healthy balance between screen time and live time, we need to make a conscious effort to model and discuss that balance. Even if we are overwhelmed by the expanse of influences and exposure our kids are experiencing, we need to stay involved by having conversations about what they are consuming. This is not to say we have to know everything they engage in and everyone they connect with, but we need to stay informed about their lives and continue talking about our values, even if they resist. We have to fully embrace our role as our kids' primary sexuality educators to help them make sense of the cultural messages they are bombarded with. Talking to kids early and often about bodies, relationships, sexuality, friendships, and alcohol and drugs is an investment in readying our kids for the long term. It is tricky to maintain awareness of the future and stay present with the day-to-day interactions with our kids, especially when the path is not smooth. Don't aim for smooth. Embrace the random effortless moments and keep having conversations despite the rough patches.

Parents who try to dodge the tough stuff in an attempt to "enjoy them while they are here" may miss the deeper connections that develop when these conversations are woven in and around the fun parts. I believe connecting with kids requires keeping expectations manageable and grooving through the daily routines, ready to soak up the morsels of wonder that wash up on occasion. Loving our children is easy, but liking them every day can be a challenge. Sometimes I feel like my only feature is that I have keys to a car that will get them where they need to go. Instead of bossing them into showing gratitude and noticing all I have sacrificed to get them to lacrosse practice, I drive on, listen, and try to appreciate the beauty of the sky while they bicker about the injustices of who got the front seat or smelly farts.

Making memories with our kids means we have to be open to being redirected. I used to anticipate "family joy" with giddiness as we embarked on a hike, outing, vacation, or dinner out together as a family. It wasn't too far into our parenting journey that I learned how expectations, hopes, and agendas can turn special time together into a slog. A day of skiing together or a visit to a cool place could implode over nothing. It was so disappointing to leave a restaurant with a snarky kid (or two or three) and salty parents. By the time kids were trying to brush their teeth around our *one* family sink, way past their bedtimes, they were shopping for opportunities to blame, cry, and take up the most psychic space, all of them jacked up on carbs from a dinner of bread and pasta. One of them would end up hurt and collapsed in a puddle on the floor of the bathroom over almost nothing. Bruce and I would play rock, paper, scissors to see who would help encourage the puddle kid to get in bed rather than sleep on the dirty bath mat. We always played two out of three. We would make big statements that we were never going out for dinner ever again because it always ended in fighting and irritation. We would forget and get fired up for a family hike to a favorite spot. Somewhere along the trail, one or all would end up dropping anchor for one reason or another, and the vibe would be off the rails even though it didn't need to be.

After lots of repetition and watching patterns emerge, we started to secretly find humor in these inevitable scenes and stopped engaging with the anchor dropper or the puddle kid by focusing on the kid who was pointing out the beautiful sky or noticing the small bug struggling to makes its way. We developed the ability to stay present and keep moving. Not engaging as much meant anchors dropped less and kid puddles got back up more often because no one wants to miss the fun stuff. It is human nature to want to connect, but we all have our own way of connecting. When we slow down and pay attention, we will find the circuits to make connections more often. Over time, we don't remember the bickering and the tears as much as the sky and the bugs.

I decided that planning family joy is impossible. Family joy sneaks around and lurks, popping up in random ten-minute windows. If we stayed receptive to the unexpected conversation, observation, question, or silence together, we would find the joy. Sometimes it happens on an outing, but it is more likely that family joy shows up in the middle of mundane moments such as cleaning up after dinner. You can't wait for it, expect it, or force it, but when it slips in to shine on your family, you want the presence of mind to bask in it before someone steps on his sister's snack and all hell breaks loose in the backseat. I used to dream of a bigger bathroom with two sinks. Luckily, it never happened, because that one sink shared by five people gives us so many opportunities to wrangle for space, cooperate, and practice patience, and to get to the other side of juicy battles over toothpaste—and still love each other. These situations are training for our kids and the relationships they will have throughout their lives. In this time, when devices distance us from one another, we need to create more opportunities to connect. Find one sink, and gather up.

NOTES

Introduction

1. Vicki Hoefle, *Duct Tape Parenting: A Less is More Approach to Raising Respectful, Responsible, and Resilient Kids* (Brookline, MA: Bibliomotion, 2012), 110.

Chapter 1

1. Catherine Steiner-Adair, *The Big Disconnect: Protecting Childhood and Family Relationships in the Digital Age* (New York: HarperCollins, 2014), 135.
2. Tamara Lewin, "If Your Kids Are Awake, They're Probably Online," *New York Times* online edition, January 20, 2010, accessed May 5, 2015, http://www.nytimes.com/2010/01/20/education/20wired.html?_r=0.
3. Hannah Richardson, "Limit Children's Screen Time, Expert Urges," BBC News online edition, October 9, 2012, accessed January 10, 2015, http://www.bbc.com/news/education-19870199.
4. Jenny Brundin, "Waldorf's 4th Graders Gain Insight from Media Fast," Colorado Public Radio transcript, February 9, 2013, accessed January 12, 2015 http://www.denverwaldorf.org/tag/npr/.
5. Dr. Marty Klein, "Want to Watch a Lot of Porn AND Have Good Sex?" *Sexual Intelligence* blog, November 11, 2014, accessed December 15, 2014, https://sexualintelligence.wordpress.com/2014/11/11/want-to-watch-a-lot-of-porn-and-have-good-sex/.
6. Austin Tedesco, "BC Students Read Offensive Yik Yak Posts," *The Heights* blog, May 6, 2014, accessed March 1, 2015, http://bcheights.com/blog/2014/bc-students-read-offensive-yik-yak-posts/.
7. Rachel Simmons, *Odd Girl Out: The Hidden Culture of Aggression in Girls* (Boston and New York: Mariner Books, a division of Houghton Mifflin Harcourt, 2002), 321.

8. Clifford Nass, interview by Ira Flatow, "The Myth of Multitasking," *Science Friday*. National Public Radio, May 10, 2013, accessed December 29, 2014, http://www.npr.org/2013/05/10/182861382/the-myth-of-multitasking.

9. Dara Kerr, "One-fifth of Third Graders Own Cell Phones," CNet online version, April 9, 2012, accessed January 10, 2015, http://www.cnet.com/news/one-fifth-of-third-graders-own-cell-phones/.

10. Travis Bradberry, "Multitasking Damages Your Brain and Career, New Studies Suggest," *Forbes* online version, October 8, 2014, accessed February 24, 2015, http://www.forbes.com/sites/travisbradberry/2014/10/08/multitasking-damages-your-brain-and-career-new-studies-suggest/.

11. Steiner-Adair, *The Big Disconnect*, 4.

12. Gunilla Norris, *Inviting Silence* (Katonah, NY: Bluebridge, 2004), 7.

Chapter 2

1. Frances Jensen, interview by Terry Gross, "Why Teens Are Impulsive, Addiction-Prone and Should Protect Their Brains," *Fresh Air*, National Public Radio, January 28, 2015, accessed February 15, 2015, http://www.npr.org/blogs/health/2015/01/28/381622350/why-teens-are-impulsive-addiction-prone-and-should-protect-their-brains.

2. "About the Film" page for *Race to Nowhere: The Dark Side of America's Achievement Culture* (Vicki Abeles and Jessica Congdon, codirectors), March 27, 2015, http://www.racetonowhere.com/about-film.

3. Vicki Hoefle, *Duct Tape Parenting: A Less is More Approach to Raising Respectful, Responsible, and Resilient Kids* (Brookline, MA: Bibliomotion, 2012), 53.

4. Roko Belic, "The Search for Happiness," *Huffington Post*, updated March 21, 2012, accessed January 27, 2015, http://www.huffingtonpost.com/roko-belic/happy-documentary_b_1220111.html.

5. Jensen, "Why Teens Are Impulsive."

6. Jensen, "Why Teens Are Impulsive."

7. Lisa M. Schab, *The Anxiety Workbook for Teens* (Oakland, CA: Instant Help Books, Harbinger Publications, 2008), 1.

Chapter 3

1. John Arlidge, "The Dirty Secret That Drives Technology: It's Porn," *Guardian*, online edition, March 2, 2002, accessed on March 24, 2002, http://www.theguardian.com/technology/2002/mar/03/internetnews.observerfocus.

2. Allison Conner, PsyD, "Porn Habit—Indulgence or Addiction," *Psychology Today* online edition, April 13, 2014, accessed May 6, 2015, https://www.psychologytoday.com/blog/therapy-in-mind/201408/porn-habit-indulgence-or-addiction.

3. Patrick Howse, "'Pornography Addiction Worry' for tenth of 12 to 13-year-olds," BBC News, online edition, March 31, 2015, accessed March 31, 2015, http://www.bbc.com/news/education-32115162.

4. Alexandra Katehakis, "Effects of Porn on Adolescent Boys," *Psychology Today* online edition, July 28, 2011, accessed March 26, 2015, https://www.psycho logytoday.com/blog/sex-lies-trauma/201107/effects-porn-adolescent-boys. [updates made to quoted material by A. Katehakis]

5. All Pro Dad, "Pornography Statistic Sources," updated 2015, accessed, April 5, 2015, http://www.allprodad.com/pornography-statistic-sources/.

6. Enough Is Enough, "Internet Safety 101: Pornography Statistics," accessed February 12, 2015, http://www.internetsafety101.org/Pornographystatistics.htm.

7. Katehakis, "Effects of Porn." [updates made to quoted material by A. Katehakis]

8. Donna Freitas, *The End of Sex: How Hookup Culture Is Leaving a Generation Unhappy, Sexually Unfulfilled, and Confused About Intimacy* (New York: Basic Books, 2013).

9. Regan McMahon, "Porn Destroys Relationships, Lives," *SFGate, San Francisco Chronicle* online edition, February 2, 2010, accessed December 27, 2014, http://www.sfgate.com/health/article/Porn-addiction-destroys-relationships-lives-3272230.php.

10. Jonathan Lew, "All Men Watch Porn, Scientists Find," *The Telegraph* online edition, December 2, 2009, accessed, January 2015, http://www.telegraph.co.uk/women/sex/6709646/All-men-watch-porn-scientists-find.html.

11. Katehakis, "Effects of Porn." [updates made to quoted material by A. Katehakis]

12. Wyatt Myers, "Young Men Get Erectile Dysfunction, Too," *Everyday Health,* updated November 2, 2015, accessed May 7, 2015, http://www.everydayhealth.com/erectile-dysfunction/young-men-get-erectile-dysfunction-too.aspx.

13. Myers, "Young Men Get Erectile Dysfunction, Too."

14. Tyger Latham, "Does Porn Contribute to ED?" *Psychology Today* online edition, May 3, 2012, accessed May 10, 2015, https://www.psychologytoday.com/blog/therapy-matters/201205/does-porn-contribute-ed.

15. Latham, "Does Porn Contribute to ED?"

16. Latham, "Does Porn Contribute to ED?"

17. David Horsey, "Internet Porn Is an Experiment in Dehumanization," *Los Angeles Times* online edition, December 15, 2015, accessed January 10, 2015, http://www.latimes.com/opinion/topoftheticket/la-na-tt-internet-porn-20141215-story.html.

18. Enough Is Enough, "Internet Safety 101: Pornography Statistics," April 28, 2014, accessed February 12, 2015, http://www.internetsafety101.org/Pornographystatistics.htm.

19. Gail Dines, *Pornland: How Porn Has Hijacked Our Sexuality* (Boston: Beacon Press, 2010), xxvi.

20. Dines, *Pornland*, xxvi.
21. Regan McMahon, "Porn Destroys Relationships, Lives," *SFGate, San Francisco Chronicle* online edition, February 2, 2010, accessed December 27, 2014 http:// www.sfgate.com/health/article/Porn-addiction-destroys-relationships-lives -3272230.php.
22. J. Lloyd, N. S. Crouch, C. L. Minto, L.-M. Liao, and S. M. Creighton, "Female Genital Appearance: 'Normality' Unfolds," *BJOG: An International Journal of Obstetrics & Gynaecology* 112 (2005): 643–646, doi: 10.1111/j.1471-0528.2004.00517.x.
23. "About The Great Wall of Vagina," accessed April 5, 2015, http://www.great wallofvagina.co.uk/about.
24. Katehakis, "Effects of Porn." [updates made to quoted material by A. Katehakis]
25. Maura Kelly, "The Rise of Anal Sex," *Marie Clare* online edition, October 7, 2010, accessed February 25, 2015, http://www.marieclaire.com/sex-love/ a5489/rise-in-anal-sex-statistics/.
26. Katehakis, "Effects of Porn."

Chapter 4

1. Deborah Roffman, *Talk to Me First: Everything You Need to Know to Become Your Kids' "Go-To" Person about Sex* (Boston: De Capo Press, 2012),17.
2. Jodi Kantor, "Sex Ed for the Stroller Set," *New York Times* online edition, November 17, 2005, accessed February 23, 2015, http://www.nytimes. com/2005/11/17/fashion/thursdaystyles/17sex.html?pagewanted=all&_r=0.
3. Gormly, "How to Have "The Talk."
4. Catherine Buni, "The Case for Teaching Kids 'Vagina, Penis and Vulva,' " *Atlantic* online edition, April 15, 2013, accessed January, 2015, http://www .theatlantic.com/health/archive/2013/04/the-case-for-teaching-kids-vagina -penis-and-vulva/274969/.
5. Buni, "The Case for Teaching Kids 'Vagina, Penis and Vulva.' "
6. Bonnie Rochman, "Let's Talk (Frankly) About Sex," *New York Times* online edition, March 25, 2015, accessed on March 31, 2015, http://www.nytimes .com/2015/03/29/magazine/lets-talk-frankly-about-sex.html.
7. Gormly, "How to Have "The Talk."
8. Roffman, *Talk to Me First,* 13.

Chapter 5

1. Enough Is Enough, "Internet Safety 101: Pornography Statistics," April 28, 2014, accessed February 12, 2015, http://www.internetsafety101.org/ Pornographystatistics.htm.

2. Robie H. Harris, "Start Sex Education Early, Definitely Before Puberty," *New York Times* online edition, May 9, 2013, accessed January 14, 2015, http://www.nytimes.com/roomfordebate/2013/05/07/at-what-age-should -sex-education-begin/start-sex-education-early-definitely-before-puberty.

3. Tessa Berenson, "Planned Parenthood Thinks It Found a Way to Stop Middle Schoolers from Having Sex," *Time* magazine online edition, October 20, 2014, accessed February, 2015, http://time.com/3525125/planned -parenthood-sex-education/.

4. "Learn More About Get Real: Comprehensive Sex Education That Works," Planned Parenthood of Massachusetts, accessed February 10, 2015, http:// getrealeducation.org/learn-more/about-get-real.

5. "Learn More About Get Real."

6. Sarah Gibb Millspaugh, "Forty Years of UU Sexuality Education," *UUA World: Liberal Religion and Life,* Winter 2011, accessed February 25, 2015, http://www.uuworld.org/articles/40-years-sexuality-education.

7. "Our Whole Lives: Lifespan Sexuality Education," Unitarian Universalist Association, accessed February 26, 2015, http://www.uua.org/re/owl/.

8. Advocates For Youth, "An Explanation of the Circles of Sexuality," adapted from *Life Planning Education: A Youth Development Program, 2007,* accessed May 14, 2015 http://www.advocatesforyouth.org/for-professionals/lesson -plans-professionals/200.

9. Lee Che Leong, "Testimony: NYC DOE Must Provide Comprehensive Sex Education," NYCLU, n.d., accessed March 24, 2015, http://www.nyclu.org/ content/testimony-nyc-doe-must-provide-comprehensive-sex-education.

10. Jill Burke, "More Body Hair Removal Tips for the Renaissance Women," *Jill Burke's Blog,* March 13, 2014, accessed March 1, 2015, https://renresearch .wordpress.com/.

11. Jill Burke, "Did Renaissance Women Remove Their Body Hair?" *Jill Burke's Blog,* December 9, 2012, accessed March 1, 2015, https://renresearch.word press.com/2012/12/09/did-renaissance-women-remove-their-body-hair/.

12. Jesse Bering, "A Bushel of Facts About the Uniqueness of Human Pubic Hair," *Scientific American* online version, March 1, 2010, accessed February 27, 2015, http://blogs.scientificamerican.com/bering-in-mind/2010/03/01/ a-bushel-of-facts-about-the-uniqueness-of-human-pubic-hair/.

13. Scott M. Butler, Nicole K. Smith, Erika Collazo, Lucia Caltabiano, and Debby Herbenick, "Pubic Hair Preferences, Reasons for Removal, and Associated Genital Symptoms: Comparisons Between Men and Women, *Journal of Sexual Medicine* 11 (2014), accessed March 1, 2015, http://onlinelibrary. wiley.com/doi/10.1111/jsm.12763/full.

14. Bering, "A Bushel of Facts."

15. Bill Albert, *With One Voice 2004: America's Adults and Teens Sound Off About Teen Pregnancy* (Washington, DC: National Campaign to Prevent Teen Pregnancy, 2004), 5, https://thenationalcampaign.org/sites/default/files/resource-primary-download/wov_2004.pdf.

Chapter 6

1. Jessica Samakow, "Let Toys Be Toys Compares 1970s Toy Catalogue to Toy Marketing Today," *Huffington Post,* June, 7, 2013, accessed March 30, 2015, http://www.huffingtonpost.com/2013/06/07/let-toys-be-toys_n_3402972.html.

2. Elizabeth Sweet, "Toys Are More Divided by Gender Now Than They Were 50 Years Ago," *Atlantic* online edition, December 9, 2014, accessed February 24, 2015, http://www.theatlantic.com/business/archive/2014/12/toys-are-more-divided-by-gender-now-than-they-were-50-years-ago/383556/.

3. "Get Girls Active!," Women's Sports Foundation, June 20, 2011, accessed May 14, 2015, http://www.womenssportsfoundation.org/home/get-inspired/get-active/get-girls-active/get-girls-active.

4. Al Vernacchio, *For Goodness Sex: Changing the Way We Talk to Teens About Sexuality, Values, and Health* (New York: HarperCollins, 2014), 118.

5. Caroline Bologna, "12 Brilliant Kids' Clothing Lines That Say No to Gender Stereotypes," *Huffington Post,* April 7, 2015, accessed May 14, 2015, http://www.huffingtonpost.com/2015/04/07/kids-clothing-lines-break-gender-stereotypes_n_6925592.html.

6. Vernacchio, *For Goodness Sex,* 163.

7. Caroline Heldman, "The Sexy Lie," *Everyday Feminism*, February 9, 2014, accessed February 13, 2015, http://everydayfeminism.com/2014/02/the-sexy-lie/.

8. Dove "Our Research" page, Unilever, accessed March 23, 2015. http://www.dove.us/Our-Mission/Girls-Self-Esteem/Our-Research/default.aspx.

Chapter 7

1. Caroline Heldman, "The Sexy Lie," *Everyday Feminism*, February 9, 2014, accessed February 13, 2015, http://everydayfeminism.com/2014/02/the-sexy-lie/.

2. Heldman, "The Sexy Lie."

3. Mary Pipher, *Reviving Ophelia: Saving the Selves of Adolescent Girls* (New York: The Berkley Publishing Group, 1994), 12.

4. Lauren Greenfield (director), "Always#LikeAGirl" video, "Always: Change the Rules" campaign, Procter & Gamble, YouTube video, accessed March 25, 2015, https://www.youtube.com/watch?v=XjJQBjWYDTs.

5. Megan Grassell, "The Yellowberry Story," Yellowberry Company, accessed January 24, 2015, http://www.yellowberrycompany.com/ABUS.html.

6. "Dove: Legacy," Unilever, September 30, 2014, accessed April 30, 2015, http://www.dove.co.uk/en/Tips-Topics-and-Tools/Latest-Topics/Legacy.aspx.

7. "Dove: Legacy."

8. Jennifer Siebel Newsom (director), *Miss Representation* extended trailer, uploaded to YouTube October 13, 2011, accessed January 14, 2015, https://www.youtube.com/watch?v=S5pM1fW6hNs.

9. "Our Mission," The Representation Project, 2015, accessed April 20, 2015, http://therepresentationproject.org/about/mission/.

10. "Help Us Create the #NotBuyingIt App!," The Representation Project, You-Tube video, published August 21, 2014, accessed February 8, 2015. https://www.youtube.com/watch?v=ucFl3LiO1GU.

11. "Help Us Create the #NotBuyingIt App!"

12. Elise Hu, "Seventeen Magazine Takes No-Photoshop Pledge After 8th-Grader's Campaign," *The Two Way,* National Public Radio, July 5, 2012, accessed February 10, 2015, http://www.npr.org/blogs/thetwo-way/2012/07/05/156342683/seventeen-magazine-takes-no-photoshop-pledge-after-8th-graders-campaign.

13. "About Girls Leadership," Girls Leadership, 2015, March 27, 2015, http://girlsleadership.org/about/.

Chapter 8

1. Dan Kindlon and Michael Thompson, *Raising Cain: Protecting the Emotional Life of Boys* (New York: Ballantine Books, 2000), 20.

2. Kindlon and Thomson, *Raising Cain*, 36.

3. Leonard Sax, *Boys Adrift* (New York: Basic Books, 2007).

4. Yalda T. Uhls, Minas Michikyan, Jordan Morris, Debra Garcia, Gary W. Small, Eleni Zgourou, Patricia M. Greenfield, "Five Days at Outdoor Education Camp Without Screens Improves Preteen Skills with Nonverbal Emotion Cues," *Computers in Human Behavior,* October 2014, 387–392, http://www.sciencedirect.com/science/article/pii/S0747563214003227.

5. Rosalind Wiseman, *Masterminds and Wingmen: Helping Our Boys Cope with Schoolyard Power, Locker-Room Tests, Girlfriends, and the New Rules of Boy World* (New York: Harmony, 2013), 14.

6. Wiseman, *Masterminds,* 14.

7. William Pollack, *Real Boys: Rescuing Our Sons from the Myths of Boyhood* (New York: Henry Holt and Company, 1999), chapter 1, https://www.nytimes.com/books/first/p/pollack-boys.html.

8. Andi Diehn, "Recess Chat at the Willow School," *Kid Stuff,* April–May 2012, 4–7.

9. "Meet Joe—Joe's Videos," Coach for America, February 24, 2015. http://www.coachforamerica.com/meet-joe/videos-of-joe.

10. Jennifer Siebel Newsom (director), *The Mask You Live In* trailer, published to YouTube December 18, 2013, January 24, 2015, https://www.youtube.com/watch?v=hc45-ptHMxo.

Chapter 9

1. Brené Brown, *The Gifts of Imperfection: Let Go of Who You Think You're Supposed to Be and Embrace Who You Are,* (Center City, Minnesota: Hazelden Publishing, 2010), 49–124.

2. Brené Brown, *Daring Greatly* (New York: Gotham/Penguin, 2013), 109.

3. "Quick Facts About Video Games," Education.com, accessed February 10, 2015, http://www.education.com/facts/quickfacts-video-games/average-amount-playing/.

4. "Understanding and Raising Boys: Active or Aggressive Boys?," PBS Parents, accessed April 2, 2015, http://www.pbs.org/parents/raisingboys/aggression.html.

5. Leonard Sax, *Boys Adrift* (New York: Basic Books, 2007), 51.

6. "Essential Facts About the Computer and Video Game Industry: 2014 Sales, Demographic, and Usage Data," Entertainment Software Association, February 10, 2015, www.theesa.com/wp-content/uploads/2014/10/ESA_EF_2014.pdf.

7. Eddie Makuch, "Percentage of Female Developers Has More than Doubled Since 2009," Gamespot, June 24, 2014, accessed February 10, 2015, http://www.gamespot.com/articles/percentage-of-female-developers-has-more-than-doubled-since-2009/1100-6420680/.

8. Edward L. Swing, Douglas A. Gentile, Craig A. Anderson, "Learning Processes and Violent Video Games," in *Handbook of Research on Effective Electronic Gaming in Education,* ed. Richard E Ferdig (New York: Information Science Reference, 2009), 876-892.

9. "About Us," Quest to Learn Upper School, February 23, 2015, http://upperschool.q2l.org/about-us/.

10. Michael Kimmel, *Guyland: The Perilous World Where Boys Become Men* (New York: HarperCollins, 2008), 47–48.

11. Kimmel, *Guyland,* 21.

Chapter 10

1. Frances Jensen, interview by Terry Gross, "Why Teens Are Impulsive, Addiction-Prone and Should Protect Their Brains," *Fresh Air,* January 30,

2015, accessed February 28, 2015, http://www.npr.org/player/v2/mediaPlayer. html?action=1&t=1&islist=false&id=381622350&m=382175999.

2. Jensen, "Why Teens Are Impulsive."

3. Social Development Research Group/Seattle Children's Hospital, *Parent's Guide to Preventing Underage Marijuana Use* (Seattle: Seattle Children's Hospital, 2014), 2, accessed March 2, 2015, http://learnaboutmarijuanawa.org/ parentpreventionbooklet2014.pdf.

4. William Brangham, "Is Pot Getting More Potent?" *PBS Newshour* online, April 2, 2014, accessed March 1, 2015, http://www.pbs.org/newshour/ updates/pot-getting-potent/.

5. David. G. Newman, "Cannabis and Its Effects on Pilot Performance and Flight Safety: A Review," released in accordance with s.25 of the Transport Safety Investigation Act, 2003, 8-10, accessed February 2015, http://www.northstar behavioral.com/Cannabis%20and%20its%20Effects%20on%20Pilot %20Performance%20and%20Flight%20Safety%20%28Australian %20Transportation%20Safety%20Bureau%202004%29%20%281% 29.pdf.

6. National Institute of Drug Abuse, "Is Marijuana Addictive?" updated April 2015, accessed April 3, 2015, http://www.drugabuse.gov/publications/ research-reports/marijuana/marijuana-addictive.

7. National Institute on Alcohol Abuse and Alcoholism, "College Drinking," July 2013, accessed April 3, 2015, http://pubs.niaaa.nih.gov/publications/ CollegeFactSheet/CollegeFactSheet.pdf.

8. Student Health Services University of Pennsylvania, "Alcohol," 2015, accessed April 3, 2015. http://www.vpul.upenn.edu/shs/alcohol.php.

9. Elissa R. Weitzman, Toben F. Nelson, and Henry Wechsler, "Taking Up Binge Drinking in College: The Influences of Person, Social Group, and Environment," *Journal of Adolescent Health* (2003): 29, accessed April 3, 2015, http:// archive.sph.harvard.edu/cas/Documents/uptake/uptake1.pdf.

10. Linda Thrasybule, "Pre-Gaming Risky for Young Adults," *Livescience,* November 9, 2012, accessed February 28, 2015, http://www.livescience .com/36730-pre-gaming-alcohol-risky-young-adults.html.

11. United States Department of Justice, "Sexual Assault," April 2, 2015, accessed May 18, 2015, http://www.justice.gov/ovw/sexual-assault.

12. Student Health Services University of Pennsylvania, "Alcohol," 2015, accessed April 3, 2015, http://www.vpul.upenn.edu/shs/alcohol.php.

13. RAINN (Rape, Abuse & Incest National Network), "Who Are the Victims?," accessed February 20, 2015, https://www.rainn.org/get-information/ statistics/sexual-assault-victims.

14. Jackson Katz, *"Violence and Silence,"* February 11, 2013, accessed May 10, 2015, https://www.youtube.com/watch?v=KTvSfeCRxe8

15. Gina Kirkland, "Girls Fight Back," Kirkland Productions, March 29, 2015, http://www.girlsfightback.com/.

16. Emma Sulcowicz, "Carry That Weight," *Columbia Daily Spectator,* September 2, 2014, accessed February 15, 2015, https://www.youtube.com/watch?v=l9hHZbuYVnU.

Chapter 11

1. Cole Moreton, "Children and the Culture of Pornography: Boys Will Ask You Every Day Until You Say Yes," *Telegraph,* January 27, 2013, accessed January 22, 2015, http://www.telegraph.co.uk/women/sex/9828589/Children-and-the-culture-of-pornography-Boys-will-ask-you-every-day-until-you-say-yes.html.

2. Donna Freitas, *The End of Sex: How Hookup Culture Is Leaving a Generation Unhappy, Sexually Unfulfilled, and Confused About Intimacy* (New York: Basic Books, 2013), 112.

3. Al Vernacchio, *For Goodness Sex: Changing the Way We Talk to Teens About Sexuality, Values, and Health* (New York: HarperCollins, 2014), 191.

4. Vernacchio, *For Goodness Sex,* 158.

5. Freitas, *The End of Sex,* 112.

6. Student Health Services University of Pennsylvania, "Alcohol," 2015, accessed April 3, 2015, http://www.vpul.upenn.edu/shs/alcohol.php.

7. Alexandra Katehakis, "Effects of Porn on Adolescent Boys," *Psychology Today* online edition, July 28, 2011, accessed February 20, 2015, https://www.psychologytoday.com/blog/sex-lies-trauma/201107/effects-porn-adolescent-boys. [updates made to quoted material by A. Katehakis]

REFERENCES

Advocates for Youth. "An Explanation of the Circles of Sexuality." Adapted from *Life Planning Education: A Youth Development Program*. Washington, DC: Advocates for Youth, 2007. http://www.advocatesforyouth.org/for -professionals/lesson-plans-professionals/200.

Albert, Bill. *With One Voice 2004: America's Adults and Teens Sound Off About Teen Pregnancy*. Washington, DC: National Campaign to Prevent Teen Pregnancy, December 2004. https://thenationalcampaign.org/sites/default/files/ resource-primary-download/wov_2004.pdf.

All Pro Dad. "Pornography Statistic Sources." All Pro Dad. Updated 2015. Accessed, April 5, 2015. http://www.allprodad.com/pornography-statistic -sources/.

Arlidge, John. "The Dirty Secret That Drives Technology: It's Porn." *Guardian* online edition, March 2, 2002. Accessed March 24, 2002. http://www .theguardian.com/technology/2002/mar/03/internetnews.observerfocus.

Belic, Roko. "The Search For Happiness." *Huffington Post*, March 21, 2012. Accessed January 27, 2015. http://www.huffingtonpost.com/roko-belic/ happy-documentary_b_1220111.html.

Berenson, Tessa. "Planned Parenthood Thinks It Found a Way to Stop Middle Schoolers from Having Sex." *Time* magazine online edition, October 20, 2014. Accessed February, 2015. http://time.com/3525125/planned-parenthood -sex-education/.

Bering, Jesse. "A Bushel of Facts about the Uniqueness of Human Pubic Hair." *Scientific American* online edition, March 1, 2010. Accessed February 27, 2015. http://blogs.scientificamerican.com/bering-in-mind/2010/03/01/a-bushel-of -facts-about-the-uniqueness-of-human-pubic-hair/.

Bologna, Caroline. "12 Brilliant Kids' Clothing Lines That Say No to Gender Stereotypes." *Huffington Post* online edition, April 7, 2015. Accessed May 14, 2015.

http://www.huffingtonpost.com/2015/04/07/kids-clothing-lines-break-gender-stereotypes_n_6925592.html.

Bradberry, Travis. "Multitasking Damages Your Brain and Career, New Studies Suggest." *Forbes* online edition, October 8, 2014. Accessed February 24, 2015. http://www.forbes.com/sites/travisbradberry/2014/10/08/multitasking-damages-your-brain-and-career-new-studies-suggest/.

Brangham, William. "Is Pot Getting More Potent?" PBS *Newshour* online, April 2, 2014. Accessed March 1, 2015. http://www.pbs.org/newshour/updates/pot-getting-potent/.

Brown, Brené. *Daring Greatly: How the Courage to Be Vulnerable Transforms the Way We Live, Love, Parent, and Lead.* New York: Gotham Books, 2012.

Brundin, Jenny. "Waldorf's 4th Graders Gain Insight from Media Fast." Colorado Public Radio transcript, February 9, 2013. Accessed February 15, 2015. http://www.denverwaldorf.org/tag/npr/.

Buni, Catherine. "The Case for Teaching Kids 'Vagina, Penis and Vulva.'" *Atlantic* online edition, April 15, 2013. Accessed January 23, 2015. http://www.theatlantic.com/health/archive/2013/04/the-case-for-teaching-kids-vagina penis-and-vulva/274969/.

Burke, Jill. "Did Renaissance Women Remove Pubic Hair?" *Jill Burke's Blog.* December 9, 2012. Accessed March 1, 2015. https://renresearch.wordpress.com/2012/12/09/did-renaissance-women-remove-their-body-hair/.

Burke, Jill. "More Body Hair Removal Tips for the Renaissance Women." *Jill Burke's Blog,* March 13, 2014. Accessed March 3, 2015. https://renresearch.wordpress.com/.

Butler, Scott M., Nicole K. Smith, Erika Collazo, Lucia Caltabiano, and Debby Herbenick. "Pubic Hair Preferences, Reasons for Removal, and Associated Genital Symptoms: Comparisons Between Men and Women." *The Journal of Sexual Medicine,* November 14, 2014. Accessed March 1, 2015. http://onlinelibrary.wiley.com/doi/10.1111/jsm.12763/full.

Diehn, Andi. "Recess Chat at the Willow School." *Kid Stuff* April–May 2012.

Dines, Gail. *Pornland: How Porn Has Hijacked Our Sexuality.* Boston: Beacon Press, 2010.

Education.com, "What Is the Average Amount of Time Per Week American Children Play Video Games?" Education.com. Accessed April 5, 2015. http://www.education.com/facts/quickfacts-video-games/average-amount-playing/.

Enough Is Enough. "Internet Safety 101: Pornography Statistics." April 28, 2014. Accessed February 12, 2015 http://www.internetsafety101.org/Pornographys tatistics.htm.

Masters, Kim. *The Keys to the Kingdom: The Rise of Michael Eisner and the Fall of Everybody Else.* New York: HarperCollins, 2001.

Fisher, B.S., F.T. Cullen, and M.G. Turner. "The Sexual Victimization of College Women." National Institute of Justice, Bureau of Justice Statistics, 2000. Accessed, January 28, 2015. http://www.nsvrc.org/saam/campus-resource-list# Stats.

Freitas, Donna. *The End of Sex: How Hookup Culture Is Leaving a Generation Unhappy, Sexually Unfulfilled, and Confused About Intimacy.* New York: Basic Books, 2013.

Girls Leadership. "About Girls Leadership." Accessed February 25, 2015. http://girlsleadership.org/about/.

Gormly, Kellie B. "How to Have 'The Talk.'" *Pittsburgh Tribune Review* (on Robie H. Harris's website). January 9, 2007. Accessed January 10, 2015. http://robieharris.com/?page_id=108.

Hamkins, SuEllen, and Renée Schultz, *The Mother-Daughter Project.* New York: Hudson Street Press, 2007.

Harris, Robie H. "Start Sex Education Early, Definitely Before Puberty." *New York Times* online edition, May 9, 2013. Accessed January 14, 2015. http://www.nytimes.com/roomfordebate/2013/05/07/at-what-age-should-sex-education-begin/start-sex-education-early-definitely-before-puberty.

Heldman, Caroline. "The Sexy Lie." *Everyday Feminism*, February 9, 2014. Accessed February 13, 2015. http://everydayfeminism.com/2014/02/the-sexy-lie/.

Hoefle, Vicki. *Duct Tape Parenting: A Less Is More Approach to Raising Respectful, Responsible, and Resilient Kids.* Brookline, MA: Bibliomotion, 2012.

Horsey, David. "Internet Porn Is an Experiment in Dehumanization." *Los Angeles Times* online edition, December 15, 2015. Accessed: January 10, 2015. http://www.latimes.com/opinion/topoftheticket/la-na-tt-internet-porn-20141215-story.html.

Howse, Patrick. "'Pornography Addiction Worry' for Tenth of 12 to 13-Year Olds." BBC News online edition, March 31, 2015. Accessed March 31, 2015. http://www.bbc.com/news/education-32115162.

Huffington Post. "Porn Sites Get More Visitors Each Month Than Netflix, Amazon and Twitter Combined." *Huffington Post,* May 4, 2013. Accessed February 26, 2015. http://www.huffingtonpost.com/2013/05/03/internet-porn-stats_n_3187682.html.

Hu, Elise. "Seventeen Magazine Takes No-Photoshop Pledge After 8th-Grader's Campaign." *The Two Way.* National Public Radio. July 5, 2012. Accessed February, 2015. http://www.npr.org/blogs/thetwo-way/2012/07/05/156342683/seventeen-magazine-takes-no-photoshop-pledge-after-8th-graders-campaign.

Jensen, Frances. *The Teenage Brain: A Neuroscientist's Survival Guide to Raising Adolescent and Young Adults.* New York: Harper, 2015.

Jensen, Frances. "Why Teens Are Impulsive, Addiction-Prone and Should Protect Their Brains." Interview by Terry Gross. *Fresh Air.* National Public Radio, January 28, 2015. Accessed February 15, 2015. http://www.npr.org/blogs/health/2015/01/28/381622350/why-teens-are-impulsive-addiction-prone-and-should-protect-their-brains.

Kantor, Jodi, "Sex Ed for the Stroller Set." *New York Times* online edition. November 17, 2005. Accessed February 23, 2015. http://www.nytimes.com/2005/11/17/fashion/thursdaystyles/17sex.html?pagewanted=all&_r=0.

Katehakis, Alexandra. "Effects of Porn on Adolescent Boys." *Psychology Today* online edition, July 28, 2011. Accessed March 26, 2015. https://www.psychologytoday.com/blog/sex-lies-trauma/201107/effects-porn-adolescent-boys.

Katz, Jackson. *The Macho Paradox: Why Some Men Hurt Women and How All Men Can Help.* Naperville, Illinois: Sourcebooks, 2006.

Katz, Jackson. "Violence and Silence." Youtube video, February 11, 2013. Accessed May 10, 2015. https://www.youtube.com/watch?v=KTvSfeCRxe8.

Kelly, Maura. "The Rise of Anal Sex." *Marie Claire* online edition, October 7, 2010. Accessed February 24, 2015. http://www.marieclaire.com/sex-love/a5489/rise-in-anal-sex-statistics/.

Kerr, Dara. "One-Fifth of Third Graders Own Cell Phones." CNet online version, April 9, 2012. Accessed January 10, 2015. http://www.cnet.com/news/one-fifth-of-third-graders-own-cell-phones/.

Kimmel, Michael. *Guyland: The Perilous World Where Boys Become Men.* New York: Harper Collins, 2008.

Kindlon, Dan, and Thompson, Michael. *Raising Cain: Protecting the Emotional Life of Boys.* Ballantine Books: New York, 2000.

Kirkland, Gina. "Girls Fight Back." Kirkland Productions. Accessed April 20, 2015. http://www.girlsfightback.com/.

Klein, Dr. Marty. "Want to Watch a Lot of Porn AND Have Good Sex?" *Sexual Intelligence* blog, November 11, 2014. Accessed December 15, 2014. https://sexualintelligence.wordpress.com/2014/11/11/want-to-watch-a-lot-of-porn-and-have-good-sex/.

Latham, Tyger. "Does Porn Contribute to ED?" *Psychology Today* online edition, May 3, 2012. Accessed May 10, 2015. https://www.psychologytoday.com/blog/therapy-matters/201205/does-porn-contribute-ed.

Leong, Lee Che. "Testimony: NYC DOE Must Provide Comprehensive Sex Education." NYCLU, n.d. http://www.nyclu.org/content/testimony-nyc-doe-must-provide-comprehensive-sex-education.

Lewen, Tamara. "If Your Kids Are Awake, They're Probably Online." *New York Times* online edition, January 20, 2010. http://www.nytimes.com/2010/01/20/education/20wired.html?_r=0.

Lew, Jonathan. "All Men Watch Porn, Scientists Find." *Telegraph* online edition, December 2, 2009. Accessed January 15, 2015. http://www.telegraph.co.uk/women/sex/6709646/All-men-watch-porn-scientists-find.html.

Lloyd, Jillian, Naomi Crouch, Catherine L. Minto, Lih-Mei Liao, and Sarah M. Creighton, "Female Genital Appearance: 'Normality' Unfolds." *BJOG: An International Journal of Obstetrics & Gynaecology* 112 (2005): 643–646. http://onlinelibrary.wiley.com/doi/10.1111/j.1471-0528.2004.00517.x/full.

Masters, Kim. *The Keys to the Kingdom: The Rise of Michael Eisner and the Fall of Everybody Else.* New York: HarperCollins, 2001.

McMahon, Regan. "Porn Destroys Relationships, Lives." *SFGate, San Francisco Chronicle* online edition, February 2, 2010. Accessed December 27, 2014. http://www.sfgate.com/health/article/Porn-addiction-destroys-relationships-lives-3272230.php.

Millspaugh, Sarah Gibb. "Forty Years of UU Sexuality Education." *UUWorld: Liberal Religion and Life,* Winter, 2011. Accessed February 24, 2015. http://www.uuworld.org/articles/40-years-sexuality-education.

Moreton, Cole. "Children and the Culture of Pornography: Boys Will Ask You Every Day Until You Say Yes." *Telegraph,* January 27, 2013. Accessed January 19, 2015.

Myers, Wyatt. "Young Men Get Erectile Dysfunction, Too." *Everyday Health,* updated November 2, 2015. Accessed May 7, 2015. http://www.everydayhealth.com/erectile-dysfunction/young-men-get-erectile-dysfunction-too.aspx.

Nass, Clifford. "The Myth of Multitasking." Interview by Ira Flatow. *Science Friday.* National Public Radio, May 10, 2013. Accessed December 29, 2014. http://www.npr.org/2013/05/10/182861382/the-myth-of-multitasking.

National Institute on Alcohol Abuse and Alcoholism. "College Drinking: College Fact Sheet." National Institute on Alcohol Abuse and Alcoholism. July 2013. Accessed April 3, 2015. http://pubs.niaaa.nih.gov/publications/CollegeFactSheet/CollegeFactSheet.pdf.

National Institute of Drug Abuse. "Is Marijuana Addictive?" National Institute of Drug Abuse. Updated April, 2015. Accessed, April 3, 2015. http://www.drugabuse.gov/publications/research-reports/marijuana/marijuana-addictive.

Newman, David. G. "Cannabis and Its Effects on Pilot Performance and Flight Safety: A Review," released in accordance with s.25 of the Transport

Safety Investigation Act, 2003, 8-10. Accessed February 29, 2015. http://www.northstarbehavioral.com/Cannabis%20and%20its%20Effects%20on%20Pilot%20Performance%20and%20Flight%20Safety%20%28Australian%20Transportation%20Safety%20Bureau%202004%29%20%281%29.pdf.

Newsom, Jennifer Siebel, director. *Miss Representation* (extended trailer). Uploaded on October 13, 2011. Accessed March 2, 2015. https://www.youtube.com/watch?v=S5pM1fW6hNs.

Norris, Gunilla. *Inviting Silence*. Katonah, NY: Bluebridge, 2004.

PBS Parents. "Understanding and Raising Boys: Active or Aggressive Boys?" http://www.pbs.org/parents/raisingboys/aggression.html.

Pettitt, Jessica. "I Am Social Justice." Accessed May 1, 2015. http://www.jessica pettitt.com/index.htm.

Planned Parenthood of Massachusetts. "Learn More About Get Real: Comprehensive Sex Education That Works." March 26, 2015. http://getrealeducation. org/learn-more/about-get-real.

Pollack, William. *Real Boys: Rescuing Our Sons from the Myths of Boyhood*. New York: Henry Holt and Company, 1999.

Pipher, Mary. *Reviving Ophelia: Saving the Selves of Adolescent Girls*. New York: Berkley Publishing Company, 1994.

Quest to Learn. "About Us." Quest to Learn Upper School website, accessed February 5, 2015. http://upperschool.q2l.org/about-us/.

Race to Nowhere: The Dark Side of America's Achievement Culture (Vicki Abeles and Jessica Congdon, codirectors) "About the Film." Accessed March 2, 2015. http://www.racetonowhere.com/about-film.

RAINN: Rape, Abuse, and Incest National Network, Effects of Rape. "Who Are the Victims?" RAINN, 2009. Accessed February, 2015. https://www.rainn .org/get-information/statistics/sexual-assault-victims.

Richardson, Hannah. "Limit Children's Screen Time, Expert Urges." BBC News online edition, October 9, 2012. Accessed January 10, 2015. http://www.bbc .com/news/education-19870199.

Rochman, Bonnie. "Let's Talk (Frankly) About Sex." *New York Times* online edition, March 25, 2015. Accessed March 31, 2015. http://www.nytimes. com/2015/03/29/magazine/lets-talk-frankly-about-sex.html?_r=0.

Roffman, Deborah. *Talk to Me First: Everything You Need to Know to Become Your Kids' "Go-To" Person about Sex*. Boston: De Capo Press, 2012.

Samakow, Jessica. "Let Toys Be Toys Compares 1970s Toy Catalogue to Toy Marketing Today." *Huffington Post*, June, 7, 2013. Accessed March 30, 2015. http://www.huffingtonpost.com/2013/06/07/let-toys-be-toys_n_3402972.html.

Sax, Leonard. *Boys Adrift*. New York: Basic Books, 2007.

Sax, Leonard, *Girls on the Edge*. New York: Basic Books, 2010.

Schab, Lisa M., *The Anxiety Workbook for Teens*. Oakland, CA: Harbinger Publications, 2008.

Simmons, Rachel. *Odd Girl Out: The Hidden Culture of Aggression in Girls*. Boston and New York: Mariner Books, an imprint of Houghton Mifflin Harcourt, 2002.

Social Development Research Group/Seattle Children's Hospital. *Parent's Guide to Preventing Underage Marijuana Use*. Seattle: Seattle Children's Hospital, 2014. Accessed March 2, 2015. http://learnaboutmarijuanawa.org/parent preventionbooklet2014.pdf.

Steiner-Adair, Catherine. *The Big Disconnect: Protecting Childhood and Family Relationships in the Digital Age*. New York: Harper Collins, 2013.

Sulkowicz, Emma. "Carry That Weight." *Columbia Daily Spectator,* September 2, 2014. Accessed February 15, 2015. https://www.youtube.com/watch?v=l9hHZbuYVnU.

Sweet, Elizabeth. "Toys Are More Divided by Gender Now Than They Were 50 Years Ago." *Atlantic* online edition. December 9, 2014. Accessed February 24, 2015. http://www.theatlantic.com/business/archive/2014/12/toys-are-more -divided-by-gender-now-than-they-were-50-years-ago/383556/.

Swing, Edward L., Douglas A. Gentile, and Craig A. Anderson. "Learning Processes and Violent Video Games." In *Handbook of Research on Effective Electronic Gaming in Education,* edited by Richard E. Ferdig. New York: Information Science Reference, 2009.

Tedesco, Austin. "BC Students Read Offensive Yik Yak Posts." *The Heights* online edition, May 6, 2014. Accessed March 1, 2015. http://bcheights.com/ blog/2014/bc-students-read-offensive-yik-yak-posts/.

Thrasybule, Linda. "Pre-Gaming Risky for Young Adults." *Livescience*, November 9, 2012. Accessed February 28, 2015. http://www.livescience.com/36730 -pre-gaming-alcohol-risky-young-adults.html.

Unitarian Universalist Association. "Our Whole Lives: Lifespan Sexuality Education." Unitarian Universalist Association. Accessed February 10, 2015. http:// www.uua.org/re/owl/.

United States Department of Justice. "Sexual Assault." April 2, 2015. Accessed May 18, 2015. http://www.justice.gov/ovw/sexual-assault.

Vernacchio, Al. *For Goodness Sex: Changing the Way We Talk to Teens About Sexuality, Values, and Health*. New York: HarperCollins, 2014.

Weitzman, Elissa R., Toben F. Nelson, and Henry Wechsler. "Taking Up Binge Drinking in College: The Influences of Person, Social Group, and Environment."

Journal of Adolescent Health (2003): 26–35. Accessed April 3, 2015. http://
  archive.sph.harvard.edu/cas/Documents/uptake/uptake1.pdf.

Wiseman, Rosalind, *Masterminds and Wingmen: Helping Our Boys Cope with
  Schoolyard Power, Locker-Room Tests, Girlfriends, and the New Rules of Boy
  World*. New York: Harmony, 2013.

Wiseman, Rosalind. *Queen Bees and Wannabes; Helping Your Daughter Survive
  Cliques, Gossip, Boyfriends, and the New Realities of Girl World*. New York:
  Three Rivers Press, 2009 edition.

Women's Sports Foundation. "Get Girls Active!" January 20, 2011. Accessed
  May 14, 2015. http://www.womenssportsfoundation.org/home/get-inspired/
  get-active/get-girls-active/get-girls-active.

INDEX

ACKNOWLEDGMENTS

It is amazing how the universe aligns. Thanks to Laura Alden Kamm for helping me connect with my life's purpose and for knowing this book was going to happen before I could even imagine such a thing.

Many thanks to my dear friend Vicki Hoefle, for her friendship, for helping us find our way as parents, and for connecting me to the amazing Bibliomotion team.

Thanks to Jill Friedlander and Erika Heilman for your support, guidance, and belief in this message. Bibliomotion is a wonderful community of authors, thanks to the two of you.

Huge thanks to Susan Lauzau for her attention to detail, thoroughness, and stamina.

Thanks to Jill Schoenhaut for helping me bring this home.

Thanks to the Bibliomotion team: Shevaun Betzler, Ari Choquette, Sue Ramin, and Alicia Simons.

Thanks to my editing team: Eric Barthold, Sarah Callaway, Jane Esselstyn, Connor Gibson, Vicki Hoefle, Jane LeMasurier, Leslie MacGregor, Edie Thys Morgan, Josiah Proietti, and Brook Raney.

Thanks for engaging in conversations and contributing wisdom to this book: Terri Ashley, Eric Barthold, Mary Bender, David Cook, Jane Esselstyn, Lucia Gagliardone, Connor Gibson, Jonathan Kalin, Elizabeth Keene, Michael Lyons, Sabina McMahon, Leslie MacGregor, Stacy Nadeau, Riley

O'Connor, William Okin, Sohier Perry, Jessica Pettitt, Josiah Proietti, Brook Raney, Sara Oneto Rose, Mindy Schorr, Chris Seibel, Sara Shea, Robbie Tanner, and Al Vernacchio.

Thanks to the Arc. Angels for building the fire, and thanks to Kristi Graham for lighting the match. I am grateful to all of you for getting me on this path.

Thanks to Lianne Moccia and Mindy Schorr for being positive forces in so many people's lives and for encouraging me to keep telling stories.

Thanks to Michael Livingston and Christa Wurm for trusting me with your students first.

Thanks to Kristin Brown, Jane Esselstyn, Elizabeth Keene, and Pennie Rand. The Coven feeds my soul.

Thanks to my aunt, Nancy Pierce Williamson. Her career as a journalist was impressive. She inspired me to write a family newspaper at twelve and to never shy away from tough questions. Also, thanks to Nancy for showing me how to throw a perfect spiral.

Thanks to my mom for always speaking her mind even when it makes people nervous. We are all grateful for our big, amazing family. I love you all!!

My deepest thanks and love go to my husband, Bruce, and our three wonderful kids, Zander, Sadie, and Colter.

ABOUT THE AUTHOR

CINDY PIERCE is a comic storyteller and sexuality educator who has been engaging audiences with her message about making healthy choices and navigating cultural pressures since 2004. She is a college speaker represented by Kirkland Productions. Cindy frequently presents to parents, educators, and high school students, and has been performing comic solo shows around New England, Colorado, New York, and on the West Coast for more than ten years. She is the coauthor of *Finding the Doorbell: Sexual Satisfaction for the Long Haul*. Cindy and her husband, Bruce, own and run Pierce's Inn in Etna, New Hampshire, where they are raising their three kids.